Linux Programming:
A Beginner's Guide

Linux Programming:
A Beginner's Guide

Richard Petersen

Osborne/**McGraw-Hill**

Berkeley New York St. Louis San Francisco
Auckland Bogotá Hamburg London Madrid
Mexico City Milan Montreal New Delhi Panama City
Paris São Paulo Singapore Sydney Tokyo Toronto

Osborne/**McGraw-Hill**
2600 Tenth Street
Berkeley, California 94710
U.S.A.

For information on translations or book distributors outside the U.S.A., or to arrange
bulk purchase discounts for sales promotions, premiums, or fund-raisers, please contact
Osborne/**McGraw-Hill** at the above address.

Linux Programming: A Beginner's Guide

1234567890 CUS CUS 01987654321

ISBN 0-07-212743-0

Publisher   Brandon A. Nordin
Vice President & Associate Publisher   Scott Rogers
Acquisitions Editor   Jane Brownlow
Project Editor   Lisa Theobald
Acquisitions Coordinator   Ross Doll
Technical Editor   James Couzens
Copy Editors   Andy Carroll and Lisa Theobald
Proofreader   Linda Medoff
Indexer   Karin Arrigoni
Computer Designers   Gary Corrigan, Tara Davis, Elizabeth Jang
Illustrator   Michael Mueller
Series Design   Gary Corrigan
Cover Designer   Pattie Lee

This book was composed with Corel VENTURA™ Publisher.

To my godson,
Dylan

About the Author

Richard Petersen, M.L.I.S., is the author of *Linux: The Complete Reference,* now in its third edition; *Linux: Programmer's Reference,* now in its second edition; and *Red Hat Linux: The Complete Reference.* Richard also teaches UNIX and C/C++ courses at the University of California at Berkeley.

About the Technical Editor

James Couzens is the Systems Administrator for Market News Publishing, an electronic news wire service based in Vancouver, Canada. He is a Linux programmer who has been working with computers for more than 13 years.

Contents at a Glance

Contents

PART 1
Shell Programming

PART 2
Higher Level Languages

PART 4

Appendix

Acknowledgments

I would like to thank all those at Osborne/McGraw–Hill who made this book a reality, particularly Jane Brownlow, acquisitions editor, for her continued encouragement and analysis as well as management of such a complex project; James Couzens, the technical editor, whose analysis and suggestions proved very insightful and helpful; Ross Doll, Acquisitions Coordinator, who provided needed resources and helpful advice; Andy Carroll, copy editor, for his excellent job editing as well as insightful comments; and project editor Lisa Theobald, who incorporated the large number of features found in this book as well as coordinating the intricate task of generating the final version. Thanks also to Scott Rogers, who initiated the project.

Special thanks to Linus Torvalds, the creator of Linux, and to those who continue to develop Linux as an open, professional, and effective operating system accessible to anyone. Thanks also to the academic community, whose special dedication has developed UNIX as a flexible and versatile operating system. I would also like to thank professors and students at the University of California, Berkeley, for the experience and support in developing new and different ways of understanding operating system technologies.

I would also like to thank my parents, George and Cecelia, and my brothers, George, Robert, and Mark, for their support and encouragement with such a difficult project. Also Valerie and Marylou and my nieces and nephews, Aleina, Larisa, Justin, Christopher, and Dylan, for their support and deadline reminders.

Introduction

The Linux operating system has become one of the major operating systems, bringing to the PC all the power and flexibility of a UNIX workstation as well as a complete set of Internet applications and a fully functional desktop interface. What many may not realize is that all standard Linux systems support a wide range of programming languages that allow users to create their own programs easily. Keep in mind that Linux was based on UNIX, which was designed as a research platform upon which researchers could quickly develop customized applications. In this spirit, all Linux distributions include a large selection of programming platforms, including support for numerous kinds of shell programming, a variety of higher level languages like Perl and Tcl/Tk, and extensive GUI programming for desktops like GNOME and KDE. Once Linux is installed, you can start creating your own programs.

This book is designed as a beginner's guide to programming on Linux. It covers numerous programming platforms and the languages that are currently available on Linux. You can begin to work with most of these with no prior programming experience, with the exception of the GUI platforms covered at the end of the book. GUI programming does assume a working knowledge of C and C++ programming.

This book identifies three major Linux programming topics: shell programming, the higher level languages, and GUI programming. Writing shell programs and the higher level languages do not necessarily require that you have any prior programming experience. Part 1 of the book covers BASH and TCSH shell programming. BASH and TCSH are shell environments on Linux that have programming features. From within a BASH shell, you can create simple programs that you can execute easily. BASH shell programming is organized into two modules, one on the basics and the other on control structures. Control structures allow you to control the execution of a program so that you can repeat commands or select commands to execute. TCSH shell programs use a different syntax, although they work in much the same way.

Part 2 covers higher level languages, including GAWK, Perl, and Tcl/Tk. Each of these languages allows you to create very complex programs using a few powerful commands. They each have control structures, many of which operate in similar ways. With GAWK, you can easily process data, generating modified versions of the original. Perl lets you access files and manipulate strings as well as manage arrays. Tcl performs many of the same tasks as Perl. Tk is an extension of Tcl that lets you create GUIs. With just a few commands, you can create your own windows with menus and buttons. Tk supports a wide range of GUI objects.

Part 3 provides an introduction to programming in GNOME and KDE. The module on GNOME, Module 9, is meant as a brief introduction and does require an understanding of C programming. The module on KDE, Module 10, also provides an introduction, although programming in KDE requires that you have an understanding of C++ programming, particularly class hierarchies. For those of you with this background, these modules may prove helpful. Those without this background will still gain an understanding of what is needed to develop applications for these desktops. The book does not cover the lower level Linux system calls. These are often used for systems programming, developing applications such as device drivers. They require an understanding of the underlying structure of the Linux operating system, including processes, scheduling, and file structure. This is beyond the scope of a beginner's book, though, and is best handled at an intermediate level. This book focuses on programming that any beginner can do, without having to know how operating systems are built.

Part 1

Shell Programming

Module 1

Introduction to Linux Programming

The Goals of This Module

- Learn about the programming languages available on Linux
- Get an overview of Linux setup
- Learn about Linux history
- Study the available Linux distributions
- Find online resources for Linux programming

L inux is an operating system for PCs and workstations that features a fully functional graphical user interface—a GUI that's similar to the GUI used by Windows and Macintosh platforms (although Linux is more stable). Linux has become the predominant platform for Internet services, such as Web servers, e-commerce, and database support. Since Linux was developed in the early 1990s by Linus Torvalds, the program has been amended and improved over the years by other programmers around the world. As an operating system, Linux performs many of the same functions performed by UNIX, Macintosh, Windows, and Windows NT machines. However, Linux is distinguished by its power and flexibility. As part of their basic configuration, all Linux systems provide extensive support for programming. You can install Linux on your system and start programming in any number of languages at no extra cost or effort.

Linux programming can be classified into four general categories: shell programming languages, higher level languages, graphical user interface (GUI) programming, and standard programming using system calls. This book concentrates on the commonly used and easy-to-understand shell and higher level languages, with introductory chapters on GUI programming. Shell and higher level programming do not require that you have previous programming knowledge, although some understanding of programming principles will help. GUI programming *does* require that you know the C and C++ programming languages. Standard programming consists of C and C++ programs that can access lower level Linux operations, such as file access and process scheduling. Such programming is often used to create administration applications such as device drivers. This kind of programming is well beyond the scope of this book.

Higher level programming languages include two of the most commonly used languages in Linux: Perl and Tcl/Tk, which are discussed in later modules in this book. With Perl you can easily create complex applications to manage files and manipulate text. With Tcl/Tk, you can create applications with GUIs that make use of windows, menus, and toolbars. Higher level languages are easy to learn, and they use simple commands to generate operations that would normally require extensive and complex C programs. As part of their free standard installation, all Linux distributions include support for shell programming, GAWK, Perl, Tcl/Tk, C and C++ programming, as well as the development support for GNOME and KDE (K Desktop Environment).

1

Note

The programming support may not be automatically installed on your computer when you install a distribution. Major distributions, such as Red Hat, Caldera, and SuSE, let you install programming support when you install the distribution software, as part of a development class of applications.

Because this is a Linux programming text that assumes many readers are already familiar with the basics of using Linux, this module begins with a discussion of various programming languages available in Linux. If you're new to Linux and want to learn more about the operating system before you dive deeper, you might want to start in the middle of this module at the section "More About Linux," and then you can come back to the beginning to learn more. Later on in the module, online resources for documentation, distributions, software, and newsgroups as well as Web sites with the latest news and articles on Linux are also presented. Near the end of the module, you'll find a table containing Web site listings. Here you can find sites for distributions, Linux publications, software repositories, and Linux programming development.

Linux Programming

Linux has been developed as a cooperative effort over the Internet. No company or institution controls Linux, and the software developed for Linux reflects this. Linux software development has always operated in an Internet environment. It is global in scope, enlisting programmers from around the world. The only thing you need to start a Linux-based software project is a Web site. Development often takes place when Linux users decide to work on a project together. When completed, the software is posted at an Internet site, where any user can access and download the software. Because of this active development environment, growth of new and increasingly functional Linux-based software is explosive.

Most Linux software is copyrighted under a GNU (which stands for GNU's not UNIX) public license provided by the Free Software Foundation and is often referred to as *GNU software* (see **www.gnu.org**). GNU software is distributed free and has proven to be very reliable and effective. Many of the popular Linux utilities, such as C compilers, shells, and editors, are GNU software applications.

Before it can be executed by the operating system, a Linux program needs to be transformed into lower level machine-language commands known as *binary code*. For example, when programming, you create a set of instructions using ordinary words that then need to be translated into binary code, which all fits together as an executable *application*. This translation can be carried out on the fly by an *interpreter,* or it can be explicitly generated all at once by a *compiler*. Most of the programming languages described in this book use an *interpreter*. The shell programming languages BASH, TCSH, GAWK, Perl, Tcl, and Tk use their own interpreters. Programs developed in these languages can be run directly as though the programs were application files. A compiler will create a separate application file containing the binary code that you can then execute—but we won't be dwelling on compilers in this book.

GNOME and KDE programming, which are also covered in this book, differ from this model greatly. GNOME and KDE programs are really C and C++ programs that need to be first compiled with the *gcc compiler* (the GNU C and C++ compiler). The gcc compiler will create an executable application file that you can then run. This means that you will need to know how to program in C if you want to use GNOME and for KDE you need to know C++.

BASH Shell Programming

A *shell program* combines Linux commands in such a way as to perform a specific task. The BASH shell provides many programming tools that you can use to create shell programs. You can define variables and assign values to them, and you can also define variables in a script file and have a user interactively enter values for them when the script is executed. The shell provides *loop* and *conditional control structures* that repeat Linux commands or make decisions on which commands you want to execute. You can also construct expressions that perform arithmetic or comparison operations. All these BASH shell programming tools operate similar to those found in other programming languages. You can find out more about BASH from your online Linux manual (at the command prompt, enter the **man** command with the term **bash**—like this: **man bash**) and from the GNU Web site at **www.gnu.org** (BASH is a GNU software product).

Two modules in this book deal with shell programming: one on shell programming basics such as declaring variables and running scripts, and the other on shell control structures that shows you how to use loops and

1

conditions to create complex programs. Usually, the instructions making up a shell program are entered into a script file that can then be executed. To run the shell program, you execute its script file. You can even distribute your program among several script files, one of which will contain instructions to execute others. You can think of variables, expressions, and control structures as tools you use to bring together several Linux commands into one operation. In this sense, a shell program is a new, complex Linux command that you have created.

You can control the execution of Linux commands in a shell program with control structures that allow you to repeat commands and select certain commands over others. A control structure consists of two major components: a *test* and *commands*. If the test is successful, the commands are executed. In this way, you can use control structures to make decisions about whether commands should be executed.

TCSH Shell Programming

The TCSH shell, like the BASH shell, also has programming language capabilities. You can

● Define variables and assign values to them.

● Place variable definitions and Linux commands in a script file and then execute that script.

● Use loop and conditional control structures to repeat Linux commands or make decisions on which commands you want to execute.

● Place traps in your program to handle interrupts.

You can find out more about TCSH from your online Linux manual (at the command prompt, enter the **man** command with the term **tcsh** (like so: **man tcsh**).

The TCSH shell differs from other Linux shells in that its control structures conform more to a programming language format. For example, the **test** condition for a TCSH shell's control structure is an expression that evaluates to true or false, not to a Linux command. In addition, a TCSH shell expression uses the same operators as those found in the C programming language, so you can perform a variety of assignment, arithmetic, relational, and bitwise operations. The TCSH shell also allows you to declare numeric variables that easily can be used in such operations.

GAWK

GAWK is a programming language designed to let Linux users create their own *filters*. A filter reads information from an input source such as a file or the standard input, modifies or analyzes that information, and then outputs the results. Results can be a modified version of the input or an analysis. For example, the **sort** filter reads a file and then outputs a sorted version of it. The **wc** filter reads a file and then calculates the number of words and lines in it, outputting just that information.

With GAWK, you can design and create your own filters—in effect creating your own Linux commands. You can instruct GAWK to display lines in a text file much like **cat** or to search for patterns like **grep**, or even to count words like **wc**. In each case, you could add your own customized filtering capabilities to your programs. You could, for example, display only part of each line, search for a pattern in a specific field, or count only words that are capitalized.

The GAWK utility has all the flexibility and complexity of a programming language. GAWK has a set of operators that allows you to program it to make decisions and calculations. You can also declare variables and use them in control structures to control how lines are to be processed. Many of the programming features are taken from the C programming language and share the same syntax. All of this makes for a very powerful programming tool. You can find out more about GAWK from your online Linux manual (enter the **man** command with the term **gawk**), and from the GNU's Web site at **www.gnu.org/software.gawk**.

Perl

Perl (Practical Extraction and Report Language) is a scripting language that was originally designed to operate on files to generate reports and handle very large files. You can think of Perl as the successor of GAWK and the BASH shell programming language. It includes many of the same capabilities but with greater power and flexibility. Perl was designed as a core program to which features could be easily added, and over the years, Perl's capabilities have been greatly enhanced. It can now control network connections and process interactions, and it even supports a variety of database management files. With Perl you can easily access files and manipulate strings, as well as manage arrays. At the same time, Perl remains completely portable—a Perl script will run on any Linux system. You can find out more about Perl at **www.perl.com.**

1

Tool Command Language (Tcl)

Tcl is a general-purpose command language developed by John Ousterhout in 1987 at the University of California, Berkeley. Originally designed to customize applications, it has become a fully functional language in its own right. As with Perl and GAWK, you can write Tcl scripts, developing your own Tcl programs. Tcl is a simple language to use. You can find out more about Tcl at **dev.scriptics.com**.

Tk and Expect are applications that extend the capabilities of the Tcl language. The Tk application allows you to easily develop graphical interactive applications. You can create your own windows and dialog boxes with buttons and text boxes of your choosing. The Expect application provides easy communication with interactive programs such as ftp and telnet.

Tcl is often used in conjunction with Tk to create graphical applications. Tk is used to create the graphical elements, while Tcl performs programming actions, such as managing user input. Like Java, Tcl and Tk are cross-platform applications. This means that a Tcl/Tk program will run on any platform that has the Tcl/Tk interpreter installed. Currently, Tcl/Tk versions exist for Windows, Macintosh, and UNIX systems, including Linux. You can write a Tcl application on Linux and run the same code in Windows or on a Macintosh.

Tcl is an *interpreted language* that operates, like Perl, within its own shell. To invoke the Tcl shell, you use the **tclsh** command. Within this shell, you can then execute Tcl commands. You can also create files within which you can invoke the Tcl shell and list Tcl commands, effectively creating a Tcl program.

Tk

The Tk application extends Tcl with commands for creating and managing graphical objects such as windows, icons, buttons, and text fields using the X Window System. You can find out more about Tk at **dev.scriptics.com.**

Within the X Window System, Tk uses its own shell, called the *wish shell*, to execute Tk commands. To run Tk programs, you must first start the X Window System and then start the wish shell using the command **wish**. You'll see a window in which you can then run Tk commands. If you are using a GUI such as Open Look or Motif, X Windows is automatically available.

GNOME Programming

The GNU Network Object Model Environment known as GNOME provides a powerful and easy-to-use desktop consisting primarily of a panel, a desktop, and a set of GUI tools with which you can construct program interfaces. Its aim is not just to provide a consistent interface, but also to provide a flexible platform for the development of powerful applications. You can find out more about GNOME programming at **developer.gnome.org**.

GTK+ is the *widget set* used for GNOME applications. Widgets are the buttons, icons, fields, and other objects that appear within an application's GUI. GTK+'s look and feel was originally derived from the Motif GUI (more about Motif later in this module), and this widget set was designed with power and flexibility in mind. For example, buttons can have labels, images, or any combination thereof. Objects can be dynamically queried and modified at run time. GTK+ also includes a *theme engine* that lets users change the look and feel of applications using the widgets. Even with all this capability, the GTK+ widget set remains small and efficient. It is entirely free under the Library General Public License (LGPL), which allows developers to use the set with proprietary as well as free software.

A GNOME program is essentially a C program that includes GTK+ functions as well as GNOME functions. Although not as easy to use as Tk, GNOME requires that you use only a few basic functions to create simple user interfaces. GNOME programming makes use of an extensive set of functions and structures contained in many libraries, which make up the different components that go into a GNOME application. You can think of GTK+ functions as lower level operations and GNOME functions as easy-to-use higher level operations. The GNOME functions usually incorporate several GTK+ functions, making GUI tasks easier to program. This module will provide only a general overview of these libraries and how you use them to create GNOME programs.

KDE Programming

KDE (the K Desktop Environment) is organized on a C++ object model: that is, C++ objects contain functions with which you can modify the object. Many of the functions are inherited, and others are defined for a particular type of object. In a KDE program, you define an object and then use its public and private functions to modify it. For example, you can create a menu object and then use the menu object's functions to add new menu items to it. As a C++ object-oriented program, KDE uses an extensive set of hierarchical object classes contained in the KDE and Qt libraries. Classes lower in the hierarchy will inherit members from connected classes higher in the hierarchy. You can create your own classes and they can inherit members (functions) from the predefined KDE classes. KDE uses the Qt toolkit and currently relies on it directly. (Qt is a toolkit of GUI functions developed and maintained by Trolltech.) The Qt Free Edition is used in KDE. Unlike GNOME, which can have its lower level functions managed by any toolkit, KDE relies solely on the Qt toolkit; in fact, KDE programming is essentially Qt programming.

For a complete listing of the KDE user interface classes, consult the documentation provided on the KDE developer's site, **developer.kde.org**. This site includes a detailed tutorial, and complete reference materials for the KDE API, as well as KOM (KDE Object Manager) documentation and Qt reference materials. Each class is described in detail along with the class type declaration, including its member function declarations and definitions. In addition, you should consult the KDE and Qt header files. The **.h** files contain a complete listing of the KDE and Qt classes along with detailed comments describing their member functions.

Ask the Expert

Question: What is the easiest way to create programs that use desktop elements like windows and menus?

Answer: Use Tk, the Tcl extension that supports GUI elements such as windows and toolbars. Enter the Tk commands in a script. Unlike GNOME and KDE programming, you do not need to know C or C++.

Question: What is the easiest way to write programs to manage text files?

Answer: Use Perl. It has excellent file handling capabilities. With a few simple commands, you can create, read from, or update files.

Question: What BASH shell commands would I use to create my own shell filters?

Answer: You would not use BASH shell commands to create shell filters. Use GAWK instead. GAWK is designed to work like a filter, but it includes a full range of programming capabilities.

1-Minute Drill

- **Do Linux shells provide programming capability?**
- **What languages can you use to create more complex programs?**
- **If you were interested in GUI programming on Linux, what would you use?**

More About Linux

An *operating system* is a program that manages computer hardware and software for the user. Operating systems were originally designed to perform repetitive hardware tasks that centered around managing files, running programs, and receiving commands from the user. You interact with an operating system through a *user interface*. This user interface allows the operating system to receive and interpret instructions sent by the user. An operating system's user interface can be as simple as entering commands on a line or as complex as selecting menus and icons on a desktop.

An operating system also manages software applications. To perform different tasks, such as editing documents or performing calculations, specific software applications are needed. An editor is an example of a software application. An editor allows you to edit a document, making changes and adding new text. The editor is a program that consists of instructions to be executed by the computer. To use the program, it must be loaded into computer memory and then its instructions executed. The operating system controls the loading and execution of all programs, including any software applications. When you want to use an editor, you simply instruct the operating system to load the editor application and execute it.

File management, program management, and user interaction are traditional features common to all operating systems. Linux, like all versions of UNIX, adds two features: the multitasking and multiuser features. As a multitasking system, you can ask the system to perform several tasks

---

- **Yes; both BASH and TCSH are discussed in this book.**
- **GAWK, Perl, and Tcl.**
- **Tk, GNOME, and KDE.**

simultaneously. For example, you can edit a file while another file is being printed. As a multiuser system, several users can log in to the system at the same time, each interacting with the system through his or her terminal.

Operating systems were originally designed to support hardware efficiency. When computers were first developed, their capabilities were limited and the operating system had to make the most of them. In this respect, operating systems were designed with the hardware in mind, not the user. Operating systems tended to be rigid and inflexible, forcing the user to conform to the demands of hardware efficiency.

Linux, on the other hand, is designed to be flexible, reflecting its UNIX roots. This flexibility allows Linux to be an operating system that is accessible to the user. Rather than the user being confined to limited and rigid interactions with the operating system, the operating system provides a set of highly effective tools for the user. This user-oriented philosophy means that you can configure and program the system to meet your specific needs. With Linux, the operating system becomes an *operating environment*.

Linux is a PC version of the UNIX operating system that has been used for decades on mainframes and minicomputers and is currently the system of choice for workstations. Linux brings the speed, efficiency, and flexibility of UNIX to your PC, taking advantage of all the capabilities that today's personal computers can provide. Along with its UNIX capabilities, Linux offers powerful networking features, including support for Internet, intranet, Windows, and AppleTalk networking. As a standard, Linux is distributed with fast, efficient, and stable Internet servers such as the Web, FTP, and mail servers, along with domain name, proxy, news, mail, and indexing servers. In other words, Linux has everything you need to set up, support, and maintain a full functional network.

Now with the inclusion of both GNOME and the KDE, Linux also provides GUIs with an extremely high level of flexibility and power: unlike Windows and the Mac, you can choose the interface you want and then customize it, adding panels, applets, virtual desktops, and menus—all with full drag-and-drop capabilities and Internet-aware tools. On your desktop, a file manager window can access any Internet site, letting you display Web pages and download files with a few simple mouse operations.

Linux does all this at a great price: it is *free*, including the network servers and GUI desktops. Unlike the official UNIX operating system, Linux is distributed freely under a GNU General Public License as specified by the

Free Software Foundation, and it's available to anyone who wants to use it. Although Linux is copyrighted, its GNU public license basically makes Linux in the public domain. The license is designed to ensure that Linux remains free and, at the same time, standardized, so there is only one *official* Linux. The GNU project was initiated and is managed by the Free Software Foundation to provide free software to users, programmers, and developers. The list of software available under the GNU Public License is extensive, and it includes environments, programming languages, Internet tools, and text editors.

Before Linux, There Was UNIX

To truly appreciate Linux, you need to understand the special context in which the UNIX operating system was developed. Unlike most other operating systems, UNIX was developed in a research and academic environment. In universities and research laboratories, UNIX is the system of choice. Its development paralleled the entire computer and communications revolution that has occurred over the past several decades. Computer professionals often developed new computer technologies on UNIX, such as those developed for the Internet. Though a very sophisticated system, UNIX was designed from the beginning to be flexible. The UNIX system can be easily modified to create different versions. In fact, many vendors maintain their own official versions of UNIX: IBM, Sun, and Hewlett-Packard all sell and maintain their own versions. People involved in research programs will often create their own versions of UNIX, tailored to their own special needs. This inherent flexibility in the UNIX design in no way detracts from its quality; in fact, it attests to its ruggedness, allowing it to adapt practically to any environment.

Ask the Expert

Question: Because Linux is free, does this indicate that it is not as good as other operating systems, like Windows?

Answer: Definitely not. The fact that Linux is free sometimes gives people the mistaken impression that it is somehow less than a professional operating system. Linux is, in fact, a PC and workstation version of UNIX. Many consider it far more stable and much more powerful than Windows. It is this power and stability that has made it an operating system of choice as a network server.

It is in this context that Linux was developed. Linux is, in this sense, another version of UNIX—a version for the PC. Its development by computer professionals working in a research-like environment reflects the way UNIX versions have usually been developed.

─┤Note ──────────────────────────

The fact that Linux is publicly licensed and free reflects the deep roots that UNIX has in academic institutions, with their sense of public service and support. Linux is a top-rate operating system accessible to everyone, free of charge.

How UNIX Came to Be

As a version of UNIX, Linux's history naturally begins with UNIX. The story begins in the late 1960s during a concerted effort to develop new operating system techniques. In 1968, a consortium of researchers from General Electric, AT&T Bell Laboratories, and the Massachusetts Institute of Technology carried out a special operating system research project called MULTICS (MULTiplexed Information Computing System). MULTICS incorporated many new concepts in multitasking, file management, and user interaction. In 1969, Ken Thompson, Dennis Ritchie, and the researchers at AT&T Bell Laboratories developed the UNIX operating system, incorporating many of the features developed by the MULTICS research project. They tailored the system for the needs of a research environment, designing it to run on minicomputers. From its inception, UNIX was an affordable and efficient multiuser and multitasking operating system.

The UNIX system became popular at Bell Labs as more and more researchers started using the system. In 1973, Ritchie and Thompson rewrote the programming code for the UNIX system in the C programming language. Ritchie developed the C programming language as a flexible tool for program development. One of the advantages of C is that it can directly access the hardware architecture of a computer with a generalized set of programming commands. Until this time, an operating system had to be specially rewritten in a hardware-specific assembly language for each type of computer. The C programming language allowed the researchers to write only one version of the UNIX operating system that could then be compiled by C compilers on different computers. In effect, the UNIX operating system became transportable—able to run on a variety of different computers with little or no reprogramming.

UNIX gradually grew from one person's tailored design to a standard software product distributed by many different vendors, such as Novell and IBM. Initially, UNIX was treated as a research product. The first versions of UNIX were distributed free to the computer science departments of many noted universities. Throughout the 1970s, Bell Labs began issuing official versions of UNIX and licensing the systems to different users. One of these users was the Computer Science department of the University of California, Berkeley. UC Berkeley added many new features to the system that later became standard. In 1975, UC Berkeley released its own version of UNIX, known by its distribution arm, Berkeley Software Distribution (BSD). This BSD version of UNIX became a major contender to the AT&T Bell Labs version. Other independently developed versions of UNIX sprouted up. In 1980, Microsoft developed a PC version of UNIX called Xenix. AT&T developed several research versions of UNIX, and in 1983 it released its first commercial version, called System 3. This was later followed by System V, which became a supported commercial software product.

At the same time, the BSD version of UNIX was developing through several releases. In the late 1970s, BSD UNIX became the basis of a research project by the Department of Defense's Advanced Research Projects Agency (DARPA). As a result, in 1983, Berkeley released a powerful version of UNIX called BSD release 4.2. It included sophisticated file management as well as networking features based on TCP/IP network protocols—the same protocols now used for the Internet. BSD release 4.2 was widely distributed and adopted by many vendors, such as Sun Microsystems.

The proliferation of different versions of UNIX led to a need for a UNIX standard. Software developers had no way of knowing what versions of UNIX their programs would actually run on. In the mid-1980s, two competing standards emerged, one based on the AT&T version of UNIX and the other on the BSD version. In bookstores today you will see many different books on UNIX for one or the other version. Some specify System V UNIX, while others focus on BSD UNIX.

AT&T moved UNIX to a new organization, called UNIX System Laboratories, that could focus on developing a standard system, integrating the different major versions of UNIX. In 1991, UNIX System Laboratories developed System V release 4, which incorporated almost all the features found in the System V release 3, BSD release 4.3, SunOS, and Xenix. In response to System V release 4, several other companies, such as IBM and Hewlett-Packard, established the Open Software Foundation (OSF) to create their own standard version of UNIX. There were then two commercial standard versions of UNIX—the OSF version and System V release 4. In 1993, AT&T sold off its interest in UNIX to Novell, and UNIX Systems Laboratories became part of Novell's UNIX Systems Group. Novell issued its own versions of UNIX based on System V release 4, called UnixWare, designed to interact with Novell's NetWare system. UNIX Systems Laboratories is currently owned by the Santa Cruz Operation. With Solaris, Sun has introduced System V release 4 onto its Sun systems. Two competing GUIs for UNIX, called Motif and Open-Look, have been merged into a new desktop standard called the Common Desktop Environment (CDE).

Throughout much of its development, UNIX remained a large and demanding operating system requiring a workstation or minicomputer to be effective. Several versions of UNIX were designed primarily for the workstation environment. SunOS was developed for Sun workstations, and AIX was designed for IBM workstations. However, as personal computers became more powerful, efforts were made to develop a PC version of UNIX. Xenix and System V/386 are commercial versions of UNIX designed for IBM–compatible PCs. AUX is a UNIX version that runs on the Macintosh. It is a testament to UNIX's inherent portability that it can be found on almost any type of computer: workstations, minicomputers, and even supercomputers. This inherent portability made possible an effective PC version of UNIX.

Enter Linux

Linux was originally designed specifically for Intel-based personal computers. It started out as a personal project of a computer science student named Linus Torvalds at the University of Helsinki. At that time, students were making use of a program called Minix that highlighted different UNIX features. Minix was created by Professor Andrew Tannebaum and was widely distributed over the Internet to students around the world. Torvalds's intention was to create an effective PC version of UNIX for Minix users. He called it Linux, and in 1991 released version 0.11.

Linux was widely distributed over the Internet, and in the following years other programmers refined and added to it, incorporating most of the applications and features now found in standard UNIX systems. All the major window managers have been ported to Linux. Linux has all the Internet utilities, such as FTP, telnet, and SLIP. It also has a full set of program development utilities, such as C++ compilers and debuggers.

Note

Given all its features, the Linux operating system remains small, stable, and fast. In its simplest format, it can run effectively on just 4MB of memory.

Though Linux has developed in the free and open environment of the Internet, it adheres to official UNIX standards. Due to the proliferation of UNIX versions in the previous decades, the Institute of Electrical and Electronics Engineers (IEEE) developed an independent UNIX standard for the American National Standards Institute (ANSI). This new ANSI-standard UNIX is called the Portable Operating System Interface for Computer Environments (POSIX). The standard defines how a UNIX-like system needs to operate, specifying details such as system calls and interfaces. POSIX defines a universal standard to which all UNIX versions must adhere. Most popular versions of UNIX are now POSIX compliant. Linux was developed from the beginning according to the POSIX standard.

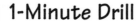

1-Minute Drill

● **How much does Linux cost?**

● **Can more than one user work on a single Linux system at the same time?**

● **What operating system was Linux based on?**

Linux Anatomy: Shells, Directories, and Desktops

Like UNIX, Linux can be divided into three major components: the kernel, the shell, and the file structure. The *kernel* is the core program that runs other programs and manages hardware devices such as disks and printers. The *environment* provides an interface for the user. It receives commands from the user and sends those commands to the kernel for execution. The *file structure* organizes the way files are stored on a storage

---

● **It's free**
● **Yes, it is multi-user**
● **UNIX**

device such as a disk. Files are organized into directories. Each directory may contain any number of subdirectories, each holding files. Together, the kernel, the environment, and the file structure form the basic operating system structure. With these three, you can run programs, manage files, and interact with the system.

An environment provides an interface between the kernel and the user. It can be described as an interpreter. It interprets commands entered by the user and sends them to the kernel. Linux provides several kinds of environments: desktops, window managers, and command line shells. Users can tailor their environments to their own special needs, whether they be shells, window managers, or desktops. In this sense, for the user, the operating system functions more as an operating environment that the user can control.

The shell interface is very simple. It usually consists of a prompt at which you type a command and then press ENTER on the keyboard. In a sense, you are typing the command on the *command line*. You will find that the commands entered on the command line can become very complex. Over the years, several different kinds of shells have been developed. Currently, there are three major shells: Bourne, Korn, and C-shell. The Bourne shell was developed at Bell Labs for System V. The Korn shell is a further enhancement of the Bourne shell. The C-shell was developed for the BSD version of UNIX. Current versions of UNIX, including Linux, incorporate all three shells, allowing you to choose the one you prefer. However, Linux uses enhanced or public domain versions of these shells: the Bourne Again shell, the TC-shell, and the Public Domain Korn shell, among others. When you start your Linux system, you will be placed in the Bourne Again shell, an updated version of the Bourne shell. From there, you can switch to other shells as you wish.

As an alternative to a command line interface, Linux provides both desktops and window managers. These use GUIs based on the X Window System developed for UNIX by the Open Group consortium (**www.opengroup.org** and **www.X11.org**). A window manager is a reduced version of a desktop that supports only window operation but still lets you run any application. A desktop provides a complete GUI, much like Windows and the Mac. You have windows, icons, and menus, all managed through mouse controls. Currently, two desktops are freely available and included with most distributions of Linux: GNOME and KDE.

In Linux, files are organized into directories, much as they are in Windows. The entire Linux file system is one large interconnected set of directories, each containing files. Some directories are standard directories reserved for system use. You can create your own directories for your own files, as well as easily move files from one directory to another. You can even move entire directories and share directories and files with other users on your system. With Linux, you can also set permissions on directories and files, allowing others to access them or restricting access to you alone.

The directories of each user are in fact ultimately connected to the directories of other users. Directories are organized into a hierarchical tree structure, beginning with an initial root directory. All other directories are ultimately derived from this first root directory. You can actually travel throughout the system, entering any directory that may be open to you. This interconnectivity of the file structure makes it easy to share data—several users could access the same files.

The root directory is a special directory that you will need to make use of when you first set up your Linux system. Linux is a multiuser system: several users can share the same operating system. However, the operating system itself resides in programs placed in special directories beginning with the root directory. These are sometimes referred to as *system directories*.

With the KDE and GNOME, Linux now has a completely integrated GUI. You can perform all your Linux operations entirely from either interface. Previously, Linux did support window managers that provided some GUI functionality, but they were usually restricted to window operations. KDE and GNOME are fully operational desktops supporting drag-and-drop operations, letting you drag icons to your desktop and set up your own menus on an Applications panel. Both rely on an underlying X Window System, which means that as long as they are both installed on your system, applications from one can run on the other desktop. You can run KDE programs, such as the KDE mailer or newsreader, on the GNOME desktop. GNOME applications such as the Gftp FTP client can run on the KDE desktop. You can even switch file managers, running the KDE file manager on GNOME—you will lose some desktop functionality, such as drag-and-drop operations, but the applications will run fine.

Both desktops can run any X Window System program as well as any cursor-based program such as Emacs and Vi, which were designed to work in a shell environment. At the same time, a great many applications were written just for those desktops and included with your distributions.

1

The K Desktop has a complete set of Internet tools along with editors and graphics, multimedia, and system applications. GNOME has slightly fewer applications, but a great many are currently in the works. Check their Web sites at **www.gnome.org** and **www.kde.org** for new applications. As new versions are released, they will include new software.

1-Minute Drill

● **What are the three major components that make up the Linux operating system?**

● **What are the desktops most often used on Linux systems?**

● **How are directories organized?**

Linux Distributions

Although there is only one standard version of Linux, there are actually several different releases. Different companies and groups have packaged Linux and Linux software in slightly different ways. Each company or group then releases the Linux package, usually on a CD-ROM. Later releases may include updated versions of programs or new software. Some of the more popular releases are Red Hat, OpenLinux, SuSE, and Debian.

Note

Several distributions, such as Caldera and Red Hat, also offer their systems bundled with commercial software.

Red Hat

Red Hat Linux is currently the most popular Linux distribution. It originated the RPM package system used on several distributions that automatically installs and removes software packages. Red Hat is also providing much of the software development for the GNOME desktop. However, it also supports KDE. Its distribution includes both GNOME

● **Kernel, environment, and file structure**
● **GNOME and KDE**
● **Tree structure**

and KDE. Red Hat, like Caldera OpenLinux, maintains software alliances with major companies like Oracle, IBM, and Sun. The Red Hat distribution of Linux is available online at **www.redhat.com**.

OpenLinux

Caldera OpenLinux is designed for corporate commercial use. OpenLinux Linux system and software packages including all the GNU software packages, as well as the X Windows managers, Internet servers, WordPerfect, and the K Desktop. However, it does not presently include GNOME. It is POSIX compliant, adhering to UNIX standards. Caldera distributes its OpenLinux system free of charge. Caldera also offers a line of commercial and proprietary Linux packages. Such proprietary, licensed software packages are not freely distributable. They include such products as Partition Magic, Star Office, AdabasD database, and the Novell NetWare client. See the Caldera Web site at **www.calderasystems.com** for more information. Presently, it supports only the Intel platform.

SuSE

Originally a German language–based distribution, SuSE has become very popular throughout Europe and is currently one of the fastest growing distributions worldwide. Its current distribution includes both KDE and GNOME. Its distributions include WordPerfect, Star Office, and KOffice. It also bundles commercial products like AdabasD and the Linux Office Suite. Currently, it supports only Intel platforms. For more information, see **www.suse.com**.

Debian

Debian Linux is an entirely noncommercial project, maintained by a group of volunteer programmers. It does, however, incorporate support for commercial products in its distribution. Debian currently maintains software associations with Corel and Sun, among others. Currently it supports Alpha, Intel, Mac 86K, and Sparc platforms. For more information, see **www.debian.org**.

Slackware

Slackware is available from numerous Internet sites, and you can order the CD from Walnut Creek Software. It includes both GNOME and KDE.

1

The Slackware distribution takes special care to remain as closely UNIX compliant as possible. Currently, it supports only Intel platforms. See **www.slackware.com** for more information.

Infomagic

The Infomagic distributes bundled sets of Linux software. The Linux Developers Resource set includes the four major distributions: Red Hat, OpenLinux, SuSE, and Slackware. The Linux Archive set contains mirrors of Linux archive sites including KDE, GNOME, XFree86, and GNU. Currently it supports only the Intel platform. See **www.infomagic.com** for more information.

LinuxPPC

The LinuxPPC distribution provides versions of Linux designed exclusively for use on PowerPC machines. The distribution will run on any PowerPC machine, including IBM, Motorola, and Apple systems (including G4 and iMac machines). It provides support for the USB on Mac systems. Its current distribution includes the GNOME desktop and the Enlightenment window manager. See **www.linuxppc.com** for more information.

TurboLinux

TurboLinux is distributed by Pacific HiTech, providing English, Chinese, and Japanese versions. It includes several of its own packages such as TurboPkg for automatically updating applications, the TurboDesk desktop, and the Cluster Web Server. Like Red Hat, it supports RPM packages. It is currently widely distributed in East Asia. Currently, TurboLinux supports only the Intel platform, but a PowerPC version is in development. See **www.turbolinux.com** for more information.

Mandrake

Mandrake Linux is another popular Linux distribution with many of the same features as Red Hat. It focuses on providing up-to-date enhancements and an easy-to-use installation and GUI configuration. You can learn more about Mandrake at **www.linux-mandrake.com**.

Linux Resources

Extensive online resources are available on almost any Linux topic. The following tables list sites where you can obtain software, display documentation, and read articles on the latest developments. Different sites of interest are listed for Linux programming, including Perl, Tcl/Tk, and the GNOME and KDE sites (see Table 1-1). For BASH and GAWK, you can find online documentation and information at the GNU Web site at **www.gnu.org**. At **www.linuxprogramming.com** and at **www.linuxworld.com** you can find recent articles on Linux programming topics.

Distribution FTP and Web sites such as **www.calderasystems.com** and **www.redhat.com** provide extensive Linux documentation and software (see Table 1-2). You can find other sites through resource pages that hold links to other Web sites.

Linux documentation has also been developed over the Internet (as shown in Table 1-3). Much of the documentation currently available for Linux can be downloaded from Internet FTP sites. A special Linux project called the Linux Documentation Project (LDP), headed by Matt Welsh, is currently developing a complete set of Linux manuals. The documentation, at its current level, is available at the LDP home site at **http://metalab.unc.edu/LDP/**. The documentation includes a user's guide, an introduction, and administration guides. They are available in text, PostScript, or Web page format. Table 1-3 lists these guides. You can find briefer explanations in what are referred to as HOW-TO documents. HOW-TO documents are available for different subjects, such as installation, printing, and e-mail. The documents are available at Linux FTP sites, *usually* in the directory **/pub/Linux/doc/HOW-TO**.

Many Linux Web sites provide news, articles, and information about Linux. Several are based on popular Linux magazines such as *Linux Journal* (**www2.linuxjournal.com/**) and *Linux Gazette* (**http://isisesc.supelec.fr/lg/**) (see Table 1-4). Others operate as Web portals for Linux, such as **www.linux.com**, **www.linuxworld.com**, and **www.linux.org**. Some specialize in particular topics like **www.kernelnotes.org** for news on the Linux kernel and **www.linuxgames.com** for the latest games ported for Linux. The **www.gnome.org** site holds software and documentation for the GNOME desktop, and **www.kde.org** holds software and documentation for the KDE desktop.

URL	Internet Sites
www.gnu.org	GNU Web site with support for BASH and GAWK
www.perl.com	Perl Web site with Perl software
dev.scriptics.com	Tk and Tcl development and resources
developer.gnome.org	GNOME developers Web site
developer.kde.org	Developer's library for KDE
www.blackdown.org	Sun's Java Development Kit for Linux
www.openprojects.nu	Open Projects Network
www.linuxprogramming.org	Linux programming resources

Table 1-1   Linux Programming Sites

Through your Internet connection, you can also access Linux newsgroups
to read the comments of other Linux users and post messages of your own.
There are several Linux newsgroups, each beginning with **comp.os.linux**.
One of particular interest to the beginner is **comp.os.linux.help**, where
you can post questions. For programming topics, you can find information
on **comp.os.linux.development**. There are also an extensive number
of development newsgroups beginning with **linux.dev**, such as
linux.dev.admin and **linux.dev.doc**. Table 1-5 lists the different
Linux newsgroups available on Usenet.

URL	Internet Site
www.redhat.com	Red Hat Linux
www.calderasystems.com	Caldera OpenLinux
www.suse.com	SuSE Linux
www.debian.org	Debian Linux
www.infomagic.com	Infomagic
www.linuxppc.com	LinuxPPC (Mac PowerPC version)
www.turbolinux.com	TurboLinux (Pacific Hi-Tech)
www.slackware.com	Slackware Linux Project
www.kernel.org	The Linux Kernel
www.linux-mandrake.com	Mandrake
java.sun.com	Sun Java Web site

Table 1-2   Linux Distributions and Kernel Sites

Sites	Description
http://metalab.unc.edu/LDP/	LDP Web site
ftp://metalab.unc.edu/pub/linux/docs/LDP/	LDP FTP site
Guides	**Document Format and Web Sites**
Linux Installation and Getting Started Guide	DVI, PostScript, LaTeX, PDF, and HTML
Linux User's Guide	DVI, PostScript, HTML, LaTeX, and PDF
Linux System Administrator's Guide	PostScript, PDF, LaTeX, and HTML
Linux Network Administrator's Guide	DVI, PostScript, PDF, and HTML
Linux Programmer's Guide	DVI, PostScript, PDF, LaTeX, and HTML
The Linux Kernel	HTML, LaTeX, DVI, and PostScript
Linux Kernel Hacker's Guide	DVI, PostScript and HTML
Linux HOWTOs	HTML, PostScript, SGML, and DVI
Linux FAQs	HTML, PostScript, and DVI
Linux Man Pages	Man page format

Table 1-3   Linux Documentation Project Sites and Guides

URL	Internet Site
www.linuxdoc.org/	Web site for Linux Documentation Project
www.lwn.net	Linux Weekly News
www.linux.com	Linux.com
www.linuxtoday.com	Linux Today
www.linuxpower.org	Linux Power
www.linuxfocus.org	Linux Focus
www.linuxmagazine.com	Linux Magazine
www.linuxworld.com	Linux World
www.linuxmall.com	Linux Mall
www2.linuxjournal.com	Linux Journal
http://isisesc.supelec.fr/lg/	Linux Gazette
www.linux.org	Linux Online
www.li.org	Linux International Web site
www.linux.org.uk	Linux European Web site
www.kernelnotes.org	Latest news on the Linux kernel
www.slashdot.org	Linux forum
www.webwatcher.org	Linux Web site watcher

Table 1-4   Linux Information and News Sites

1

Newsgroup	Content
linux.dev.*group*	There are an extensive number of development newsgroups beginning with **linux.dev**, such as **linux.dev.admin** and **linux.dev.doc**
comp.os.linux.devlopment	For programmers developing Linux applications
comp.os.linux.devlopment.apps	For programmers developing Linux applications
comp.os.linux.devlopment.system	For programmers working on the Linux operating system
comp.os.linux.announce	Announcements of Linux developments
comp.os.linux.hardware	Linux hardware specifications
comp.os.linux.admin	System administration questions
comp.os.linux.misc	Special questions and issues
comp.os.linux.setup	Installation problems
comp.os.linux.answers	Answers to command problems
comp.os.linux.help	Questions and answers for particular problems
comp.os.linux.networking	Linux network questions and issues

Table 1-5   Usenet Newsgroups

Mastery Check

1. What are the four general categories of Linux programming?

2. Can you create GUI programs without programming desktops like GNOME and KDE?

3. What programming language would you use to create filters?

4. What programming tasks require that you know another language?

5. What institution created Linux?

Module 2

BASH Shell Scripts

The Goals of This Module

- Develop BASH shell programs
- Manage shell input and output
- Use shell operators for arithmetic, comparison, and assignment operations
- Manage shell arguments and their options
- Develop a shell program using multiple scripts
- Learn to export variables to subshells

A *shell program* combines Linux commands in such a way as to perform a specific task. A shell is like a command interpreter—it serves as a liaison between the user and the operating system. When you log in to your account, your Linux system generates your user shell. The primary shell used on Linux systems is the BASH shell. BASH stands for Bourne Again Shell and is based on the original Bourne shell used in UNIX systems.

The BASH shell provides many programming tools that you can use to create shell programs. You can define variables and assign values to them. You can also define variables in a script file and have a user interactively enter values for them when the script is executed. The shell provides loop and conditional control structures that repeat Linux commands or make decisions on which commands you want to execute. You can also construct expressions that perform arithmetic or comparison operations. All these BASH shell programming tools operate in ways similar to those found in other programming languages, so if you're already familiar with coding, you might find BASH simple to learn.

This module will cover the basics of creating a shell program using the BASH shell, the shell used on most Linux systems. You will learn how to create your own scripts, define shell variables, and develop user interfaces, as well as the more difficult task of combining control structures to create complex programs. Tables throughout the module list BASH shell commands and operators, while numerous examples show how they are implemented.

Usually, the instructions making up a shell program are entered into a script file that can then be executed. To run the shell program, you execute its script file. You can even distribute your program among several script files, one of which will contain instructions on how to execute others. You can think of variables, expressions, and control structures as tools you use to bring together several Linux commands into one operation. In this sense, a shell program is a new and complex Linux command that you have created.

The BASH shell has a flexible and powerful set of programming commands that allow you to build complex scripts. It supports variables that can be either local to the given shell or exported to other shells. You can pass *arguments* from one script to another. The BASH shell has a complete set of control structures, including loops and if statements, as well as case structures—all of which you'll learn about as you read this book. All shell commands interact easily with redirection and piping operations that allow them to accept input from the standard input or send it to the standard output. Unlike the Bourne shell, the first shell used for UNIX, BASH incorporates many of the features of the TCSH and Z shells. Arithmetic operations in particular are easier to perform in BASH.

Shell Scripts: Commands and Comments

A *shell script* is a text file that contains Linux commands that you enter using any standard editor, such as vi, emacs, WordPerfect, or any of the GNOME or KDE text editors. There are several ways to run a shell script. One way to do this is to precede the name of the shell script with a period, as shown next. The shell will read the commands in shell scripts and execute them. In this example, the name of the script is *hello*. The period (.) symbol instructs Linux to execute this script.

```
$ . hello.
```

You can also make the script file itself executable, or "runable," and use its name directly on the command line in the same way that you would use the name of any command.

The following shows the *hello* script (in bold) and its output. Script and output will be shown in this way throughout this book.

```
$ hello
Hello, how are you
$
```

You may have to specify that the script you are using is in your current working directory. You do this by prefixing the script name with a period and slash combination, **./**, as in **./hello**. The following example shows how you would execute the *hello* script.

```
$ ./hello
Hello, how are you
$
```

In a script file, it is often helpful to include short explanations describing the file's task as well as the purpose of certain commands and variables. You can enter such explanations using *comments*. A comment can appear in any line or part of a line—with the exception of the first line—and is preceded by a number sign (#). You can't use comments in the first line of your script file, because this line is reserved for shell identification. Any characters entered following a number sign will be ignored by the shell. In the next example, a comment describing the name and function of the script is placed at the head of the file.

The content of the *hello* script with an initial command line is shown here:

```
# The hello script says hello

echo "Hello, how are you"
```

Setting Permissions: Permission Symbols

Before you can run a script directly, you need to make it executable. You do this by turning on the script's execute permission. Each file in Linux has a set of three possible permissions: read, write, and execute. You can turn these on or off using the **chmod** command and the appropriate options. These options are the characters *r*, *w*, and *x* for read, write, and execute, respectively. Any of these permissions can be added or removed. The symbol used to add a permission is the plus sign (+). The symbol to remove a permission is the minus sign (−). In the next example, the **chmod** command adds the execute permission and removes the write permission for the *mydata* file. The read permission is not changed.

```
$ chmod +x-w mydata
```

There are also permission symbols that specify each user category. The owner, group, and others categories are represented by the *u*, *g*, and *o* characters, respectively. Notice that the owner category is represented by a *u* and can be thought of as the user. The symbol for a category is placed before the read, write, and execute permissions. If no category symbol is used, all categories are assumed, and the permissions specified are set for the user, group, and others. In the next example, the first **chmod** command sets the permissions for the group to read and write. The second **chmod** command sets permissions for other users to read. Notice that there are no spaces between the permission specifications and the category. The permissions list is simply one long phrase, with no spaces.

```
$ chmod g+rw mydata
$ chmod o+r mydata
```

A user may remove permissions as well as add them. In the next example, the read permission is set for other users, but the write and execute permissions are removed.

```
$ chmod o+r-wx hello
```

Another permission symbol, *a*, represents all the categories. The *a* symbol is the default. In the next example, both commands are equivalent. The read permission is explicitly set with the *a* symbol, denoting all types of users: other, group, and user.

```
$ chmod a+r hello
$ chmod +r hello
```

The executable permission indicates that a file contains executable instructions and can be directly run by the system. In the next example, the file **lsc** has its executable permission set and then executed.

```
$ chmod u+x hello
$ hello
Hello, how are you
$
```

The **chmod** commands and options are shown in Table 2-1.

Command	Execution
chmod	Changes the permission of a file or directory.
Options	
+	Adds a permission.
−	Removes a permission.
r	Sets read permission for a file or directory. A file can be displayed or printed. A directory can have the list of its files displayed.
w	Sets write permission for a file or directory. A file can be edited or erased. A directory can be removed.
x	Sets execute permission for a file or directory. If the file is a shell script, it can be executed as a program. A directory can be changed to and entered.
u	Sets permissions for the user who created and owns the file or directory.
g	Sets permissions for group access to a file or directory.
o	Sets permissions for access to a file or directory by all other users on the system.
a	Sets permissions for access by the user, group, and all other users.

Table 2-1   chmod **Commands and Options**

Ask the Expert

Question: Can I run a BASH shell script in a different shell, such as the TCSH shell?

Answer: Yes, you can. You may want to be able to execute a script that is written for one of the Linux shells while you are working in another. Suppose, for example, that you are currently working in the TCSH shell and you want to execute a script you wrote in the BASH shell that contains BASH shell commands. First you would have to change to the BASH shell using the **sh** command, and then you could execute the script and change back to the TCSH shell.

You can, however, automate this process by placing the number and exclamation point characters (**#!**) as the first characters in your script, followed by the path name for the shell program on your system. This signals to the TCSH shell that you want to switch and issue BASH shell commands while still working in the TCSH shell. Here's an example:

```
#!/bin/bash
```

Question: **How does the script know what shell it should use?**

Answer: Your shell always examines the first character of a script to determine what type of script it is, such as BASH, PDKSH, or TCSH shell script. Here's the lowdown on each of the characters that can begin a script:

- **Single space**   The script is assumed to be either a BASH or PDKSH shell script.

- **#**   The script is a TCSH shell script.

- **#!**   Your shell reads the path name of a shell program that follows.

The characters **#!** should always be followed by the path name of a shell program that identifies the type of shell the script works in. If you are currently working in a different shell, that shell will read the path name of the shell program, change to the indicated shell, and execute your script. If you are in a shell other than BASH or TCSH, the single space or **#** character alone is not enough to identify the type of script. Such identification works only within the BASH or TCSH shell, respectively. To identify a script from a different shell, you must include the **#!** characters followed by a path name for the shell.

For example, if you include **#!/bin/sh** at the beginning of the first line of the *hello* script, you could execute this BASH shell code directly from the TCSH shell. The script will change to the BASH shell, execute its commands, and then return to the TCSH shell (or whatever type of shell it was executed from). In the next example, the *hello* script includes the **#!/bin/sh** command. The script is executed while the programmer is still working in the TCSH shell.

```
#!/bin/bash

# The hello script says hello

echo "Hello, how are you"
```

Variables and Scripts

Within the shell, you can create shell programs (programs within the program) using variables and scripts. When you execute a script file, you initiate a new process that has its own shell. Within this shell, you can define variables, execute Linux commands, and even execute other scripts.

A *variable* is a reference to a location that contains data that can be modified during program execution. Within a shell program, you can define variables and assign values to them. A variable is defined in a shell the first time you use the variable's name. Following are the rules for using a variable:

- A variable name may be any set of alphabetic characters, including the underscore character.

- The name may also include a number.

- A variable name may not include any other type of character, such as an exclamation point, ampersand, or even a space. Such symbols are reserved by the shell for its own use.

- A variable name may not include more than one word, because a shell uses spaces to parse commands, delimiting command names and arguments.

Variable definitions are used in shell programs for many purposes. Variables are used extensively in script input and output operations. The **read** command, for example, allows the user to interactively enter a value for a variable. Often, **read** is combined with a prompt notifying the user when to enter a response.

Evaluation of Variables: = and $

You assign a value to a variable with the *assignment operator*. Type the variable name, the assignment operator, and the equal sign (=), and then enter the

2

value assigned. Any set of characters can be assigned to a variable. In this example, the greeting variable is assigned the string "Hello":

```
$ greeting="Hello"
```

Note

Do not use spaces around an assignment operator.

Once you have assigned a value to a variable, you can use that variable to reference the value. For example, you might often use the values of variables as arguments for a command. You can reference the value of a variable using the variable name preceded by the dollar sign (**$**) operator. The dollar sign is a special operator that uses a variable name to reference a variable's value—in effect, *evaluating* the variable. Evaluation retrieves a variable's *value*—a set of characters. This set of characters replaces the variable name on the command line. Thus, wherever a **$** is placed before the variable name, the variable name is replaced with the value of the variable.

In the next example, the shell variable *greeting* is evaluated and its contents, "Hello," are then used as the argument for an **echo** command. (The **echo** command simply echoes or prints a set of characters to the screen.)

```
$ echo $greeting
Hello
```

Hint

You can obtain a list of all the defined variables by using the **set** command. If you decide that you do not want a certain variable, you can remove it with the **unset** command.

Variable Values: Strings

You know that the values that you assign to variables may consist of any set of characters. These characters may be a *character string* that you explicitly type in, or they may appear as the result of executing a Linux command. In most cases, you will need to surround these values with single quotes, double quotes, backslashes, or back quotes to set them apart from executable code.

Quoting Strings and Characters with Double Quotes, Single Quotes, and Backslashes

Although variable values can comprise any characters, problems occur when you include characters that are also used by the shell as *operators*. Your shell uses special characters in evaluating the command line. For example,

Character	Purpose in the Shell
Space	Parses arguments on the command line
Asterisk (*), question mark (?), and brackets ({ and })	Generate lists of file names
Period (.)	Represents the current directory
Dollar sign ($)	Evaluates variables
Greater-than (>) and less-than (<) characters	Redirect the standard input and output
Ampersand (&)	Executes background commands
Vertical bar pipe (I)	Pipes output from one command to another

If you want to use any of these characters as part of the value of a variable, you must first *quote* them (enclose them in double or single quotes, or backslashes). Quoted special characters are *not* evaluated by the shell.

By surrounding these characters with double and single quotes, you can quote several special characters at a time. Any special characters that fall within double or single quotes are not evaluated. If you want to assign more than one word to a variable, you must also quote the spaces separating the words. You can do this by enclosing the words within double quotes. You can think of this as creating a character string to be assigned to the variable.

If you want to quote a single character, you use a backslash before and after that character. The following examples show three ways of quoting strings. In the first example, the double quotes enclose words separated by spaces. Because the spaces are enclosed within double quotes, they are treated as *characters*, not as separators used to parse command line arguments.

```
$ notice="The meeting will be tomorrow"
$ echo $notice
"The meeting will be tomorrow"
```

In this example, single quotes enclose a sentence with a period, so the period will be treated as just a character.

```
$ message='The project is on time.'
$ echo $message
The project is on time.
```

In the next example, an asterisk is enclosed within the double quotes. The asterisk is considered just another character in the string and is not evaluated.

```
$ notice="You can get a list of files with ls *.c"
$ echo $notice
You can get a list of files with ls *.c
```

Asterisk is not evaluated

Hint

Double quotes are not used to quote the dollar sign—the operator that evaluates variables. A dollar sign that precedes a variable name enclosed within double quotes ("**$**variable") will still be evaluated, replacing the variable name with its value. The *value* of the variable, not the variable name, will then become part of the string.

There may be times when you want a quoted variable to be evaluated. In the next example, the double quotes are used so that the winner's name will be included in the notice.

```
$ winner=dylan
$ notice="The person who won is $winner"
$ echo $notice
The person who won is dylan
```

Variable is evaluated

On the other hand, there may be times when you do not want a variable within quotes to be evaluated. In that case, you would use single quotes. Single quotes suppress any variable evaluation and treat the dollar sign, or anything else inside the quotes, as just another character. In the next example, single quotes prevent the evaluation of the winner variable.

```
$ winner=dylan                        Variable is not evaluated
$ result='The name is in the $winner variable'
$ echo $result
The name is in the $winner variable
```

You can quote any special character, including the **$** operator, by preceding it with a backslash. The backslash is useful when you want to evaluate variables within a string and also include a regular dollar sign ($) character. In the next example, the backslash is placed before the $ so that a dollar sign character will appear, like so: **\$**. At the same time, the variable *$winner* is evaluated, since double quotes do not quote the $ operator that precedes the variable.

```
$ winner=dylan
$ result="$winner won \$100.00""
$ echo $result
dylan won $100.00
```

Obtaining Values from Linux Commands Using Back Quotes

Although you can create variable values by typing in characters or character strings, you can also obtain values using other Linux commands. However, to assign the result of a Linux command to a variable, you first need to execute the command. If you place a Linux command within back quotes (`) on the command line, that command is first executed and its result becomes an argument on the command line. In the case of assignments, the result of a command can be assigned to a variable by placing the command within back quotes. Think of back quotes as a kind of expression that contains both a command to be executed and its result, which is then assigned to the variable. The characters making up the command itself are not assigned.

In the next example, the command **ls** *.c is executed and its result is then assigned to the variable *listc*. The command **ls** *.c generates a list of all files with a .c extension; this list of files will then be assigned to the *listc* variable.

```
$ listc=`ls *.c`        Command is executed first
$ echo $listc
main.c prog.c lib.c
```

Single Quotes vs. Back Quotes   Keep in mind the difference between the single quote (') and the back quote (`). Single quotes tell Linux to treat a command as a set of characters. Back quotes force execution of the Linux command.

There may be times when you accidentally enter single quotes when you intend to use back quotes. The following examples illustrate the difference. In the first example, the assignment for the *lscc* variable uses single quotes, not back quotes, placed around the **ls** *.c command. In this case, the characters **ls** *.c are to be assigned to the variable *lscc*.

```
$ lscc='ls *.c'        Defines a string
$ echo $lscc
ls *.c
```

Next, back quotes are placed around the **ls** *.c command, forcing evaluation of the command. A list of file names ending in .c is generated and assigned as the value of *lscc*.

```
$ lscc=`ls *.c`        Executes command
$ echo $lscc
main.c  prog.c
```

Quoting Commands Using Single Quotes

Adding single quotes allows you to assign the written command to a variable. You can then use that variable name as another name for the Linux command. Entering the variable name preceded by the **$** operator on the command line will execute the command. In the next example, a shell variable is assigned the characters that make up a Linux command to list files, **'ls –F'**. Notice the single quotes around the command. When the shell variable is evaluated on the command line, the Linux command that it contains will become a command line argument and will be executed by the shell.

```
$ lsf='ls -F'
$ $lsf
mydata /reports /letters
$
```

1-Minute Drill

● **Do you need to define a variable before you use it?**

● **Can you assign the value of one variable to another?**

● **How would you assign the result of a Linux command to a variable?**

Script Input and Output: **echo**, **read**, and **<<**

Within a script, you can use the **echo** command to output data and the **read** command to read input into variables. In addition, you can create a *Here document* to specify data within the script and redirect it to a command.

Within a script, the **echo** command will send data to the standard output. The data is in the form of a string of characters. As you have seen in an earlier example, the **echo** command can output variable values as well as string constants.

The **read** command reads in a value for a variable. It allows a user to interactively input a value for a variable. The **read** command literally reads the next line in the standard input. Everything in the standard input up to the carriage return is read in and assigned to a variable. In shell programs, you can combine the **echo** command with the **read** command to prompt the user to enter a value and then read that value into a variable.

● **No; assigning a value or otherwise using a variable automatically defines it.**

● **Yes. Use the dollar sign ($) in front of the variable whose value you want to assign, as in** Address=$Newaddress.

● **Place back quotes around the Linux command.**

greetvar

Project 2-1: User Input

In the *greetvar* script, the user is prompted to enter a value for the greeting variable. The **read** command then reads the value the user typed and assigns it to the greeting variable.

Step-by-Step

1. Create a file called *greetvar* using a standard text editor such as Vi, Emacs, WordPerfect, or any of the GNOME or KDE text editors.

2. Enter a prompt using the **echo** command.

3. Enter a **read** input command with the **greeting** variable. Anything the user types in on a line will be placed in the **greeting** variable.

4. Enter an output command using **echo** to output the line that the user typed in. This will be held in the **greeting** variable.

5. Save and close the file.

6. Change the permission of the *greetvar* file to executable, **chmod u+x greetvar**.

7. Run the script by entering the script name *greetvar* on the Linux command line and pressing the ENTER key.

8. Be sure to type in a greeting at the prompt.

The *greetvar* script is shown here.

```
echo Please enter a greeting:
read greeting

echo "The greeting you entered was $greeting"
```

A sample run of the *greetvar* script follows:

```
$ greetvar
Please enter a greeting:
hi
The greeting you entered was hi
$
```

When dealing with user input, you must consider the possibility that the user may enter shell *special characters*. Any special characters in a Linux command, whether within a script or not, will be evaluated unless it's quoted. If the value of a variable is a special character and the variable's value is referenced with a **$**, the special character will be evaluated by the shell. However, placing the evaluated variable within quotes prevents any evaluation of special characters such as **$**.

In the *greetvar* script in Project 2-1, **$greeting** was placed within a quoted string, preventing evaluation of any special characters. However, if **$greeting** is not quoted, any special characters it contains will be evaluated.

At times, you'll want special characters to be evaluated. Suppose, for example, that you want to retrieve the list of files beginning with characters entered by the user. In this case, any special characters entered by the user need to be evaluated. In the *listfiles* script that follows, any special characters for generating file lists will be expanded. Notice that **$fref** is not quoted.

```
echo Please enter a file reference:
read fref

echo The files you requested are: $fref
```

A sample run of the *listfiles* script follows:

```
$ listfiles
Please enter a file reference:
*.c
The files you requested are: calc.c lib.c main.c
```

Normally, a shell script contains a series of commands. However, there may be times when you need to enter data as well as commands. For such a case, you may want to type lines of data into the shell script and use the data as input for one of the commands. The *Here operation* allows you to do this. This operation redirects data within a shell script into a command. It is called *Here* because the redirected data is here in the shell script, not somewhere else in another file.

The Here operation is signaled by two less–than signs (**<<**), which can be thought of as a kind of redirection operator, redirecting lines in a shell script as input to a command. The **<<** operator is placed *after* the command to which input is being redirected. Lines following the **<<** operator are then taken as input to the command. Whereas the end of the input can be specified by an end-of-file character (press CTRL-D), you can specify your own delimiter with a word following the **<<** operator on the same line. This word is taken to be the ending delimiter for the input lines. The delimiter can be any set of symbols. All lines up to the delimiter are read as input to the command.

In the next example, a message is sent to the user **mark**. The input for the message is obtained from a Here operation. The delimiter for the Here operation is the word *myend*. The name of the script file is *mailmark*.

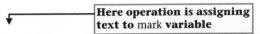
Here operation is assigning text to mark **variable**

```
mail mark << myend
Did you remember
the meeting
    robert
myend
```

1-Minute Drill

- **Can you use a shell script to start an application?**
- **Could a Here operation be used to hold commands?**

- Shell scripts are often used as startup script for applications, letting you check the status or configuration of your system before you start an application.
- For applications like editors that read commands, you could use the Here operation to list a set of application commands within the shell script. In effect, you have a program within a program.

Script Command Line Arguments

A shell script, like Linux commands, can take arguments. When you invoke a script, you can enter arguments on the command line after the script name. Each argument can then be referenced within the script using the **$** operator and the number of the command line in which it appears. Arguments on the command line are sequentially numbered starting with 1. The first argument is referenced with **$1**, the second with **$2**, and so on. The **$0** is a special variable that contains the name of the shell script, the first word on the command line.

These argument references can be thought of as *referencing read-only variables*. If you're familiar with programming terminology, you can think of words on the command line as arguments that are passed into argument variables, **$1** through **$9**. The argument variables are read-only variables, and you cannot assign values to them. Once given their initial values, they cannot be altered. In this sense, argument variables function more like *constants* (values that don't change—sort of the opposite of variables) that are determined by the command line arguments. Each word on the command line is parsed into an argument unless it is quoted. If you enter more than one argument, you can reference each argument with its corresponding argument number. In the next example, four arguments are entered on the command line. The content of the *greetargs* script is shown here:

```
echo "The first argument is: $1"
echo "The second argument is: $2"
echo "The third argument is: $3"
echo "The fourth argument is: $4"
```

A run of the *greetargs* script follows.

```
$ greetargs Hello Hi Salutations "How are you"
The first argument is: Hello
The second argument is: Hi
The third argument is: Salutations
The fourth argument is: How are you
$
```

2

The special variables used for shell script arguments are shown in Table 2-2 on the following page.

Ask the Expert

Question: **Is there a way to reference all the arguments at once?**

Answer: Yes, there is. The special variable **$*** references all the arguments in a command line. The operator **$@** also references all the arguments on the command line but allows you to separately quote each one. The difference between **$*** and **$@** is not clear until you use them to reference arguments using the **for-in** control structure. For this reaso1n, they are discussed only briefly here and are covered more extensively in Module 3.

Question: **Is there a way to detect the number of arguments that the user entered?**

Answer: Yes there is. The **$#** special variable contains the number of arguments entered on the command line. This variable is useful when you need to specify a fixed number of arguments for a script.

In the *sargs* script that follows, for example, the command line arguments are displayed first using the **$*** special variable and then using **$@**. The number of arguments is displayed using the **$#** special variable.

```
echo $*
echo $@
echo "There are $# arguments "
```

A run of the *sargs* script follows:

```
$ sargs Hello Hi Welcome
Hello Hi Welcome
Hello Hi Welcome
There are 3 arguments
```

Command Line Arguments	Description
$0	Name of Linux command
$n	The nth command line argument beginning from 1, $1–$n; you can use **set** to change them
$*	All the command line arguments beginning with 1; you can use **set** to change them
$@	The command line arguments individually quoted
$#	The count of the command line arguments

Table 2-2 Shell Command Line Arguments

Export Variables and Script Shells

If you execute another script from within the script currently running, the current script suspends execution and control is transferred to the other script. All the commands in this other script are first executed before continuing with the suspended script. The process of executing one script from another operates much like a function or procedure call in other programming languages. Think of a script calling another script. The calling script waits until the called script finishes execution before continuing with its next command.

Any variable definitions that you place in a script will be defined within the script's shell and known only within that script's shell. Variable definitions are local to their own shells. In a sense, the variable is hidden within its shell. Suppose, however, you want to be able to define a variable within a script and use it in any scripts it may call. You cannot do this directly, but you can export a variable definition from one shell to another using the **export** command. When the **export** command is applied to a variable, it will instruct the system to define a copy of that variable for each new *subshell* generated. Each new subshell will have its own copy of the exported variable. In the next example, the **myname** variable is defined and exported.

```
$ myname="Charles"
$ export myname
```

As described earlier in this module, when you log in to your account, your Linux system generates your user shell. Within this shell, you can issue commands and declare variables. You can also create and execute shell scripts. However, when you execute a shell script, the system generates a subshell. You then have two shells: the one you logged into and the one generated for the script. Within the script shell, you could execute another shell script, which would have its own shell. When a script has finished execution, its shell terminates and you return to the shell from which it was executed. In this sense, you can work with many shells, each nested within the other. Variables that you define within a shell are local to it. If you define a variable in a shell script, then, when the script is run, the variable is defined with that script's shell and is local to it. No other shell can reference it. In a sense, the variable is hidden within its shell.

To illustrate this situation more clearly, the next example will use two scripts, one of which is called from within the other. When the first script executes, it generates its own shell. From within this shell, another script is executed, which, in turn, generates its *own* shell. In the next example, the user first executes the *dispfirst* script, which displays a first name. When the *dispfirst* script executes, it generates its own shell and then, within that shell, defines the *firstname* variable. After it displays the contents of *firstname*, the script then executes another script, called *displast*. When *displast* executes, it generates its own shell. It defines the **lastname** variable within its shell and then displays the contents of **lastname**. The *displast* script then tries to reference **firstname** and display its contents. But it cannot do so because **firstname** is local to *dispfirst*'s shell and cannot be referenced outside it. As a result, an error message is displayed, indicating that for the *displast* shell, **firstname** is an undefined variable. Figure 2-1 illustrates how each variable is hidden within its own shell.

The content of the *dispfirst* script is shown here:

```
firstname="Charles"
echo "First name is $firstname"     Execute the displast
displast ◄──────────────────────── script from within
                                    the dispfirst script
```

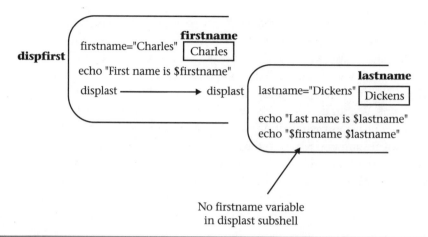

No firstname variable
in displast subshell

Figure 2-1 Attempted reference of a variable from a subshell

The content of the *displast* script is shown here:

```
lastname="Dickens"
echo "Last name is $lastname"
echo "$firstname $lastname"
```

A run of the *dispfirst* and *displast* script follows:

```
$ dispfirst
First name is Charles
Last name is Dickens
Dickens
sh: firstname: not found
$
```

Environment Variables

If you want the same value of a variable used both in a script's shell and a subshell, you could simply define the variable twice—once in each script—and assign it the same value. Better yet, what if you want to define a variable in one shell and have its value referenced in any subshell? For example, suppose that you want to define the **myfile** variable in the *dispfile* script and have its value, "List", referenced from within the *printfile* script, rather than explicitly defining another variable in *printfile*. Since variables are local to the shell in which they are defined, there is no way you can do this with ordinary variables. However, you can use an *environment variable*, which allows its value to be referenced by any subshells. Environment variables constitute an environment for the shell and any subshell it generates, no matter how deeply nested.

In the BASH shell, environmental variables are exported. That is, a copy of an environmental variable is made in each subshell. In a sense, if the **myfile** variable were exported, a copy would be automatically defined in each subshell for you. To make an environment variable, you apply the **export** command to a variable you have already defined. The **export** command instructs the system to define a copy of that variable for each new subshell generated. Each new subshell will have its own copy of the environment variable. This process is called *exporting variables*. In the TCSH shell, on the other hand, an environmental variable is defined only once and can be directly referenced by any subshell.

dispfile

Project 1-2: Exporting Variables

In the *dispfile* program, the variable **myfile** is defined. It is then turned into an environment variable using the **export** command. Consequently, the **myfile** variable will be exported to any subshells, such as the one generated when *printfile* is executed.

Step-by-Step

1. Create a file called *dispfile* using a text editor.

2. Define the variable **myfile** and assign it the name of a file, in this case, "**List**". The file name can be any simple file you have created using a simple text editor.

3. Export the **myfile** variable using the **export** command.

4. Output the value of **myfile**.

5. Display the contents of the file using the **cat** command.

6. Enter the **printfile** command to invoke the *printfile* script.

7. Create a new script called *printfile*.

8. Display the contents of the **myfile** variable (do *not* define **myfile**; it will inherit its definition from *dispfile*).

9. Enter the command to print **myfile**.

10. Change the permissions for both files to make them executable.

11. Run them by entering the **dispfile** command on your command line.

The content of the *dispfile* script is shown here:

```
myfile="List"
export myfile
echo "Displaying $myfile"
cat -n $myfile
printfile
```

The content of the *printfile* script is shown here:

```
echo "Printing $myfile"
lp $myfile &
```

A run of the *dispfile* script follows:

```
$ dispfile
Displaying List
1 screen
2 modem
3 paper
Printing List
$
```

As shown in the following illustration, when *printfile* is executed, it will be given its own copy of **myfile** and can reference that copy within its own shell. You no longer need to explicitly define another **myfile** variable in *printfile*.

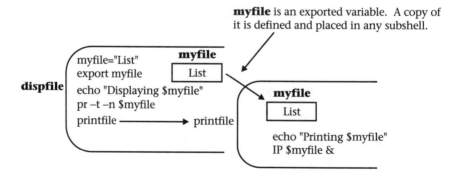

Arithmetic Shell Operations: **let**

The **let** command is the BASH shell command used for performing operations on arithmetic values. By using **let**, you can compare two values or perform arithmetic operations, such as addition or multiplication, on them. Such operations are often used in shell programs to manage control structures or perform necessary calculations. The **let** command can be indicated either with the keyword **let** or with a set of double parentheses. The syntax consists of the keyword **let** followed by two numeric values, separated by an arithmetic or relational operator, as shown here:

```
$ let value1 operator value2
```

Here's an example using double parentheses:

```
$ (( value1 operator value2 ))
```

The **let** command automatically assumes that operators are arithmetic or relational. You do not have to quote shell-like operators. The **let** command also automatically evaluates any variables and converts their values to arithmetic values. This means that you can write your arithmetic operations as simple arithmetic expressions. In the next example, the **let** command multiplies the values 2 and 7. The result is output to the standard output and displayed.

```
$ let 2*7
14
```

If you want to have spaces appear between operands in the arithmetic expression, you must quote the expression, as shown here. The **let** command expects one string.

```
$ let "2 * 7"
```

You can also include assignment operations in your **let** expression. In the next example, the result of the multiplication is assigned to *res*.

```
$ let "res = 2 * 7"  ◄────  Assignment combined with
                            arithmetic operation
$ echo $res
14
```

─┤*Note*

You can also use any of the relational operators to perform comparisons between numeric values, such as determining whether one value is less than another.

You can use as your operator any of those listed in Table 2-3.

Arithmetic Operators	Function
*	Multiplication
/	Division
+	Addition
−	Subtraction
%	Modulo—results in the remainder of a division
Relational Operators	
>	Greater than
<	Less than
>=	Greater than or equal to
<=	Less than or equal to
=	Equal in **expr** command
==	Equal in **let**
!=	Not equal
&	Logical AND
|	Logical OR
!	Logical NOT

Table 2-3   Expression Operators: let

1-Minute Drill

●   **Could you create complex programs using several shell scripts?**

●   **What kind of value is held in a variable after a** let **arithmetic assignment operation?**

2

☑ *Mastery Check*

1. How can you run a BASH shell script from within the TCSH shell?

2. What would a **read** command in a shell script input if the script argument is *?

3. Could you assign the text of several lines to a variable?

4. How do you reference different arguments of a script as a single argument?

5. Can you define global variables?

6. What is the difference between == and = ?

●   Yes; just be sure to export any needed variables a script might use.
●   A string that represents a number.

Module 3

BASH Shell Control Structures

The Goals of This Module

- Learn how to construct tests for control structures
- Implement complex conditions with nested **if** statements
- Check for different options using a **case** statement
- Implement standard loops as well as **read** arguments with a **for** loop
- Automatically read any option a user enters
- Handle shell redirection and pipe operations in shell scripts
- Learn to check for certain signals, such as an interrupt signal to stop a program

This module will cover the basics of creating a shell program using the BASH shell, the shell used on most Linux systems. You will learn how to create your own scripts, define shell variables, develop user interfaces, and master the more difficult task of combining control structures, to create complex programs. Tables in this module list BASH shell commands and operators, while numerous examples show you how they are implemented.

The BASH shell has a complete set of control structures, including loops and **if** statements as well as **case** structures. All the shell commands interact easily with redirection and piping operations that allow them to accept input from the standard input or to send to the standard output.

You can control the execution of Linux commands in a shell program with *control structures*. Control structures allow you to repeat commands and select certain commands over others. A control structure consists of two major components: a test and commands. If the test is successful, the commands are executed. In this way, you can use control structures to make decisions as to whether commands should be executed.

Two types of control structures are used in shell programs: *loops* and *conditions*. A loop repeats commands, while a condition executes a command when certain conditions are met. The BASH shell has three loop control structures—**while**, **for**, and **for-in**—and two condition structures—**if** and **case**.

The **while** and **if** control structures are used for general purposes, such as performing iterations and making decisions using a variety of different tests.

The **case** and **for** control structures are more specialized. The **case** structure is a restricted form of the **if** condition and is often used to implement menus. The **for** structure is a limited type of loop. It runs through a list of values, assigning a new value to a variable with each iteration.

The **if** and **while** control structures test the execution of a Linux command. All Linux commands return an exit status after they have finished executing. If a command is successful, its exit status will be 0. If the command fails for any reason, its exit status will be a positive value referencing the type of failure that occurred. The **if** and **while** control structures check to see whether the exit status of a Linux command is 0 or some other value. In the case of the **if** and **while** structures, if the exit status is a 0 value, the command was successful and the structure continues.

3

The **test** Command

Often you may need to perform a test that compares two values; yet the test used in control structures is a Linux command, not a relational expression. There is, however, a Linux command called **test** that can perform such a comparison of values. The **test** command compares two values and returns as its exit status a 0 if the comparison is successful.

Using the **test** command, you can compare integers and strings, and you can even perform logical operations. The command (its syntax is shown following) consists of the keyword *test* followed by the values being compared, which are separated by an *option* that specifies what kind of comparison is taking place. You can think of the option as the operator, but it is written, like other options, with letter codes preceded by a minus sign. For example, **–eq** is the option that represents the equality comparison. The syntax for the **test** command is shown here:

```
test value –option value
test string = string
```

Be aware that two string operations actually use an operator instead of an option. When you compare two strings for equality, you use the equal sign (=). For inequality, you use **!=**. In the next example, two integer values are compared to determine whether they are equal. In this case, you need to use the equality option, **–eq**. The exit status of the **test** command is examined to determine the result of the **test** operation. The shell special variable **$?** holds the exit status of the most recently executed Linux command.

```
$ num=5
$ test $num -eq 10
$ echo $?
1
```

Alternatively, instead of using the keyword *test* for the **test** command, you can use enclosing brackets (**[** and **]**). The command test **$greeting = "hi"** can also be written like this:

String comparison

```
$ [ $greeting = "hi" ]
```

Similarly, the **test** command **test $num −eq 10** can be written in this way:

```
$ [ $num -eq 10 ]          Arithmetic test
```

—|Note

You must surround the brackets with white space by pressing the SPACEBAR, TAB, or ENTER key. Without the spaces, this command would be invalid.

—Hint

The **test** command is used extensively as the Linux command in the test component of control structures. Be sure to keep in mind the different options used for strings and integers. Do not confuse string comparisons and integer comparisons. To compare two strings for equality, you use the equal sign (=); to compare two integers, you use the option **−eq**.

Table 3-1 lists all the options and operators used by **test**.

Integer Comparisons	Function
−gt	Greater than
−lt	Less than
−ge	Greater than or equal to
−le	Less than or equal to
−eq	Equal
−ne	Not equal
String Comparisons	
−z	Tests for empty string
−n	Tests for string value
=	Equal strings
!=	Not equal strings
Str	Tests to see whether string is not a null string
Logical Operations	
−a	Logical AND
−o	Logical OR
!	Logical NOT

Table 3-1 Test Command Operations

File Tests	Function
–f	File exists and is a regular file
–s	File is not empty
–r	File is readable
–w	File can be written to, modified
–x	File is executable
–d	File name is a directory name
–h	File name is a symbolic link
–c	File name references a character device
–b	File name references a block file

Table 3-1   Test Command Operations *(continued)*

Conditions: **if**, **if-else**, **elif**, and **case**

The BASH shell has a set of conditional control structures that allow you to choose which Linux commands to execute. Many of these structures are similar to conditional control structures found in programming languages, with some differences. The **if** condition tests the success of a Linux command, not an expression. Furthermore, the end of an **if-then** command must be indicated with the keyword *fi*, and the end of a **case** command is indicated with the keyword *esac*. The condition control structures are listed in Table 3-2.

The **if-then** Structure

The **if** structure places a condition on commands. That condition is the exit status of a specific Linux command. If a command is successful, returning an exit status of 0, the commands within the **if** structure are executed. If the exit status is anything other than 0, the command has failed and the commands within the **if** structure are not executed.

The **if** command begins with the keyword *if* and is followed by a Linux command whose exit condition will be evaluated. This command is

Condition Control Structures	**Function**
if *command* then *command* fi	**if** executes an action if its **test** command is true

if *command* then
    command
else
    command
fi
	if-else executes an action if the exit status of its **test** command is true; if false, the **else** action is executed

if *command* then
    command
elif *command* then
    command
else
    command
fi
	elif allows you to nest **if** structures, enabling selection among several alternatives; at the first true **if** structure, its commands are executed and control leaves the entire **elif** structure

case *string* in *pattern*) *command;;* esac	**case** matches the string value to any of several patterns; if a pattern is matched, its associated commands are executed
command && *command*	The logical AND condition returns a true 0 value if both commands return a true 0 value; if one returns a nonzero value, the AND condition is false and also returns a nonzero value
command ‖ *command*	The logical OR condition returns a true 0 value if one or the other command returns a true 0 value; if both commands return a nonzero value, the OR condition is false and also returns a nonzero value
! *command*	The logical NOT condition inverts the return value of the command

Table 3-2   BASH Shell Conditions

always executed. After the command, the keyword is placed on a line by itself. Any set of commands may then follow. The keyword *fi* ends the command. Often, you need to choose between two alternatives based on whether or not a Linux command is successful. The *else* keyword allows an **if** structure to choose between two alternatives. If the Linux command

3

is successful, those commands following the *then* keyword are executed. If the Linux command fails, those commands following the *else* keyword are executed. The syntax for the **if–then–else** command is shown here:

```
if Linux command
   then
       commands
   else
       commands
fi
```

The *elsels* script in the next example executes the **ls** command to list files with two different possible options, either by size or with all file information. If the user enters an **s**, files are listed by size; otherwise, all file information is listed.

```
echo Enter s to list file sizes,
echo otherwise all file information is listed.
echo -n "Please enter option: "
read choice

if [ "$choice" = s ]
    then
          ls -s
    else
             ls -l
fi
echo Good-bye
```

A run of the *elsels* script follows:

```
$ elsels
Enter s to list file sizes,
otherwise all file information is listed.
Please enter option: s
total 2
    1 monday      2 today
$
```

Ask the Expert

Question: Can I use the if structure to test for arguments?

Answer: The **if** structure is often used to check whether the user entered the appropriate number of arguments for a shell script. The special shell variable # contains the number of arguments the user entered. Using $# in a test operation allows you to check whether the user entered the correct number of arguments.

Question What should happen if an incorrect number of arguments is detected?

Answer: If an incorrect number of arguments has been entered, you may need to end the shell script. You can do this with the **exit** command, which ends the shell script and returns an exit condition. The **exit** command takes a number argument. An argument of 0 indicates that the shell script ended successfully. Any other argument, such as 1, indicates that an error occurred.

In the next example, the *ifarg* script takes only one argument. If the user fails to enter an argument or enters more than one argument, the **if** test will be true, the error message will be printed out, and the script will exit with an error value.

```
if [ $# -ne 1 ]
    then
    echo Invalid number of arguments
    exit 1
fi

echo $1
```

The following shows the run of the *ifarg* script with no arguments. This error is detected and the error message is displayed.

```
$ ifarg
Invalid number of arguments
```

The **elif** structure allows you to nest if-then–else operations. The **elif** structure stands for "else if." The first operation is specified with the **if** structure, followed by other operations, each specified by its own **elif** structure. The operation for the last **elif** structure is specified with an **else**. If the test for the first **if** structure fails, control will be passed to the next **elif** structure, and its test will be executed. If it fails, control is passed to the next **elif** and its test checked. This continues until a test returns true. Then the true **elif** has its commands executed and control passes out of the **if** structure to the next command following the *fi* keyword.

The syntax for the **elif** structure is shown here:

```
if  Linux command
   then
         Linux commands
   elif
         Linux commands
   else
         Linux commands
fi
```

In the *elifls* script, two possible ways of listing files are presented. The last **else** is reserved for detecting invalid input—in this case, an invalid choice. Notice that only one *fi* keyword ends this entire sequence of nested **if-else** commands.

```
echo  s. List Sizes
echo  1. List All Information
echo "Please enter option: \c"
read choice
if [ "$choice" = s ]
   then
         ls -s
   elif [ "$choice" = 1 ]
         then
               ls -1
         else
               echo Invalid Option
fi
echo Goodbye
```

A run of the *elifls* script follows:

```
$ elifls
s. List Sizes
l. List All File Information
Please enter option: l
total 2
-rw-rw-r-x  1  chris weather 568  Feb 14  10:30  today
-rw-rw-r--  1  chris weather 308  Feb 17  12:40  monday
$
```

The Logical Commands: **&&** and ||

The logical commands perform logical operations on two Linux commands. The syntax is as follows:

> *command* && *command*
> *command* || *command*

In the case of the logical AND (**&&**), if both commands are successful, the logical command is successful. For the logical OR (||), if either command is successful, the OR is successful and returns an exit status of 0. The logical commands allow you to use logical operations as your test commands in control structures.

The **case** Structure

The **case** structure allows your program to choose among several possible alternatives. The choice is made by comparing a value with several possible patterns. Each possible value is associated with a set of operations. If a match is found, the associated operations are performed.

The **case** structure begins with the keyword *case*, followed by an evaluation of a variable and the keyword *in*. A set of patterns then follows. Each pattern is a regular expression terminated with a closing parenthesis. After the closing parenthesis, commands associated with this pattern are listed, followed by a double semicolon on a separate line, designating the end of those commands. After all the listed patterns, the keyword *esac* ends the **case** command. The syntax looks like this:

3

```
case string in
    pattern)
        commands
        ;;
    pattern)
        commands
        ;;
    *)
        default commands
    ;;
    esac
```

Hint

A pattern can include any shell special characters. The shell special characters are *, [,], ?, and I. You can specify a default pattern with a single * special character. The * special character matches on any pattern and, therefore, performs as an effective default option. If all other patterns do not match, the * will. In this way, the default option is executed if no other options are chosen. The default is optional, and you do not have to include it.

A **case** structure is often used to implement menus. In the program *lschoice*, in the next example, the user is asked to enter a choice for listing files in different ways. Notice the default option that warns of invalid input:

```
# Program to allow the user to select different ways of
#    listing files

echo  s. List Sizes
echo  l. List All File Information
echo  c. List C Files

echo -n "Please enter choice: "
read choice

case $choice in
    s)
        ls -s
        ;;
```

```
1)
    ls -l
    ;;
c)
    ls *.c        ┌──────────────────────────┐
    ;;            │ Matches on any character │
*) ◄──────────────│ not matched previously   │
    echo Invalid Option  └──────────────────────────┘
esac
```

A run of the *lschoice* script is shown here:

```
$ lschoice
s. List Sizes
l. List All File Information
c. List C Files
Please enter choice: c
main.c   lib.c   file.c
$
```

Hint

The use of the file-generation *metacharacters* in patterns can give you a great deal more flexibility. For example, in the previous example only the lowercase versions of the patterns were permissible. An uppercase *A* would be considered invalid input. If you use the | special character in the pattern, it will allow you to specify more than one possible match. The **a|A** pattern, for example, will match on both an uppercase *A* and a lowercase *a*. Metacharacters are discussed in most UNIX and Linux texts.

1-Minute Drill

● **What operator would you use to test for an empty string?**

● **Can you perform the same task with a** case **structure that you can perform with an** if **structure?**

● The –z **operator in a test expression.**
● **Yes; use** elif **for nested** if **structures.**

Loops: **while, until, for-in, and for**

The BASH shell has a set of loop control structures that allow you to repeat Linux commands: the **while, for**, and **for-in** structures. Like the BASH **if** structure, **while** and **until** test the result of a Linux command. However, the **for** and **for-in** structures do not perform tests. Instead, they simply progress through a list of values, assigning each value in turn to a specified variable. Furthermore, the **while** and **until** structures operate in ways similar to the corresponding structures found in programming languages, whereas the **for** and **for-in** structures are very different from their corresponding programming structures. The loop control structures are listed in Table 3-3.

Loop Control Structures	Description
while *command* do *command* done	**while** executes an action as long as its **test** command is true
until *command* do *command* done	**until** executes an action as long as its **test** command is false
for *variable* in *list-values* do *command* done	**for-in** is designed for use with lists of values; the variable operand is consecutively assigned the values in the list
for *variable* do *command* done	**for** is designed for reference script arguments; the variable operand is consecutively assigned each argument value
select *string* in *item-list* do *command* done	**select** creates a menu based on the items in the *item-list*, and then it executes the command; the command is usually a case

Table 3-3   BASH Shell Loops

The **while** loop

The **while** loop repeats commands. A **while** loop begins with the keyword *while* and is followed by a Linux command. The keyword *do* follows on the next line. The end of the loop is specified by the keyword *done*. Here is the syntax for the **while** command:

```
while Linux command
    do
        commands
    done
```

The Linux command used in **while** structures is often a test command indicated by enclosing brackets. In the *myname* script, the next example, you are asked to enter a name. The name is then printed out. The loop is controlled by testing the value of the variable again using the bracket form of the **test** command.

```
again=yes

while [ "$again" = yes ]    ◄———  Start of loop
do                                 with test
    echo -n "Please enter a name: "
    read name
    echo "The name you entered is $name"

    echo -n "Do you wish to continue? "
    read again  ◄———
done                      If user enters yes,
                          loop repeats
echo Good-bye
```

A run of the *myname* script follows:

```
$ myname
Please enter a name: George
The name you entered is George
Do you wish to continue? yes
Please enter a name: Robert
The name you entered is Robert
Do you wish to continue? no
Good-bye
```

Hint

The **while** loop is often used to perform repetitive tasks, such as inputting or outputting lines. You can combine a **while** with a **case** structure to drive a menu.

helloprg

Project 2-1: Basic Loops

Relational operations are often used to manage control structures such as loops and conditions. The *helloprg* program displays the word *hello* three times. It makes use of a **let** less-than-or-equal-to operation to manage the loop, **let "again <= 3 "**, and to increment the **again** variable, **let "again = again + 1"**. Notice that when **again** is incremented, it does not need to be evaluated. No preceding **$** is needed. The **let** command will automatically evaluate variables used in expressions.

Step-by-Step

1. Using a text editor, create a file called *helloprg*.

2. Define a variable named *again* and assign it a value of 1. This is an initialization of the variable you will use to control the loop.

3. Enter a **while** command where the Linux statement used for the test is a **let** command (see Module 2). Check to see whether the value of the *again* variable is less than or equal to 3.

4. Output the value of the *again* variable and the word *Hello*.

5. Increment the *again* variable using the **let** command with an arithmetic assignment operation.

6. End the **while** loop with the **done** command.

The *helloprg* script is shown here:

```
again=1
while let "again <= 3"
        do
        echo $again Hello
        let "again = again + 1"
        done
```

3

A run of the *helloprg* script follows:

```
$ helloprg
1 Hello
2 Hello
3 Hello
```

The **until** Structure

The **until** structure operates in much the same way as the **while** structure. However, **until** tests for the unsuccessful result of a Linux command. As long as the Linux command fails, the **until** structure continues the loop. In a sense, **until** checks for a false test condition. In this respect, the **until** structure is very different from the until structures found in programming languages. Instead, **until** is more like the operator in programming languages that tests for false expressions. Following is the syntax for the **until** structure:

```
until  Linux command
do
        commands
done
```

The **for-in** Structure

The **for-in** structure is designed to reference a list of values sequentially. It takes two operands: a variable and a list of values. Each value in the list is assigned, one by one, to the variable in the **for-in** structure. Like the **while** command, the **for-in** structure is a loop. With each iteration through the loop, the next value in the list is assigned to the variable. When the end of the list is reached, the loop stops. Like the **while** loop, the body of a **for-in** loop begins with the keyword *do* and ends with the keyword *done*. The syntax for the **for-in** loop is shown here:

```
for variable in list of values
    do
    commands
    done
```

Ask the Expert

Question   Could the for-in **loop be used to reference file names in a directory?**

Answer: Yes; in fact, the **for-in** loop is very handy for managing files. You can use special characters to generate file names for use as a list of values in the **for-in** loop. For example, the * special character, by itself, generates a list of all files and directories, and *.c lists files with the **.c** extension. The special character * placed in the **for-in** loop's value list will generate a list of values consisting of all the file names in your current directory, like so:

```
for myfiles in *
    do
```

The *cbackup* script makes a backup of each file and places it in a directory called *sourcebak*. Notice the use of the * special character to generate a list of all file names with a **.c** extension.

```
for backfile in *.c
do
    cp $backfile sourcebak/$backfile
    echo $backfile
done
```

Generates lists of files

A run of the *cbackup* script follows:

```
$ cbackup
io.c
lib.c
main.c
$
```

The **for** Structure

The **for** structure *without* a specified list of values takes as its list of values the command line arguments. The arguments specified on the command line when the shell file is invoked become a list of values referenced by the **for** command. The variable used in the **for** command is set automatically to each argument value in sequence. The first time through the loop, the variable is set to the value of the first argument. The second time, it is set to the value of the second argument.

The **for** structure without a specified list is equivalent to the list generated by **$@**. **$@** is a special argument variable whose value is the list of command line arguments. In the next example, a list of C program files is entered on the command line when the shell file *cbackuparg* is invoked. In *cbackuparg*, each argument is automatically referenced by a **for** loop. The **backfile** variable is used in the **for** loop. The first time through the loop, **$backfile** holds the value of the first argument, **$1**. The second time through, **$backfile** holds the value of the second argument, **$2**.

```
for backfile
do
    cp $backfile sourcebak/$backfile
    echo "$backfile "
done
```

A run of the *cbackuparg* script follows:

```
$ cbackuparg  main.c  lib.c  io.c
main.c
lib.c
io.c
```

You could, if you want, explicitly reference arguments using the **for-in** structure and either the **$*** or the **$@** special argument. The **for-in** structure will individually reference each argument and assign it to the **for-in** variable. However, there is a difference in the way arguments will be referenced, depending upon whether you use the **$*** or **$@** special argument. If you use the **$*** special argument, **for-in** will reference each individual word on the command line as an argument, whether it is quoted or not. In other words, for example, the arguments **hi "hello and goodbye" salutations** is read as five separate arguments. The quoted argument **"hello and goodbye"** is treated as three separate arguments. If you were to quote the **$*** argument itself, as in **"$*"**, you'd have one long, single argument. In the next example, the *indargs* script is run with only three arguments, but the **for-in** structure will reference five, ignoring the quoted argument.

```
echo "There are $# arguments "

for argf in $*
    do
            echo $argf
    done
```

A run of the *indargs* script follows:

```
$ indargs hi "hello and goodbye" salutations
There are 3 arguments
hi
hello
and
goodbye
salutations
```

The **continue** Command

The **continue** command is used with loops to pass over the remaining statements in the body of a loop and continue on with the next iteration. Use of the **continue** command can contribute to obscure programming styles. It should be used sparingly.

The **true**, **false**, and **break** Commands

The **true** command is a simple command whose exit status is always 0, always successful. Its counterpart, the **false** command, always has an exit status of 1, or always fails. You can use the **true** command as the test command in a **while** structure to implement an infinite loop. A **false** command used with the **until** structure will also implement an infinite loop. When deciding to use an infinite loop, you will need to have a way to stop it. The **break** command, when used within any loop, will transfer control out of the loop, effectively stopping it.

Hint

Often an infinite loop will contain a conditional **break** statement that, when executed, ends the loop. However, use of both the **break** command and infinite loops can contribute to sometimes obscure programming code. They should be used sparingly. It's also handy to know that the **break** command is the only way you have of stopping a **for** or **for-in** loop before it reaches the end of its list.

Ask the Expert

Question: How do I reference arguments in a for-in **structure?**

Answer: If you want your quoted arguments to be treated as one argument, you need to use the **$@** special argument. In addition, you need to place quotes around the **$@** argument, like so: **"$@"**. This will cause each argument to be treated as an individual argument as it is referenced by a **for-in** structure. In the next example, the *forargs* script displays arguments individually using a **for-in** structure and the quoted **$@** special argument.

```
echo "There are $# arguments "

    for argf in "$@"
        do
            echo $argf
        done
```

A run of *forargs* script follows:

```
$ forargs hi "hello and goodbye" salutations
There are 3 arguments
hi
hello and goodbye
salutations
```

1-Minute Drill

● **If the test in a loop is always true, would it ever stop?**

● **Is there a way to force a loop to stop?**

myindex

Project 3-2: Web page index

The *myindex* program incorporates many of the programming features commonly used in the BASH shell. The program automatically generates a Web page that can operate as an index for selecting other Web pages. It assumes that some subdirectories contain Web pages.

Step-by-Step

1. Detect directories in the current directory, and then check to determine whether any Web pages are included in them. Web pages are any files with **.html** or **.htm** extensions. The names of these files are placed in strings that consist of HTML commands, which are **hrefs** to select and display the files. The HTML references are organized into a list with the **<ul>** and **</ul>** tags, with each item preceded by a **<li>** tag. Directory names are used as headings, with the **<h1>** tag.

2. Search an HTML file for a title and use that as the link text in the index.

3. Use **grep** to search for the occurrence of a **<TITLE>** pattern. If it finds one, it returns it to the **tline** variable.

4. If you do not find the pattern, return an error level 1 to the **$?** status variable.

5. Check this variable to see whether **grep** was successful. If so, use a set of **sed** commands to strip the preceding and tailing **<TITLE>** and **</TITLE>** tags along with any other characters.

6. Assign the remaining title text to the **ntitle** variable.

● No; you would have an infinite loop.

● Yes; use the break **command.**

3

7. If **grep** does not find a **<TITLE>** line, assign the file name to **ntitle**.

8. Use **basename** to extract the file name from the path name, removing any preceding directory names.

9. Use **cut** to remove the extension (output the first field using the period as the delimiter). Both **.htm** and **.html** extensions can be removed.

10. After text is assigned for **ntitle**, use it as the link text in the **href** HTML line. This line begins with a **<li>** tag, indicating that it is a list item.

The *myindex* script is shown here:

```
#!/bin/sh

echo '<HTML>'
echo '<HEAD>'
echo '<TITLE>My Index</TITLE>'
echo '</HEAD>'
echo '<BODY>'
echo '<H1>Index of HTML Files</H1>'

for i in *
 do
     if [ -d $i ]
             then
         echo "<h2>$i</h2>"
         echo '<ul>'
         for j in $i/*.htm*
                 do
                 if [ -f $j ]
                     then
                     tline=`grep '<TITLE>' $j`
                     if [ $? -eq 1 ]
                         then
                             ntitle=`basename $j | cut -f1 -d"."`
                         else
                             ntitle=`echo $tline | sed 's/^.*<TITLE>//' | sed
                                      's/<\/TITLE>.*$//'`
                         fi
                     echo "<li><a href=$j>$ntitle</a>"
                     fi
                 done
             echo '</ul>'
     fi
done

echo '</BODY>'
echo '</HTML>'
```

The *myindex* program outputs to the standard output, so it will have to be redirected to a file to save it, using this line:

```
$ myindex > mindex.html
```

The following is an example of the *mindex.html.*

```
<HTML>
<HEAD>
<TITLE>My Index</TITLE>
</HEAD>
<BODY>
<H1>Index of HTML Files</H1>
<h2>docnotes</h2>
<ul>
<li><a href=docnotes/perlnotes.html>Why I like Perl?</a>
<li><a href=docnotes/texnotes.html>TeX and LaTeX Notes</a>
</ul>
<h2>mywebs</h2>
<ul>
<li><a href=mywebs/mypics.html>mypics</a>
<li><a href=mywebs/vacation.html>My Summer Vacation</a>
</ul>
</BODY>
</HTML>
```

Figure 3-1 displays its output, which would appear in a browser.

Figure 3-1   Display of *mindex.html* generated by *myindex* shell script

Using Redirection and Pipes with Control Structures

You can think of a control structure as a command that sends data to the standard output. This output can then be redirected or *piped* (transferred to another command), just like the output of any Linux command. In a control structure command, you can place a redirection operator immediately following the *done* keyword to redirect the output of a loop to a file. In the *mylistsave* file, for example, the **echo** command within the **for-in** loop will place the item name and the date in the standard output. These item names and dates are then redirected to a file called *foods*. The file *foods* will then hold a list of all grocery items.

```
myitems="milk cookies apples cheese"

for grocery in $myitems
    do                              ┌─────────────────────────────┐
                                    │ Output of echo command is   │
            echo "$grocery   "      │ saved in file called foods  │
    done > foods  ◄─────────────────┘─────────────────────────────┘
```

A run of the *mylistsave* script follows, along with a display of the contents of the *foods* file created by the script:

```
$ mylistsave
$ cat foods
milk
cookies
apples
cheese
```

In the next example, the *cbackupn* script has been altered to output the name of each file copied. The **echo** command within the **for-in** loop will place the names of files in the standard output. The file names are first piped to the sort filter to sort the names before redirecting them to a file. Notice that the pipe is placed to the right of the *done* keyword. The file *cnames* will then hold a list of all the C program files that have been backed up.

```
for backfile in *.c
    do
          cp $backfile sourcebak/$backfile
          echo $backfile
    done | sort > cnames
```

> **The file names output by the** echo **command are piped to the sort filter, and the sorted names are then saved in the** *cnames* **file**

A run of the *cbackupn* script follows, along with a display of the *cnames* file it creates:

```
$ cbackupn
$ cat cnames
io.c
lib.c
main.c
```

You can also redirect the standard *input* into a control structure. Just as the **echo** command outputs to the standard output, the **read** command can read from the standard input. A **read** command within a loop can read from input redirected to the loop from a file. In this way, a **read** command can read *from* a file.

In the *bookrecsR* script, the user creates a script to input records into a database file and then display those records. In the first loop, the user enters in book records that are saved to the *books* file using append redirection on the **echo** command. After all the records are entered, a second loop is used to print out only the author and title in each record. This second loop receives its data from input redirected from the *books* file to the **while** control structure.

The test command for the second loop is the **read** command. When the **read** command reads input, it will return an exit status of 0. As long as there is input, the **read** command will return true. However, when the **read** command detects an end-of-file, it returns a nonzero exit status. This means that the **while** loop will cut off when the end of the file is reached. The same principle applies to data input from the keyboard by the user. The **read** command would continue to read input until it detects a carriage return (CTRL-D) ending the input.

```
IFS=:
morerec=yes
echo "Input format is <book>:<author>:<price>:<publisher>"

while [ "$morerec" = yes ]
```

```
        do
                echo -n "Please enter book record: "
                read title author price publisher
                echo "$title\t$author\t$price\t$publisher" >> books
                echo -n "Do you wish to continue? "
                read morerec
        done

        while read title author price publisher
        do
                echo "$title $author "
        done < books
```

A run of the *bookrecsR* script follows. Here the user enters an entire record at once with fields separated by colons:

```
$ bookrecsR
Input format is <book>:<author>:<price>:<publisher>
Please enter a book record: War and peace:Tolstoy:15.75:Penguin
Do you wish to continue? yes
Please enter a book record: Christmas carol:Dickens:3.50:Academic
Do you wish to continue? yes
Please enter a book record: Iliad:Homer:10.25:Random
Do you wish to continue? yes
Please enter a book record: Raven:Poe:2.50:Penguin
Do you wish to continue? no

War and peace     Tolstoy
Christmas carol   Dickens
Iliad             Homer
Raven             Poe
$ cat books
Christmas carol   Dickens   3.50    Academic
Iliad             Homer     10.25   Random
Raven             Poe       2.50    Penguin
$
```

Trap Structures: **trap**

Another kind of control structure is a **trap**. A **trap** structure executes a command or commands when a specified event occurs. The event could occur at any time and at any point in the program. These events are commonly referred to as *signals*. When a signal is received by the system,

3

the **trap** is executed and control is passed to the commands associated with the **trap**. Below is the syntax for the **trap** structure.

```
trap 'Linux-commands' signal-numbers
```

A **trap** is designed to handle some outside event that interferes with a program. A common event signal is an interrupt signal usually sent by the user pressing CTRL-C. (If, while running a program, you press CTRL-C, you will stop the program.) Whenever your program is interrupted in this way, there are actions you or your program might want taken. A common action is to exit the program with an error value.

Each event signal is associated with a specific number by the system. You can trap for the occurrence of a specific event using that event signal's number. In the next example, the user traps for an interrupt event—i.e., a user pressing CTRL-C to stop a program. If the user presses CTRL-C, the trap will execute both an **echo** and an **exit** command. The signal number for a CTRL-C interrupt is 2.

```
trap 'echo "Goodbye"; exit 1' 2
```

The following *cbackupT* script holds a **trap** command:

```
trap 'echo Goodbye; rm cnames; exit 1' 2

for backfile in *.c
    do
        cp $backfile sourcebak/$backfile
        echo $backfile
    done | sort > cnames
```

In the next example, the user executes the *cbackupT* program and then decides to cancel it by pressing CTRL-C, indicated in the code by **^C**. At that cancellation point, the trap is executed and the commands associated with the trap are executed before the program ends.

```
$ cbackupT
^C
Goodbye
$
```

You can also use the **trap** command to prevent outside events from stopping a program. For example, suppose you do not want the user to be able to stop a program by pressing CTRL-C; you want any outside event to be ignored. The **trap** command can trap the CTRL-C event and prevent it from interfering with the execution of the program. You can do this by entering a set of empty single quotes as the **trap** command's first argument. If the **trap** command has no Linux commands to execute, it merely intercepts an event that would stop the program. The **trap** command shown next will trap all CTRL-C events and prevent a CTRL-C entered by a user from stopping your program:

```
trap '' 2
```

In the next example, the 0 signal number denotes the end-of-program events. When used with a **trap**, this number dictates that whenever your program ends, the **trap** will be executed. Should your program end due to an interruption, an **exit** command, or simply by executing the last command in the program, this **trap** will be activated and its action executed. In the next example, the "Goodbye" message will be output whenever the program ends, for any reason.

```
trap 'echo "Goodbye"' 0
```

This **trap** is entered into the *cbackupG* script, shown here, along with the other trap checking for interruptions. The CTRL-C trap, indicated by the number 2, is removed in this case to illustrate how the 0 trap works.

```
trap '' 1 3 15
trap 'echo "Goodbye"' 0

for backfile in *.c
    do
        cp $backfile sourcebak/$backfile
        echo $backfile
    done | sort > cnames
```

Two runs of the *cbackupG* script are shown here, one with a standard termination and another with a CTRL-C interrupt.

```
$ cbackupG
Goodbye
$
$ cbackupG
^C
Goodbye

$
```

Table 3-4 show the various signal numbers and a description of each.

Signals		Description
0	Program end	Program terminates
1	hang up	Disconnects communications line
2	Terminal Interrupt	Press the interrupt key—CTRL-C or DELETE
3	Quit	Press CTRL-| or CTRL-\
9	Kill	Kill a program; cannot be trapped
15	Software Kill	Use the **kill** command to end a program
24	Stop	Stop a program with a CTRL-Z; cannot be trapped

Table 3-4   **Signal Numbers**

✓ Mastery Check

1. Can you nest **if** structures?

2. How do you implement a default selection in a **case** operation?

3. How could you read the arguments of a script one by one, processing each in turn?

4. What command could you use to automatically detect options entered on the command line?

5. Could your program execute any commands after the user forces it to terminate with a CTRL-C?

Module 4

TCSH Shell Programming

The Goals of This Module

- Develop TCSH shell programs

- Define TCSH shell and environment variables

- Manage TCSH shell script input and output

- Use TCSH shell arithmetic, relational, and assignment operators

- Use TCSH control structures to implement loops and conditional tests

The TCSH shell, like the BASH shell, also has programming language capabilities. You can define variables and assign values to them. You can place variable definitions and Linux commands in a script file and then execute that script. You can use loop and conditional control structures to repeat Linux commands or make decisions on which commands you want to execute. You can also place traps in your program to handle interrupts.

The TCSH shell differs from other shells in that its control structures conform more to a programming language format. For example, the test condition for a TCSH shell's control structure is an expression that evaluates to true or false, not to a Linux command. A TCSH shell expression uses the same operators as those found in the C programming language. You can perform a variety of assignment, arithmetic, relational, and bitwise operations. The TCSH shell also allows you to declare numeric variables that can easily be used in such operations.

TCSH Shell Variables, Scripts, and Arguments

The TCSH shell uses shell variables much the same way as the BASH shell does. You can define variables in a shell and assign values to them, as well as reference script arguments. You can also define environment variables that operate much like BASH shell exported variables. The TCSH shell differs in the way it defines variables and the type of variables you can define, however. The TCSH shell defines its variables using the TCSH shell commands **set**, **@**, and **setenv**. The TCSH shell also allows you to define numeric variables and arrays. The **@** command defines a numeric variable on which you perform arithmetic operations. Parentheses and brackets allow you to define and reference arrays.

Scripts also operate in much the same way, but with several crucial differences. A TCSH shell script must begin with a number sign (#) in the first column of the first line. Also, although prompts can be output using the **echo** command, TCSH has no **read** command to handle input. Instead, you need to redirect the standard input to a variable.

TCSH Shell Variables

In the TCSH shell, you need to first declare a variable before you can use it. You declare a variable with the **set** command followed by the variable's name. Here are the rules for naming a variable:

- May be any set of alphabetic characters, including the underscore.

- May include a number, but the number cannot be the first character in the name.

- May not include any other type of character, such as an exclamation point, ampersand, or even a space. Such symbols are reserved by the shell for its own use.

The next example declares the variable greeting. You can later undefine the variable with the **unset** command.

```
set greeting
```

Note

A name may not include more than one word, since the shell parses its command line on the space. The space is a delimiter between the different elements of the command line.

You also use the **set** command to assign a value to a variable. You type in the keyword *set*; the variable name; the assignment operator, =; and then the value assigned. Any set of characters can be assigned to a variable. In the next example, the variable greeting is assigned the string "hello".

```
> set greeting="hello"
```

In the TCSH shell assignment operation, you need either to place spaces on both sides of the assignment operator or to have no spaces at all. This assignment operation

```
> set greeting ="hello"
```

will fail because there is a space before the assignment operator (**=**), but not after.

You can obtain a list of all the defined variables by using the **set** command without any arguments. The next example uses **set** to display a list of all defined variables and their values:

```
> set
greeting hello
poet  Virgil
```

As in the BASH shell, the dollar sign (**$**) is a special operator that evaluates a shell variable. Evaluation retrieves a variable's value—usually a set of characters. This set of characters then replaces the variable name. In effect, wherever a **$** is placed before a variable name, the shell replaces the variable name with the value of the variable. In the next example, the shell variable greeting is evaluated and its contents, "hello," are then used as the argument for an **echo** command. The **echo** command prints a set of characters on the screen.

```
> echo $greeting
hello
```

As with the BASH shell, double quotes, single quotes, and a backslash will suppress the evaluation of special characters. Also, back quotes can be used to assign the results of commands to variables. In the next example, the double quotes suppress the **?** special character.

```
> set notice = "Is the meeting tomorrow?."
> echo $notice
Is the meeting tomorrow?
>
```

TCSH Shell Scripts: Input and Output

You can easily define and use variables within a shell script. As in the example coming up, you can place Linux commands, such as the assignment operation and **echo**, in a file using a text editor. You can then make the file executable and invoke it on the command line as another command. Remember that to add the execute permission, you use the

chmod command with a **u+x** permission or the **700** absolute permission. Within a script, you can use the **echo** command to output data. However, input is read into a variable by redirecting the standard input using the **>** operator.

┤Note

The TCSH shell has no comparable version of the BASH shell's **read** command.

The TCSH shell examines the first character of a file to determine whether or not it is a TCSH shell script. Remember that all TCSH shell scripts must have a **#** character as the first character on the first line. This identifies the file as a TCSH shell script. Notice the **#** character at the beginning of the *greet* script. Placed anywhere in the file other than as the first character of the first line, the **#** character operates as an ordinary character.

```
#
# Script to output hello greeting

set greeting="hello"
echo The value of greeting is $greeting
```

In the following example, the *greet* script is made executable and then run.

```
> chmod u+x greet
> greet
The value of greeting is hello
```

The **set** command combined with the redirection operation, **$<**, will read whatever the user enters into the standard input. The next example reads user input into the **greeting** variable.

```
> set greeting = $<
```

You can place the prompt on the same line as the input using the **echo** command. The TCSH shell uses a special option for **echo**, the **–n** option, which eliminates the need for a carriage return at the end of the output string. The cursor remains on the same line at the end of the output string:

```
> echo -n Please enter a greeting:
```

If you wish to include a space at the end of your prompt, you need to place the output string within double quotes, including the space:

```
> echo -n "Please enter a greeting: "
```

The *greetpt* script, shown next, contains a TCSH shell version of a prompt remaining on the same line as the input.

```
#

echo -n "Please enter a greeting: "
set greeting = $<

echo "The greeting you entered was $greeting"
```

A run of the *greetpt* script follows:

```
> greetpt
Please enter a greeting: hello
The greeting you entered was hello
>
```

Arrays: ( ) and

In the TCSH shell, you can declare and use arrays, referencing each element. You declare arrays with the **set** command and a list of values for each element in the array. The list of values is enclosed within parenthesis, and each value is separated by a space. The array is as large as the number of values assigned. The next example declares an array called **weather** and assigns three values to it (see Figure 4-1). The **weather** array will have three elements, each with a corresponding value:

```
> set weather = (hot cold rain)
```

List of values

The array name by itself references all the elements in the array. The next example prints out the entire array.

```
> echo $weather
hot cold rain
```

4

You can reference each element in the array with the position of the element enclosed within brackets. Elements of the array are numbered from 1. The next example assigns a new value to the first element:

Array index

```
> set weather[1] = sunny
> echo $weather
sunny cold rain
```

You can then access the contents of an element, just like any other variable, by preceding the element reference with a dollar sign (**$**). The next example prints out the contents of the third element:

```
> echo $weather[3]
rain
```

Evaluates array element

	1	2	3
weather array	hot	cold	rain

weather[1] weather[2] weather[3]

% set weather (hot cold rain)

Figure 4-1   TCSH arrays

In the *wreport* script, the **weather** array is defined and used in a script:

```
#
set weather = (hot cold rain)
echo "The weather today is $weather[2]"
echo "Tomorrow there will be $weather[3]"
```

A run of the *wreport* script is shown here:

```
> wreport
The weather today is cold
Tomorrow there will be rain
>
```

You can specify a range of elements by specifying the beginning and end of a range, separated with a hyphen within brackets. The next example prints out the value for the second and third elements:

```
> echo $weather[2-3]
cold rain
```

Set of array elements

Ask the Expert

Question: How do I know the number of elements in an array?

Answer: In every array, a special variable holds the number of elements within that array. The variable is referenced by the array name preceded by a number sign (#). For example, the variable that holds the number of elements in the **weather** array is **#weather**. As with any variable, you can access the contents of **#weather** by preceding it with a **$**, as in **$#weather**. In this example, the number of elements in the **weather** array is printed out:

```
> echo $#weather
3
```

Argument Array: **argv**

When a shell script is invoked, all the words on the command line are parsed and placed in elements of an array called **argv**. The **argv[0]** array will hold the name of the shell script, and beginning with **argv[1]**, each element will hold an argument entered on the command line. In the case of shell scripts, **argv[0]** will always contain the name of the shell script. As with any array element, you can access the contents of an argument array element by preceding it with a **$** operator. For example, **$argv[1]** accesses the contents of the first element in the **argv** array. In the *greetarg* script, a greeting is passed as the first argument on the command line. This first argument is accessed with **$argv[1]**.

```
#
echo "The greeting you entered was: $argv[1]"
```

A run of the *greetarg* script follows:

```
> greetarg Hello
The greeting you entered was: Hello
```

Each word is parsed on the command line unless it's quoted. In the next example, the *greetarg* script is invoked with an unquoted string and then a quoted string. Notice that the quoted string, "Hello, how are you", is treated as one argument.

```
> greetarg Hello, how are you
The greeting you entered was: Hello,
> greetarg "Hello, how are you"
The greeting you entered was: Hello, how are you
>
```

If more than one argument is entered, the arguments can each be referenced with a corresponding element in the **argv** array. In the next

4

example, the *myargs* script prints out four arguments. Four arguments were then entered on the command line (see Figure 4-2).

```
#
echo "The first argument is: $argv[1]"
echo "The second argument is: $argv[2]"
echo "The third argument is: $argv[3]"
echo "The fourth argument is: $argv[4]"
```

The run of the *myargs* script is shown here:

```
> myargs Hello Hi yo "How are you"
The first argument is: Hello
The second argument is: Hi
The third argument is: yo
The fourth argument is: How are you
```

In the *wreporta* script, the *wreport* script is rewritten to use arguments. The arguments for the *wreporta* script are numbers that index the **weather** array. The first argument is 2, which is referenced by the argument variable **$argv[1]**. The second argument is 3, referenced by **$argv[2]**. The **$weather[$argv[1]]**, in this example, references **weather[2]**, cold.

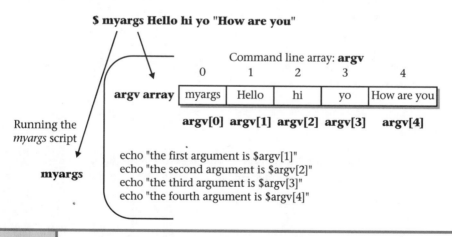

Figure 4-2 The argv **array for command line arguments**

```
#
set weather = (hot cold rain)
echo "The weather today is $weather[$argv[1]]"
echo "Tomorrow there will be $weather[$argv[2]]"
```

A run of the *wreporta* script is shown here:

```
> wreporta 2 3
The weather today is cold
Tomorrow there will be rain
>
```

4

Hint

An **argv** element can be abbreviated to the number of the element preceded by a **$** sign. **$argv[1]** can also be written as **$1**. This means TCSH shell scripts can include argument references that are very similar to BASH shell argument references.

Ask the Expert

Question: Can I reference all arguments at once?

Answer: A special argument variable **argv[*]** references all the arguments in the command line. **$argv[*]** can be abbreviated as **$***. Notice that this is the same name used in the BASH shell to reference all arguments. In the next example, the *allargs* script uses both **$argv[*]** and **$*** to reference all arguments.

```
#
echo $argv[*]
echo $*
```

The run of the *allargs* script is shown here:

```
> allargs Hello Hi Salutations
Hello Hi Salutations
Hello Hi Salutations
```

Question: Can I find out the number of arguments a user enters on the command line?

Answer: The **#argv** argument variable contains the number of arguments entered on the command line. This is useful for specifying a fixed number of arguments for a script. The number can be checked to determine whether the user has entered the correct amount. In the next example, the *argnum* script outputs the number of arguments that the user entered:

```
#
echo "The number of arguments entered is $#argv"
```

The run of the *argnum* script is shown here.

```
> argnum Hello hi salutations
The number of arguments entered is 3
```

The *arglist* script and Figure 4-3 show the use of both the **argv[*]** and **#argv** special argument variables. The user first displays the number of arguments using **#argv** and then uses **argv[*]** to display the list of arguments entered.

Number of command line arguments

```
#
echo "The number of arguments entered is $#argv"
echo "The list of arguments is: $argv[*]"
```

The list of command line arguments

The run of the *arglist* script is shown here:

```
> arglist Hello hi yo
The number of arguments entered is 3
The list of arguments is: Hello hi yo
```

Numeric Variables: @

In the TCSH shell, you can declare numeric variables using the **@** command instead of the **set** command. You can then perform arithmetic,

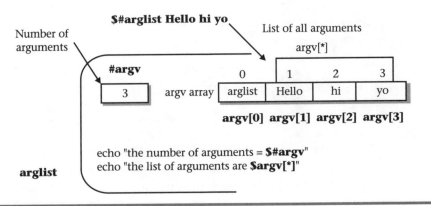

Figure 4-3 The #argv and argv[*] variables

relational, and bitwise operations on such variables (using the appropriate operators). In this respect, the TCSH shell is similar to programming languages. Numeric and string variables are two very different types of objects managed in very different ways. You cannot use the **set** command on a numeric variable. The **@** command consists of the keyword **@**, the variable name, an assignment operator, and an expression. The next example declares the numeric variable **num** and assigns the value 10 to it.

```
> @ num = 10
```

Many different assignment operators are available for you to use, such as increments and arithmetic assignment operators. They are the same as those used in GAWK (which is discussed in Module 5) and in the C programming language. The expression can be any arithmetic, relational, or bitwise expression. You can create complex expressions using parentheses. The operands in an expression should be separated from the operator by spaces; for example, 10*5 is not a valid expression and should be written with spaces, like this: 10 * 5. You can also use a numeric variable as an operand in an expression. In the next example, the variable **count** is declared as numeric and used in an arithmetic expression. Notice that **count** is evaluated with a **$** operator so that the value of **count**, 3, is used in the expression.

Assignment operation with arithmetic expression

```
> @ count = 3
> @ num = 2 * ($count + 10)
> echo $num
26
```

The TCSH shell arithmetic operators are listed in Table 4-1.

The next example uses two different assignment operators to increment the **num** variable by 1: the increment operator (**++**) and the arithmetic addition assignment operator (**+=**):

```
> @ num = $num + 1
> @ num += 1
> @ num++
```
Increment

Arithmetic Operators	Function/Description
–	Minus unary operator
+	Addition
–	Subtraction
*	Multiplication
/	Division
%	Modulo
Assignment Operators	
=	Assignment
+=	Adds to expression and then assigns
–=	Subtracts from expression and then assigns
*=	Multiplies with expression and then assigns
/=	Divides into expression and then assigns
%=	Modulo operation with expression and then assigns
++	Increment variable
–	Decrement variable

Table 4-1   **TCSH Arithmetic and Assignment Operators**

As shown in the following example, you can assign the results of an arithmetic expression to a numeric variable:

```
> @ num = 10 * 5
> echo $num
50
```

Hint

Relational operations result in the arithmetic values of 1 if true and 0 if false.

In the next example, the value of **num** will be 1 since the relational operation is true.

```
> @ count = 3
> @ num = ($count < 10)
> echo $num
1
>
```

The declaration of arrays of numeric elements is complicated by the fact that you need to use the **set** command to first declare the array. Then you can use the **@** command to assign numeric values to the individual elements of the array. In the next example, the array **degrees** is first declared and values assigned. Although these values can be any number, they are not considered *numeric* values.

```
> set degrees = (0 45 0)
```

When you use the **@** command to assign a numeric value to an element, the element is then a numeric value. You then reference the element with a number enclosed in brackets. In the next example, the first element is assigned the numeric value of 100:

```
> @ degrees[1] = 100
> echo $degrees[1]
100
>
```

4

Environment Variables: **setenv**

The TCSH shell has two types of variables: *local* variables and *environment* variables. A local variable is local to the shell it was declared in; an environment variable operates like a scoped global variable. The environment variable is known to any subshells but not to any parent shells. An environment variable is defined with the **setenv** command. You assign a value to an environment variable using the **setenv** command, the variable name, and the value assigned. There is no assignment operator. In the next example, the **greeting** environment variable is assigned the value "hello."

```
> setenv greeting hello
```

Whenever a shell script is called, it generates its own shell. If a shell script is executed from another shell script, it will have its own shell separate from that of the first script. There are now two shells: the parent shell belonging to the first script and a subshell, which is the new shell

Hint

Each shell has its own set of variables. The subshell cannot reference local variables in the parent shell, but it can reference environment variables. Any environment variables declared in the parent shell can be referenced by any subshells.

generated when the second script was executed.

In the next example, the variable **myfile** is defined as an environment variable in the *dispfile* script. Notice the use of the **setenv** command instead of **set**. The **myfile** variable can now be referenced in any subshells, such as that generated when *printfile* is executed. The user has already created a file called *List* with the entries screen, modem, and paper.

The *dispfile* script is shown here:

```
#
setenv myfile "List"
echo "Displaying $myfile"
cat -n $myfile
printfile
```

The *printfile* script is shown here:

```
#
echo "Printing $myfile"
lpr $myfile &
```

The following example shows a run of the *dispfile* script:

```
> dispfile
Displaying List
1 screen
2 modem
3 paper
Printing List
```

As shown in Figure 4-4, when *printfile* is executed, it will be able to directly access the **myfile** variable defined in the shell of the *dispfile* script.

1-Minute Drill

● **How do you assign values to a variable?**

● **How do you assign values to a numeric variable?**

● **What special array is used to hold a shell program's arguments?**

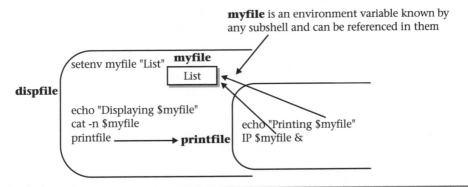

Figure 4-4   TCSH shell environment variable referenced from within a subshell

---

● Use the set **command and the assignment operator.**
● Use the @ **operator and the assignment operator.**
● The argv **array.**

Table 4-2 list commonly used TCSH commands as well as command line arguments.

TCSH Shell Commands	Function/Description
echo	Displays values.
–n	Eliminates output newline.
eval	Executes the command line.
exec	Executes a command in place of current process. Does not generate a new subshell, but uses the current one.
exit	Exits from the current shell.
setenv *var*	Makes a variable available for reference by each new subshell (call-by-reference).
printenv	Displays values of environment variables.
set	Assigns new values to variables. Used alone, lists all defined variables.
@	Assigns numeric expressions.
shift	Moves each command line argument to the left so the number used to reference it is one less than before—for example, argument **$3** would then be referenced by **$2**, and so on; **$1** is lost.
unset	Undefines a variable.
unsetenv	Undefines an environment variable.

Command Line Arguments	Description
$argv[0] $0	Name of Linux command.
$argv[n] $n	The *n*th command line argument beginning from 1, $1 to $*n*. You can use **set** to change them.
$argv[*] $*	All the command line arguments beginning from 1. You can use **set** to change them.
$#argv $#	The count of the command line arguments.

Table 4-2   TCSH Shell Commands and Variables

Control Structures and Operators: **while**, **if**, **switch**, and **foreach**

As in other shells, the TCSH shell has a set of control structures that let you control the execution of commands in a script. You can use loop and conditional control structures to repeat Linux commands or make decisions on which commands you want to execute. The **while** and **if** control structures are more general-purpose control structures that perform iterations and make decisions using a variety of different tests. The **switch** and **foreach** control structures are more specialized operations. The **switch** structure is a restricted form of the **if** condition that checks to see whether a value is equal to one of a set of possible values. The **foreach** structure is a limited type of loop that runs through a list of values, assigning a new value to a variable with each iteration.

The **while** loop and **if** conditions operate much as they do in

Hint

The TCSH shell differs from other shells in that its control structures conform more to a programming language format. The test condition for a TCSH shell control structure is an expression that evaluates to true or false, not to a Linux command. One key difference between BASH shell and TCSH shell control structures is that TCSH shell structures cannot redirect or pipe their output. They are strictly control structures, controlling the execution of commands.

programming languages. The loop continues until a test expression returns false. The **if** condition executes its commands if its test expression returns true. The test expression is a TCSH shell expression, and the operators used in a TCSH shell expression are similar to those found in the C programming language. The shell uses a wide range of assignment, arithmetic, relational, and bitwise operators, many of which are not available in the BASH or PDKSH shell. Like C program expressions, a

TCSH shell expression is true if it results in a nonzero value; it is false if it results in a 0 value.

The **switch** structure works like a restricted version of the **if** structure. The **switch** structure compares a string with a set of possible patterns. If a match is found, operations associated with that matched pattern are executed. The **switch** structure is useful for implementing menus, in which a user makes a choice from among several possible options.

The **foreach** structure runs through a list of values, assigning each value in turn to a specified variable. There is no test. The list of values can be generated by a pattern and shell special characters. For example, the asterisk (*) will generate a list of your file names. A list of values can also be specified by a set of words. Each word is then a value assigned in turn to the **for** variable. The loop will always continue until all values have been assigned.

Test Expressions

The **if** and **while** control structures use an *expression* as their test. A true test is any expression that results in a nonzero value. A false test is any expression that results in a 0 value. In the TCSH shell, relational and equality expressions can be easily used as test expressions, because they result in 1 if true and 0 if false. You can use a number of operators in an expression, as shown in Table 4-3. The test expression can also be an arithmetic or a string comparison, but strings can be compared only for equality or inequality.

Unlike the BASH and PDKSH shells, you must enclose the TCSH shell **if** and **while** test expressions within parentheses. The next example shows a simple test expression that tests to see whether two strings are equal:

```
if ( $greeting == "hi" ) then        Equality comparison
    echo Informal Greeting           expression
endif
```

The TCSH shell has a separate set of operators for testing strings against other strings or against regular expressions:

● The == and != operators test for the equality and inequality of strings.

● The =~ and !~ operators test a string against a regular expression and test to determine whether a pattern match is successful or not.

String Comparisons	Function/Description
==	Equal strings
!=	Not-equal strings
=~	Compares string to a pattern to test if equal; the pattern can be any regular expression
!~	Compares string to a pattern to test if not equal; the pattern can be any regular expression
Logical Operations	
&&	Logical AND
||	Logical OR
!	Logical NOT
File Tests	
−e	File exists
−r	File is readable
−w	File can be written to, modified
−x	File is executable
−d	File name is a directory name
−f	File is an ordinary file
−o	File is owned by user
−z	File is empty
Relational Operators	
>	Greater than
<	Less than
>=	Greater than or equal to
<=	Less than or equal to
!=	Not equal
==	Equal

Table 4-3   Test Expression Operators

The regular expression can contain any of the shell special characters. In the next example, any value of greeting that begins with an uppercase or lowercase *h* will match the regular expression, **[Hh]***:

Regular expression match

```
if ( $greeting =~ [Hh]* ) then
    echo Informal Greeting
endif
```

> **Hint**
>
> Like the BASH shell, the TCSH shell also has several special operators that test the status of files. Many of these operators are the same in both shells.

In the next example, the **if** command tests to see whether the file *mydata* is readable.

```
if ( -r mydata ) then
    echo Informal Greeting
endif
```

TCSH Shell Conditions: **if-then**, **if-then-else**, and **switch**

The TCSH shell has a set of conditional control structures with which you make decisions about what Linux commands to execute. Many of these conditional control structures are similar to conditional control structures found in the BASH shell. There are, however, some key differences. The TCSH shell **if** structure ends with the keyword *endif*. The **switch** structure uses the keyword **case** differently than it is used in the BASH shell. It ends with the keyword *endsw* and uses the keyword *breaksw* instead of the two semicolons used in the BASH shell. Furthermore, TCSH has two **if** control structures: a simple version that executes only one command, and a more complex version that can execute several commands, as well as alternative commands. The simple version of **if** consists of the keyword *if* followed by a test and a single Linux command. The complex version ends with the keyword *endif*. The TCSH shell's conditional control structures are listed in Table 4-4.

The **if-then** Structure

The **if-then** structure places a condition on several Linux commands. That condition is an *expression*. If the expression results in a value other than 0,

Control Structures	Description

if (*expression*) then
    commands
endif
	If the expression is true, the following commands are executed. You can specify more than one Linux command.

if (*expression*) then
    command
else
command
endif
	If the expression it true, the command after **then** is executed. If the expression is false, the command following **else** is executed.

switch(*string*) case *pattern*: *command* breaksw default: *command* endsw	Allows you to choose among several alternative commands.

4

Table 4-4   TCSH Conditional Control Structures

the expression is true and the commands within the **if** structure are executed. If the expression results in a 0 value, the expression is false and the commands within the **if** structure are not executed.

The **if-then** structure begins with the keyword *if* and is followed by an expression enclosed in parentheses. The keyword *then* follows the expression. You can then specify any number of Linux commands on the following lines. The keyword *endif* ends the **if** command. Notice that, whereas in the BASH shell the *then* keyword is on a line of its own, in the TCSH shell, *then* is on the same line as the test expression. The syntax for the **if-then** structure is shown here:

```
if ( expression ) then
      commands
   endif
```

The *ifls* script shown next allows you to list files by size. If you enter an **s** at the prompt, each file in the current directory is listed, followed by the number of blocks it uses. If you enter anything else at the prompt, the **if** test fails and the script does nothing.

```
#
echo -n "Please enter option: "
set option = $<

if ($option == "s") then
        echo Listing files by size
        ls -s
    endif
```

A run of the *ifls* script is shown here:

```
> ifls
Please enter option: s
Listing files by size
total 2
    1 monday      2 today
>
```

Often, you need to choose between two alternatives based on whether or not an expression is true. The *else* keyword allows an **if** structure to choose between two alternative commands. If the expression is true, those commands immediately following the test expression are executed. If the expression is false, those commands following the *else* keyword are executed. The syntax for the **if-else** command is shown here:

```
if ( expression ) then
     commands
   else
     commands
endif
```

The *elsels* script in the next example executes the **ls** command to list files with two different possible options: by size or with all file information. If the user enters an **s**, files are listed by size; otherwise, all file information is listed. Notice how the syntax differs from the BASH shell version of the *elsels* script described in Module 3.

```
#
echo Enter s to list file sizes.
echo otherwise all file information is listed.
echo -n "Please enter option : "
set option = $<

if ($option == "s") then
        ls -s
        else  ◄————— else operation
        ls -l
endif
echo Goodbye
```

4

A run of the *elsels* script follows:

```
> elsels
Enter s to list file sizes,
otherwise all file information is listed.
Please enter option: s
total 2
     1 monday      2 today
Good-bye
>
```

Ask the Expert

Question: How do I use the if **structure to check for arguments?**

Answer: The **if** structure is often used to check whether the user entered the appropriate number of arguments for a shell script. The special shell variable **#argv** contains the number of arguments the user entered. Using **$#argv** in a test operation allows you to determine whether the user entered the correct number of arguments.

If an incorrect number of arguments was entered, you may need to end the shell script. As in the BASH shell, you can do this with the **exit** command. The **exit** command ends the shell script, returning an exit condition. **exit** takes a number argument: an argument of 0 indicates that the shell script ended successfully; any other argument, such as 1, indicates that an error occurred.

In the next example, the *ifarg* script takes only one argument. If the user fails to enter an argument or enters more than one argument, the **if** test will be true, the error message will print out, and the script will exit with an error value.

```
#                         Number of arguments
if ( $#argv != 1 ) then
        echo "Invalid number of arguments"
                echo "Enter only one argument"
                exit 1
        endif

    echo $argv[1]
```

A run of the *ifarg* script follows:

```
> ifarg
Invalid number of arguments
Enter only one argument
```

Question: Can I nest the if **structures to create complex decisions?**

Answer: To nest **if-then** operations, you simply attach an **if** structure to an **else**, instead of a block. This way, you can choose between several alternatives. The first alternative is specified with the **if** structure, followed by other alternatives, each specified by its own **else-if** component. The alternative to the last **if** structure is specified with an **else**. If the test for the first **if** structure fails, control will be passed to the next **if** structure following the next **else**, and its test will be executed. If it fails, control is passed to the next **if** structure and its test checked. This continues until a test returns true. Then that **if** has its commands executed and control passes out of the **if** structure to the next command following the *endif* keyword. The following example illustrates the use of nested **else-if** operations.

```
if ($option == "s") then
        ls -s
        else if ($option == "l") then
            ls -l
            else if ($option == "d") then
                ls -F
            else
                echo "Invalid Option"
endif
```

The **switch** Structure

The **switch** structure chooses among several possible alternative commands. It is similar to the BASH shell's **case** structure in that the choice is made by comparing a string with several possible patterns. Each possible pattern is associated with a set of commands. If a match is found, the associated commands are performed.

The **switch** structure begins with the keyword *switch* followed by a test string within parentheses. The string is often derived from a variable evaluation. A set of patterns then follows—each pattern preceded by the keyword *case* and terminated with a colon. Commands associated with this choice are listed after the colon. The commands are terminated with the keyword *breaksw*. After all the listed patterns, the keyword *endsw* ends the **switch** structure. The syntax for the switch structure is shown here:

```
switch (test-string)
   case pattern:
        commands
        breaksw
   case pattern:
        commands
        breaksw
   default:
        commands
        breaksw
   endsw
```

Note

Each pattern will be matched against the test string until a match is found. If no match is found, the default option is executed. The default choice is represented with the keyword *default*. The default is optional. However, it is helpful for notifying the user of test strings with no match.

lschoice

Project 4-1: Menus with switch

A **switch** structure is often used to implement menus. In the program *lschoice*, in the next example, the user is asked to enter an option for listing files in different ways. Notice the default option that warns of invalid input. The program begins by displaying a menu of options and prompting the user to enter one. Then the **switch** structure detects the entry the user made and executes the corresponding command.

Step-by-Step

1. Create a menu of three options to list sizes, complete file information, or just C files (those with **.c** file name extensions). Use three simple **echo** commands.

2. Prompt the user to enter a choice, which is then read into the **choice** variable using the **set** command and the **$<** operator.

3. Use a **switch** structure to determine the choice that the user made. Evaluate the **choice** variable in the **switch** expression, **$choice**, and use its value to check for a match with each pattern value in the case entries.

4. Set up three case entries. The first is for the **s** pattern, which, if matched, will execute the **ls** command with the **–s** option, listing the file names with their sizes. The entry ends with the **breaksw** command.

5. Use the second case entry to hold the pattern **l**, which, if matched, will list files with all their file information, including date last changed and access permissions. The entry ends with the **breaksw** command.

6. Use the third case entry to hold the pattern ***.c**. A match here will execute the **ls *.c** command, which will display all file names ending with the character **.c** (***** is a special wildcard character that matches any pattern). The entry ends with the **breaksw** command.

7. For the default entry, display an error message "Invalid Option."
It will also end with the **breaksw** command.

8. End the switch structure with the **endsw** command.

The *lschoice* script is shown here:

```
#
echo s. List Sizes
echo l. List All File Information
echo c. List C Files

echo -n "Please enter choice: "
set choice = $<

switch ($choice)
    case s:
        ls -s
        breaksw
    case l:
        ls -l
        breaksw
    case c:
        ls *.c
        breaksw
    default:
        echo Invalid Option
        breaksw
    endsw
```

A run of the *lschoice* script follows.

```
> lschoice
s. List Sizes
l. List All File Information
c. List C Files
Please enter choice: c
io.c    lib.c    main.c
```

You can specify more than one value in a pattern. In the preceding
example, only the lowercase versions of the character choices were
permissible. An uppercase C would be considered invalid input. You can
specify more than one choice for a set of commands by using more than
one **case** structure without a **breaksw** command. You could also use the

brackets shell special characters. A pattern can use any of the shell special characters, just as the patterns in a BASH shell **case** structure can. The brackets special characters list a set of possible valid characters. The pattern **[Cc]** will match on either the uppercase or lowercase *c*.

In the next example, *lschoice* has been rewritten as *lulschoice* to include command choices for both lowercase and uppercase letters. The choice for uppercase and lowercase *c* is written as two consecutive **case** entries with no intervening **breaksw** command. However, the patterns for uppercase and lowercase *s* is written using the brackets special characters in one pattern: **[Ss]**.

```
#
echo  s. List Sizes
     echo  l. List All File Information
     echo  c. List C Files

     echo -n "Please enter choice: "
     set choice = $<

     switch ($choice)
          case [Ss]:
               ls -s
               breaksw
          case L:
          case l:
               ls -l
               breaksw
          case C:
          case c:
               ls *.c
               breaksw
          default
               echo Invalid Option
               breaksw
          endsw
```

A run of the *lulschoice* is shown here:

```
> lulschoice
s. List Sizes
l. List All File Information
c. List C Files
Please enter choice: C
main.c   lib.c   file.c
```

Loop Structures: **while, foreach**, and **repeat**

The TCSH shell has a set of loop control structures that allow you to repeat Linux commands: **while, foreach**, and **repeat**. The TCSH shell loop control structures are listed in Table 4–5.

The **while** structure operates in a way similar to corresponding structures found in programming languages. Like the TCSH shell's **if** structure, the **while** structure tests the result of an expression. The TCSH shell's **foreach** structure, like the **for** and **for-in** structures in the BASH shell, does not perform any tests. It simply progresses through a list of values, assigning each value in turn to a specified variable. In this respect, the **foreach** structure is very different from corresponding structures found in programming languages. The **repeat** structure is a simple and limited control structure. It repeats one command a specified number of times. It has no test expression, and it cannot repeat more than one command.

The **while** Structure

The **while** loop repeats commands. A **while** loop begins with the keyword *while* and is followed by an expression enclosed in parentheses.

Loop Control Structures	Description
while(*expression*) *command* end	Executes commands as long as the expression is true.
foreach *variable* (*arg-list*) *command* end	Iterates the loop for as many arguments as exist in the argument list. Each time through the loop, the variable is set to the next argument in the list; operates like **for-in** in the BASH shell.
repeat *num command*	Repeat a command the specified number of times.
continue	Jump to next iteration, skipping the remainder of the loop commands.
break	Break out of a loop.

Table 4-5   TCSH Loop Control Structures

The end of the loop is specified by the keyword *end*. The syntax for the **while** loop is shown here:

```
while ( expression )
    commands
end
```

The **while** structure can easily be combined with a **switch** structure to drive a menu. In the *lschoicew* script, notice that the menu contains a **quit** option that will set the value of **again** to no and stop the loop.

```
#
set again=yes

while ($again == yes)  ◄──── Main loop
echo "1. List Sizes"
echo "2. List All File Information"
echo "3. List C Files"
echo "4. Quit"
echo -n "Please enter choice : "
set choice = $<

switch ($choice)  ◄──── switch operation to detect user selection
    case 1:
        ls -s
        breaksw
    case 2:
        ls -l
        breaksw
    case 3:
        ls *.c
        breaksw
    case 4:
        set again = no  ◄──── Will make loop test fail
        echo Goodbye
        breaksw
    default
        echo Invalid Option
    endsw

end  ◄──── Ends main loop
```

A run of the *lschoicew* script follows:

```
> lschoicew
1. List Sizes
2. List All File Information
3. List C Files
4. Quit
Please enter choice: 3
main.c   lib.c    file.c
1. List Sizes
2. List All File Information
3. List C Files
4. Quit
Please enter choice: 4
Good-bye
>
```

The **foreach** Structure

The **foreach** structure is designed to sequentially reference a list of values. It is similar to the BASH shell's **for-in** structure. The **foreach** structure takes two operands—a variable and a list of values enclosed in parentheses. Each value in the list is assigned to the variable in the **foreach** structure. Like the **while** structure, the **foreach** structure is a loop. Each time through the loop, the next value in the list is assigned to the variable. When the end of the list is reached, the loop stops. Like the **while** loop, the body of a **foreach** loop ends with the keyword *end*. The syntax for the **foreach** loop is shown here:

```
foreach variable ( list of values )
    commands
end
```

The **foreach** loop is useful for managing files. In this structure, you can use shell special characters in a pattern to generate a list of file names for use as your list of values. This generated list of file names then becomes the list referenced by the **foreach** structure. An asterisk by itself generates a list of all files and directories. The pattern ***.c** lists files with the **.c** extension. These are usually C source code files.

The next example makes a backup of each file and places the backup in a directory called *sourcebak*. The pattern ***.c** generates a list of file names on which the **foreach** structure can operate.

```
#                    ┌─────────────────────────────────────────┐
                     │ Assigns next file in list to backfile   │
                     │ variable with each iteration            │
                     └─────────────────────────────────────────┘
foreach backfile ( *.c ) ◄────────── ┌─────────────────────────┐
     cp $backfile sourcebak/$backfile │ Generates list of all   │
                                      │ files ending in .c      │
     echo $backfile                   └─────────────────────────┘
end
```

A run of the *cbackup* script follows:

```
> cbackup
io.c
lib.c
main.c
```

The **foreach** structure without a specified list of values takes as its list of values the command line arguments. The arguments specified on the command line when the shell file was invoked become a list of values referenced by the **foreach** structure. The variable used in the **foreach** structure is set automatically to each argument value in sequence. The first time through the loop, the variable is set to the value of the first argument. The second time, it is set to the value of the second argument, and so on.

You can explicitly reference the command line argument by using the **argv[*]** special argument variable. In the next example, a list of C program files is entered on the command line when the shell file *cbackuparg* is invoked. In the **foreach** loop, **argv[*]** references all the arguments on the command line. Each argument will be consecutively assigned to the variable **backfile** in the **foreach** loop. The first time through the loop, **$backfile** is the same as **$argv[1]**. The second time through, **$backfile** is the same as **$argv[2]**. The variable **argnum** is used to reference each argument. Both the argument and the value of **backfile** are displayed to show that they are the same.

```
#

@ argnum = 1
foreach backfile ($argv[*])
```

```
    cp $backfile sourcebak/$backfile
    echo "$backfile $argv[$argnum]"
    @ argnum = $argnum + 1
end
```

A run of the *cbackuparg* script follows:

```
> cbackuparg  main.c  lib.c  io.c
main.c main.c
lib.c lib.c
io.c io.c
```

4

1-Minute Drill

- **What structure could you use to replace a** switch **structure?**

- **Can I use file matching operations like *, [ ], or ? in tests?**

- **If the variable used in a loop's test is never changed within that loop, will the program ever stop?**

The repeat Structure

The **repeat** structure is a structure that simply repeats a command a specified number of times. It can repeat only one command. The **repeat** structure begins with the keyword *repeat*, a number for the number of repetitions, and the command to be repeated. Here is the syntax:

> repeat *num command*

In this example, the **echo** command is repeated three times.

```
> repeat 3 echo "hello again"
hello again
hello again
hello again
```

- **Nested** if **structures with** else.
- **Yes.**
- **No; you have an infinite loop.**

The **continue** Command

As in the BASH shell, the TCSH shell's **continue** command is used with loops to pass over the remaining statements in the body of a loop and continue on with the next iteration.

Note

Use of the **continue** command can contribute to obscure programming styles. It should be used sparingly.

In the next example, the *loopodd* script outputs only on odd iterations of the loop by using **continue** to skip over the **echo** command on even iterations. The **continue** command literally transfers control to the *end* keyword at the end of the loop, which, in turn, continues with the next iteration of the loop.

```
#
@ num=0
while ($num < 6)
  @ num = $num + 1
  if ( ($num % 2) == 0) continue
    echo "$num iteration of loop"
  end
echo Goodbye
```

A run of the *loopodd* script follows:

```
> loopodd
1 iteration of loop
3 iteration of loop
5 iteration of loop
Goodbye
```

Infinite Loops and the **break** Command

You can implement an infinite loop in the TCSH shell by using the numeric constant 1 as the test expression in a **while** structure. If you use an infinite loop, you will need to have a way to stop it. The **break** command, when used within any loop, will transfer control out of the loop.

┤Note

Often an infinite loop will contain a conditioned **break** command that, when executed, ends the loop.

In the *loopinfinite* script that follows, the user sets up an infinite loop that outputs the number of the iteration. When **num** is greater than 3, the **break** command is executed, breaking out of the loop.

```
#
@ num=1

while ( 1 )
   if ($num > 3) break
      echo "$num iteration of loop"
   @ num = $num + 1
   end
echo Goodbye
```

A run of the *loopinfinite* script follows:

```
> loopinfinite
1 iteration of loop
2 iteration of loop
3 iteration of loop
Goodbye
```

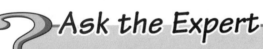

Ask the Expert

Question: Can I use the break **command to stop a** foreach **loop?**

Answer: The **break** command is the only way you have of stopping a **foreach** loop before it reaches the end of its list. In the *fnamesAM* script that follows, the user wants to output only file names that begin with the first half of the alphabet: file names beginning with *a* through *m*. The

foreach structure will output all the file names in its list. To stop it, you use the **break** command.

```
#

foreach filename ( * )
        if ( $filename =~ [n-z]* ) break
        echo $filename
    end

    echo "Goodbye"
```

A run of the *fnamesAM* script follows:

```
> ls
lib.c main.c resume termpaper
> fnamesAM
lib.c
main.c
Goodbye
```

myindext

Project 4-2: Indexing with TCSH

The *myindext* program is a TCSH shell version of the BASH *myindex* program described in Module 3. It performs the same functions, automatically generating a Web page that can operate as an index for selecting other Web pages. It assumes that there are subdirectories with Web pages in them. Many of the shell operations here are the same as those for the BASH shell program. The **grep**, **echo**, **basename**, as well as the **cut** and **sed** commands used in *myindex* are retained in *myindext*, unchanged.

The loops and **if** structures, as well as the assignments, are very different in this module's program. But there are two nested **foreach** loops in *myindext*, much like the **for** loop in the BASH program. The assignment operations use the **set** command with the = sign. The **if** conditions use parenthesis, and standard C-like operators work with them. The *then* keyword is placed on the same line as the BASH shell's test, and the **if** condition ends in the keyword *endif*.

Step-by-Step

1. Detect any directories in the current directory and then check to see whether they contain Web pages (any file with an **.html** or **.htm** extension). The names of these files are placed in strings comprising HTML commands, **href**s to select and display the files. The HTML references are organized into a list with the **<ul>** and **</ul>** tags with each item preceded by a **<li>** tag. Directory names are used as headings, **<h1>** tag.

2. Use the **foreach** command with * to match on all the file and directory names, placing each in turn in the **$i** variable.

3. If you find a directory , search for any HTML files in an inner **foreach** loop. Place HTML files in the **j** variable.

4. Search the HTML file for a title and use that as the link text in the index. Use **grep** to search for the occurrence of a **<TITLE>** pattern. If you find one, return it to the **tline** variable. If you do not find the pattern, return a 1 to the **$?** status variable.

5. Check the **$?** status variable to see whether **grep** was successful. If so, use a set of **sed** commands to strip the preceding and tailing **<TITLE>** and **</TITLE>** tags along with any other characters. The title text itself remains and is assigned to the **ntitle** variable.

6. If **grep** does not find a **<TITLE>** line, assign the file name to **ntitle**. First, use **basename** to extract the file name from the path name, removing any preceding directory names. Then use **cut** to remove the extension (outputs the first field using the period as the delimiter). Both **.htm** and **.html** extensions can be removed.

7. After assigning text to **ntitle**, use it as the link text in the **href** HTML line. This line begins with a **<li>** tag, indicating it is a list item.

The *myindext* script is shown here:

```
#!/bin/tcsh

echo '<HTML>'
echo '<HEAD>'
echo '<TITLE>My Index</TITLE>'
echo '</HEAD>'
echo '<BODY>'
echo '<H1>Index of HTML Files</H1>'

foreach i ( * )
```

```
if ( -d $i ) then
echo "<h2>$i</h2>"
echo '<ul>'
foreach j ( $i/*.htm* )
          if ( -f $j ) then
                    set tline = `grep '<TITLE>'  $j`
                    if ( $? == 1 ) then
                        set ntitle = `basename $j | cut -f1  -d"."`
                    else
                        set ntitle = `echo $tline | sed 's/^.*<TITLE>//' |
                                            sed 's/<\/TITLE>.*$//'`
                    endif
                    echo "<li><a href=$j>$ntitle</a>"
                    endif
     end
echo '</ul>'
endif
end

echo '</BODY>'
echo '</HTML>'
```

☑ *Mastery Check*

1. What command do you use to read input in a TCSH shell script?

2. Can you reference multiple elements in an array at once?

3. How can you determine the number of arguments that a user enters on the command line when running a script?

4. How can you define a variable that can be referenced in subshells?

5. What is the difference between the =, ==, and =~ operators?

6. How would you check to see whether the argument a user supplies to a script is a directory name?

Part 2

Higher Level Languages

Module 5

GAWK

The Goals of This Module

- Use GAWK for simple search operations
- Develop complex scripts using GAWK commands
- Implement search operations on text-based record files
- Use regular expressions to execute complex matching operations
- Manage GAWK basic and formatted input and output
- Learn GAWK arithmetic, relational, and assignment operators
- Use GAWK control structures to implement loops and conditional tests
- Implement both preprocessing and post-processing operations in GAWK scripts

There are two ways of thinking about GAWK. It is a filter that you can invoke on the command line, like any other filter, and it can also be used to create your own filters.

A *filter*, in Linux, reads information from an input source, such as a file or the standard input, modifies or analyses that information, and then outputs the results. Results can be a modified version of the input, or an analysis of the input. For example, the **sort** filter reads a file and then outputs a sorted version of it. The **wc** filter reads a file and then calculates the number of words and lines in it, outputting just that information. With GAWK you can design and create your own filters, in effect creating your own Linux commands. You can instruct GAWK to simply display lines in a text, much like **cat**, or to search for patterns like **grep**, or even count words like **wc**. In each case, you can add your own customized filtering capabilities. You can display only part of each line, or search for a pattern in a specific field, or count only words that are capitalized.

The GAWK utility has all the flexibility and complexity of a programming language. GAWK has a set of operators that allow it to make decisions and calculations. You can also declare variables and use them in control structures to control how lines are to be processed. Many of the programming features are taken from the C programming language and share the same syntax. All of this makes for a very powerful programming tool.

You can use GAWK directly as a filter, or you can place it within a shell file that you can then execute. In the latter case, the name of the shell file can be thought of as a new filter that you have created. This module will examine both aspects of GAWK. First, we will examine GAWK as a filter, with all its different features. Then we will see how you can use it in a shell file to define your own filters.

Note

GAWK is the GNU version of the UNIX AWK utility, which was originally created as a standard utility for the UNIX operating system. One of its creators is Brian Kernighan who helped develop the UNIX operating system. An enhanced version of AWK, called NAWK, was developed later to include file handling. With NAWK, you can access several files in the same program. GAWK is a further enhancement, including the features of NAWK as well as the standard capabilities of AWK. You can find out more about GAWK at **www.gnu.org/software/gawk**.

The **gawk** Command

The **gawk** command takes as its arguments an instruction and a list of file names. The GAWK instruction is encased in single quotes and is read as one argument.

The instruction consists of two segments, a pattern and an action, with the action enclosed in brackets. Records that match that pattern are then retrieved, and the actions in the action segment are applied to those records. The syntax of a GAWK instruction looks like this:

```
pattern {action}
```

5

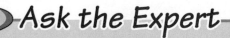

Ask the Expert

Question: Can I use the pattern segment of the GAWK instruction as a test condition?

Answer: The term "pattern" can be misleading. It is perhaps clearer to think of the *pattern* segment as a *condition*. The pattern segment can be either a pattern search or a test condition of the type found in programming languages. The GAWK utility has a full set of operators with which to construct complex conditions. You can think of a pattern search as just another kind of condition for retrieving records. Instead of simply matching patterns, as in the case of **grep**, the user specifies a condition. Records that meet that condition are then retrieved. The actions in the action segment are then applied to the retrieved records. In this respect you can think of the syntax of a GAWK instruction as

```
condition {action}
```

Question: Can GAWK operate on files?

Answer: The GAWK utility operates on either files or the standard input. You can list file names on the command line after the instruction, and if no file names are listed, the input is taken from the standard input. The following example shows the structure of the entire GAWK instruction. The invocation of GAWK consists of the *gawk* keyword followed by an instruction and file names. The instruction should be placed within single quotes to avoid interpretation by the shell. Since the condition and action are not separate arguments for GAWK, you need to enclose them both in one set of quotes. The syntax of a **gawk** command looks like this (see also the following table):

$ gawk '*pattern {action}*' *filenames*

You can think of the pattern in a GAWK instruction as operating on each line in turn. The GAWK action is then performed on each of those lines.

Options	Description
–f *filename*	With this option, GAWK will read its commands from *filename*. This option is discussed in the "GAWK Instruction Files" section, later in the module.
–Fc	This option specifies a field delimiter, **c**, for the input file. This option is discussed in the "Field Delimiters" section, later in the module.

Pattern Searches and Special Characters

A GAWK pattern search is designated with a beginning and ending slash, and it is placed in the *pattern*, or *condition*, segment of the GAWK instruction.

/pattern/ {action}

The pattern search is performed on all the lines in the file. If the pattern is found in a line, the action is performed on that line. In this respect, GAWK performs much like an editing operation. Like **sed**, a line is treated as a line of text, and the pattern is searched for throughout the line.

In the following example, **gawk** searches for any line with the pattern "Poe." When a match is found, the line is printed.

| Pattern | ➝ | ⌐ | Action |

```
$ gawk '/Poe/{print}' books
Raven        Poe        2.50    Penguin
```

The next example prints all lines with the pattern "Penguin." All records with this pattern are retrieved. The action segment in the first example contains the **print** command, which outputs the line to the standard output.

```
$ gawk '/Penguin/{print}' books
Tempest      Shakespeare  15.75   Penguin
Raven        Poe           2.50   Penguin
```

The contents of the *books* file used in this and following examples is shown here:

```
Tempest      Shakespeare  15.75   Penguin
Christmas    Dickens       3.50   Academic
Iliad        Homer        10.25   Random
Raven        Poe           2.50   Penguin
```

Both the action and pattern have defaults, so you can leave either of them out. The **print** action is the default action. If an action is not specified, the line is printed. The default pattern is the selection of every line in the text. If the pattern is not specified, the action is applied to all lines.

In this next example, there is no action segment. The default action, the **print** action, is then used.

```
$ gawk '/Penguin/' books
Tempest      Shakespeare  15.75   Penguin
Raven        Poe           2.50   Penguin
```

In the next example, the GAWK instruction has no pattern segment. In this case, all lines will have the action performed on them. The action is

5

print, which outputs a line, so this GAWK instruction effectively prints out all lines in the file.

```
$ gawk '{print}' books
Tempest     Shakespeare 15.75  Penguin
Christmas   Dickens      3.50  Academic
Iliad       Homer       10.25  Random
Raven       Poe          2.50  Penguin
```

You can use the same special characters for GAWK that are used for regular expressions. For example, the special circumflex special character (^) specifies the beginning of a line, and the **$** specifies the end of the line. The first example following searches for a pattern at the beginning of the line. The second example searches for a pattern at the end of a line, using the dollar sign special character (**$**).

Beginning-of-line special character

```
$ gawk '/^Christmas/{print}' books
Christmas   Dickens   3.50  Academic

$ gawk '/Random$/{print}' books
Iliad       Homer    10.25  Random
```

You can also use special characters to specify variations on a pattern. The period (**.**) matches any character, the asterisk (*****) matches repeated characters, and the brackets (**[ ]**)match a class of characters. In the first example that follows, the period is used to match any pattern in which a single character is followed by the characters "en."

```
$ gawk '/.en/{print}' books
Tempest     Shakespeare   15.75   Penguin
Christmas   Dickens        3.50   Academic
Raven       Poe            2.50   Penguin
```

The next example uses the brackets and asterisk to specify a sequence of numbers. The set of possible numbers is represented by the brackets enclosing the range of numeric characters, **[0–9]**. The asterisk then specifies any repeated sequence of numbers. The context for such a sequence consists of the characters .*50*. Any number ending with ".50" will be matched. Notice that the period is quoted with a backslash so that it is treated as the period character, not as a special character.

```
$ gawk '/[0-9]*\.50/ {print}' books
Christmas    Dickens    3.50  Academic
Raven        Poe        2.50  Penguin
```

GAWK also uses the extended special characters plus (**+**), question mark (**?**), and pipe (**|**). The **+** and **?** are variations on the ***** special character. The **+** matches one or more repeated instances of a character. The **?** matches zero or one instance of a character. The **|** provides alternative patterns to be searched. The next example searches for a line containing either the pattern "Penguin" or the pattern "Academic."

```
$ gawk '/Penguin|Academic/ {print}' books
Tempest      Shakespeare  15.75  Penguin
Christmas    Dickens       3.50  Academic
Raven        Poe           2.50  Penguin
```

Variables, Constants, and Functions

GAWK provides for the definition of variables. There are three types of variables: *field variables*, *special GAWK variables*, and *user-defined variables*. GAWK automatically defines both the field and special variables, and the user can define his or her own user-defined variables. The user can also define arithmetic and string constants. *Arithmetic constants* consist of numeric characters, and *string constants* consist of any characters enclosed within double quotes.

In addition to variables and constants, GAWK includes functions that can operate on the variables and constants. There are both arithmetic and string functions. For example, there are string functions that can determine the length of a string or locate the position of a character in a string.

Field Variables and Field Delimiters

Field variables are designed to reference fields in a line. A *field* is any set of characters separated by a field delimiter, and the default delimiter is a space or a tab. GAWK defines a field variable for each field in the file. A field variable consists of a dollar sign (**$**) followed by the number of the field; and as with other database filters, GAWK numbers fields starting from 1, so the field variable **$2** references the second field. The variable **$0** is a special field variable that contains the entire line.

Hint

A variable may be used in either the pattern or action segment of the GAWK instruction. If more than one variable is listed, they are separated by commas.

In the next example, illustrated in Figure 5-1, the variables **$2** and **$4** reference the second and fourth fields, so the second and fourth fields of the *books* file are printed out.

```
$ gawk '{print $2, $4}' books
Shakespeare   Penguin
Dickens       Academic
Homer         Random
Poe           Penguin
```

The *books* file used in this example follows.

```
Tempest      Shakespeare   15.75   Penguin
Christmas    Dickens        3.50   Academic
Iliad        Homer         10.25   Random
Raven        Poe            2.50   Penguin
```

In the next example, the user outputs the line with the pattern "Dickens" twice: first reversing the order of the fields, and then with the fields in order. The **$0** variable is used to output all the fields in order—the entire line.

```
$ gawk '/Dickens/ {print $4, $3, $2, $1; print $0}' books
Academic   3.50   Dickens   Christmas
Christmas  Dickens   3.50   Academic
```

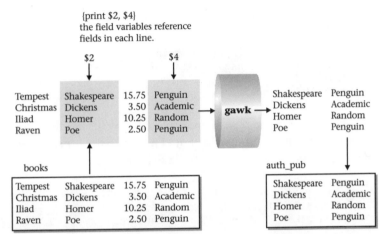

5

Figure 5-1   Field variables used to reference fields in each line

---

Hint

You can place several actions on the same line by separating them with a semicolon, as shown in the previous example:
{print $4, $3, $2, $1; print $0}.

Field Delimiters

By default, GAWK separates fields by spaces or tabs. However, if you want to use a specific delimiter, you can specify one with the **–F** option. The **–F** option actually sets a GAWK special variable called **FS**, which stands for field separator. With the **–F** option, you can specify any character you want for your delimiter.

In the next example, the *booksC* file uses a colon to separate fields. The **–F** option causes GAWK to treat the colon as a field delimiter.

```
$ gawk -F: '{print $1, $3}' booksC
War and peace 15.75
Christmas carol 3.50
Iliad 10.25
Raven 2.50
```

The contents of the *booksC* file follows.

```
War and peace:Tolstoy:15.75:Penguin
Christmas carol:Dickens:3.50:Academic
Iliad:Homer:10.25:Random
Raven:Poe:2.50:Penguin
```

The next example repeats an earlier example using the **–F** option, outputting the line with the pattern "Dickens" twice: first reversing the order of the fields, and then with the fields in order.

```
$ gawk -F\: '/Dickens/ {print $4, $3, $2, $1; print $0}' booksC
Academic  3.50  Dickens  Christmas carol
Christmas carol  Dickens   3.50   Academic
```

1-Minute Drill

● **What happens if you specify an action with no pattern?**

● **Can regular-expression pattern matching be applied to particular fields?**

GAWK Special Variables

GAWK defines a set of special variables that provide information about the line being processed. The variable **NR** contains the number of the current line. The variable **NF** contains the number of fields in the current line. There are other special variables that hold the field and record delimiters. There is even one, **FILENAME**, that holds the name of the input file. The GAWK special variables are listed in Table 5-1.

Special variables and user-defined variables do not have a dollar sign placed before them. To use such variables, you only need to specify the variable name. The following example combines the special variable **NR** with the field variables **$2** and **$4** to print out the line number of the line,

---

● **The action is applied to all lines in the file.**
● **Yes; pattern matching can be limited to individual fields.**

Variable	Description
NR	Record number of current record
NF	Number of fields in current record
$0	The entire current record
$n	The fields in the current record, numbered from 1—for example, **$1**
FS	Input field delimiter; the default delimiter is space or tab
OFS	Output field delimiter; the default delimiter is space or tab
RS	Input record delimiter; the default is a newline character
ORS	Output record delimiter; the default is a newline character
OMFT	Output format for numbers; the default delimiter is **%g**
FILENAME	Name of the current input file

Table 5-1 GAWK Special Variables

5

followed by the contents of fields two and four. The **NR** variable holds
the line number of the line being processed.

```
$ gawk '{print NR, $2, $4}' books
1 Shakespeare  Penguin
2 Dickens      Academic
3 Homer        Random
4 Poe          Penguin
```

User-Defined Variables

You can define your own variables, giving them any name you want.
Variables can be named using any alphabetic or numeric characters,
including underscores. The name must begin with an alphabetic character.
A variable is defined when you first use it, and the type of the variable is
determined by the way it is used. If you use it to hold numeric values, the
variable is considered arithmetic. If you use it to hold characters, the
variable is considered a string. You need to be consistent in the way in
which you use a variable—string variables should not be used in arithmetic
calculations, and vice versa.

You can assign a value to a variable using the assignment operator (=). The left side of an assignment operation is always a variable, and the right side is the value assigned to it. A value can be the contents of a variable, such as a field, special, or user-defined variable. It can also be a constant, as described in the next section. In this example, the user assigns the contents of the second field to the variable **myfield**.

```
$ gawk '{myfield = $2; print myfield}' books
Shakespeare
Dickens
Homer
Poe
```

Constants

Constants may be either arithmetic values or strings. Arithmetic constants are represented by digits. The number *56* represents the arithmetic value 56. String constants are any set of characters enclosed in double quotes, so a string constant for the word *edition* is **"edition"**. Keep in mind that a number with a dollar sign before it is a field variable, and a number without a dollar sign is an arithmetic constant.

Tip

Constants are used extensively with operators. GAWK has a set of relational, arithmetic, and assignment operators that can be used with variables and constants to form complex expressions. These expressions may be used in either the condition or action segments of the GAWK instruction. They are explored in depth in the following sections.

Functions

The GAWK utility provides a set of functions that can operate on fields, patterns, or variables. There are string functions and arithmetic functions. Arithmetic functions are described in the "Arithmetic and Assignment Operations" section, later in the module. Several of the more commonly used string functions are **length**, **index**, **substr**, and **split** (see Table 5-2 and "Arrays and Associative Arrays," later in this module).

The **length** function obtains the length of a string. It can be applied to any string variable, including field variables. The function call **length($2)**

String Functions	Description
length(*str*)	Returns the number of characters in a string, *str*. If length has no argument, it calculates the length of the current record in characters.
index(*str1*, *str2*)	Determines if *str1* is contained in *str2* and, if so, returns the position in *str2* where *str1* begins. If not, it returns 0.
split(*str*, *arr*, *delim*)	Copies segments of *str* that are separated by the delimiter *delim* into elements of the array *arr*. It returns the number of elements in the array (see "Arrays and Associative Arrays" later in this module).
substr(*str*, *pos*, *len*)	Returns a substring of *str*. Characters in the string are numbered from 1. The *pos* argument is a number that references the character where the substring begins. The *len* argument is a number that indicates how many characters from the *pos* character the substring will use.

5

Table 5-2	**GAWK String Functions**

returns the length of the second field. The function call **length($0)** returns the number of characters in a line, including any spaces or tabs. In the next example, the length of each line is printed out before the line.

```
$ gawk '{print length($0), $0}' books
31  Tempest      Shakespeare  15.75  Penguin
31  Christmas    Dickens       3.50  Academic
24  Iliad        Homer        10.25  Random
20  Raven        Poe           2.50  Penguin
```

The **substr** function will obtain a substring of a field or variable. The **substr** function takes three arguments. The first is the field or pattern from which the substring is copied, the second is the position from which the substring begins, and the third is the number of characters copied from the beginning position. The function call **substr($2,4,3)** returns a substring beginning from the fourth character in the second field, ending with the sixth character. The substring will consist of the characters at positions 4, 5, and 6 in the second field.

The **index** function finds the position of a pattern within a string. The position of the pattern "en" in "Dickens" is 5. In the next example, the user prints out the first word of titles containing more than one word in the *booksT* file. The *booksT* file has fields containing more than one word, with fields separated by tabs. First, **index** finds where the first word ends by looking for the first space. The position of the space is assigned to the user-defined variable **pos**. If there is no space, then the title has only one word, and index will return a 0. Then **substr** copies out the first word using the position of the space returned by **index** to determine how many characters to copy.

```
$ gawk -F\: '{pos = index($1, " ") ; print substr($1,1, pos)}'  booksC
War
Christmas
```

GAWK has an extensive number of string functions that allow you to perform operations, such as pattern substitutions (**sub** and **gsub**), pattern searches (**match**), and case changes (**tolower** and **toupper**). See Table 5-3.

Formatted Output: the **printf** Function

You can use the **printf** function to format your output. The **printf** command merely outputs strings, followed by a newline character. Suppose that you want to output several different strings on the same line, or to output numeric values to a specific decimal place. The **printf**

String Matching and Substitutions	Description
match(*str, pattern*)	Matches the pattern in the string. If found, *match* returns the position of the match; otherwise, it returns 0.
sub(*pattern, str, replacement*)	Performs a substitution operation, substituting the *pattern* in the *str* string with the *replacement* string. If no *replacement* string is specified, then $0 is used.
gsub(*pattern, str, replacement*)	Performs a global substitution on the *str* string, replacing every instance of *pattern* with *replacement*.
toupper(*str*)	Changes all lowercase characters in the *str* string to uppercase.
tolower(*str*)	Changes all uppercase characters in the *str* string to lowercase.

Table 5-3   GAWK String Matching and Substitutions

function can use a series of special control specifiers and constants to format your output. The syntax for the **printf** function follows:

printf("*format-string*", *arg1, arg2, ..., argn*)

The **printf** function takes as its first argument a format string. This is usually a string enclosed in double quotes, containing conversion specifiers or any constants you want to output. Any characters in the format string are taken as characters to be output. Nonprinting characters, such as the newline and tab, are represented with their quoted equivalents.

```
"hello\n"
```

After the format string, you list as arguments the values you want to output. These can be the values of variables, such as field variables or special variables. They can also be values that result from expressions, such as arithmetic expressions. In most cases, you will be listing variables whose values you want to output as your arguments.

For each argument that you list, you need to have a corresponding conversion specifier in the format string. A conversion specifier consists of a percent sign (%) followed by a one-letter code indicating a certain type of conversion. A conversion specifier takes the value of an argument and converts it to characters that can then be output. For example, the **%d** conversion specifier will take an integer value, such as 465, and convert it to the characters *4, 6,* and *5,* which can then be output. In most cases, you will be outputting strings, and the conversion specifier for a string is **%s**. The conversion specifiers are listed in Table 5-4.

Conversion specifiers in your format string match up sequentially to the arguments that you list. The first conversion specifier in the format string will convert the first argument, the second conversion specifier will convert the second argument, and so on. In the next example, the user outputs the integer value 23 and the string "visitors" using first a **%d** and then a **%s** conversion specifier.

```
printf("%d %s", 23, "visitors");
```

Conversion Specifiers	Description
%d	Decimal, integer
%f	Floating point
%e	Exponential notation
%g	Uses whatever floating-point notation is shorter, **f** or **e**
%o	Octal representation of an integer
%x	Hexadecimal representation
%s	Character string

Table 5-4   printf Conversion Specifiers

You can also include within the format string any constant characters that you want to output. In fact, you can use **printf** to output just a string of characters using only the format string without arguments. In the next example, the user first prints just the string "Visitors Report." Then, in the next **printf**, the user prints the values 23 and "visitors" preceded by "There were."

```
printf("Visitors Report ");
printf("There were %d %s", 23, "visitors.");

Visitors Report There were 23 visitors.
```

Hint

Notice that the output comes out all on one line. The **printf** function does not output a carriage return unless it's explicitly instructed to do so with a newline constant.

Within the format string, you can enter special constants, such as newlines or tabs, that control output. Such special constants consist of a backslash and a code letter. The special constant **\n** is a newline constant that will output a carriage return; **\t** is a tab constant that will output a tab. You can also output any octal value for any character in the character set by preceding the octal number with a backslash and a zero. **\007** will output the character in the ASCII character set that rings the bell. These special constants are listed in Table 5-5.

Special Constants	Description
\n	Newline
\t	Tab
\0*num*	Octal equivalent of a character, such as **\007**
\x*num*	Hexadecimal equivalent of a character, such as **\x7**

Table 5-5 printf Special Constants

In the next example, the user enters **\n** at the end of the **printf** format strings in order to output a newline.

```
printf("Visitors Report\n");
printf("There were %d %s\n", 23, "visitors.");

Visitors Report
There were 23 visitors.
```

In the next example, the **printf** function is used instead of the **print** command to format output. Notice the **\n** at the end of the format string.

```
$ gawk '{printf("The author is %s published by %s\n", $2, $4) }' books
The author is Shakespeare published by Penguin
The author is Dickens published by Academic
The author is Homer published by Random
The author is Poe published by Penguin
```

The **printf** function works equally well with special variables and user-defined variables. The next example formats the output for the **NR** special variable. The **NR** variable requires a **%d** conversion specifier because it is an integer.

```
                        ┌──── Conversion specifier for NR
$ gawk '{printf("Record %d\t%s\t%s\n", NR, $2, $4) }' books
Record 1    Shakespeare    Penguin
Record 2    Dickens        Academic
Record 3    Homer          Random
Record 4    Poe            Penguin
```

In addition to conversion specifiers, the **printf** function also has conversion modifiers, as listed in Table 5-6. Conversion modifiers govern field length, decimal placement, and justification. A number placed

printf Modifiers	Description
.num	Floating-point decimal placement modifier. The period is used to format floating-point values and specifies the number of places to the right of the decimal to be displayed. For example, **%.2f**.
Num	Field length modifier. Any number modifying the format specifier sets the minimum field width of the value being formatted. For example, **%5s**.
–	Left justification (right justification is the default). For example, **%–10s** for a left-justified number with 10 digits.

Table 5-6   Conversion Modifiers

between the percent sign (%) and the conversion letter code will determine the minimum field length of an output field. If a value is less than the field length, the output will be padded with spaces. This ensures that columns in the output will line up correctly. The field length modifier, however, does not truncate values that are too large.

The decimal placement modifier for floating-point conversions is used quite often. The decimal place modifier determines how many places after the decimal a floating-point value will be printed. The modifier consists of a period followed by number, and it is placed between the percent sign (%) and the conversion letter code. The conversion specifier **%.2f** will output a floating-point value with only two decimal places. The value 3.4528 would be output as 3.45, with the last place being rounded off.

Pattern Segment as a Condition

The pattern segment of a GAWK instruction can be thought of as a test condition. Control structures in programming languages have test expressions that are tested for truth or falsity, and if the test is true, the control structure's statements are executed. In the same way, a pattern in GAWK can be considered a test expression—if the pattern makes a successful match, then it is true and its GAWK action is executed. In this respect, a pattern is a condition for the action's execution. The operators you can use for creating such tests are listed in Table 5-7. Also included are special patterns that specify certain conditions. For example, the BEGIN and END patterns will execute code before and after the main code.

Equality Operators	Description
==	Equal
!=	Not equal
Relational Operators	
>	Greater than
<	Less than
>=	Greater than or equal
<=	Less than or equal
Logical Operators	
&&	Logical AND
||	Logical OR
!	Logical NOT
Pattern Search Operators	
str ~ regular expr	Matches a regular expression; the right operand is a regular expression
str !~ regular expr	Does not match a regular expression; the right operand is a regular expression
Special Patterns	
BEGIN	Executes operations before GAWK begins processing
END	Executes operations after GAWK finishes processing
Range Patterns	
first-condition, second-condition	References a range of lines beginning with the line that meets the first condition and ending with the next line that meets the second condition

Table 5-7   The GAWK Operators and Special Patterns

Equality and Relational Operators

You can construct simple conditions using equality operators, field variables, and constants. The equality operators are the same as those in the C programming language. The equality operator consists of two equal symbols (==), which is slightly different from other programming languages. A single equal symbol is the assignment operator (=). It is easy to confuse the two. The inequality operator is the exclamation point with the equal symbol (!=).

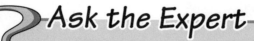

Ask the Expert

Question: How complex can expressions be?

Answer: In programming languages, test expressions can be made up of complex subexpressions using relational and logical operators, as well as arithmetic expressions and function calls. Like such test expressions, a GAWK pattern can contain subpatterns using relational, logical, and even arithmetic operations. In this sense, a pattern can be thought of as an expression.

However, in programming languages, the operands used in expressions are numbers or characters, but in the GAWK pattern, the operands are considered patterns. In GAWK, a relational operation compares a value to a pattern, so a logical operation will have subexpressions that compare patterns. In fact, the subexpressions are technically referred to as patterns, and a complex logical operation can be referred to as a compound pattern. To avoid confusion between the terms *expression* and *pattern*, an entire pattern will be referred to here as a *condition*. Bear in mind that the operands in any condition are patterns.

In the next example, only those lines whose last field is equal to the string "Penguin" are printed. Notice that a string constant is used here instead of a pattern encased in slashes. A pattern within slashes is a pattern search operation looking for the occurrence of any pattern in the field, whereas a string is a simple value comparing the entire field to the string value.

```
$ gawk '$4 == "Penguin" {print}' books
Tempest    Shakespeare  15.75  Penguin
Raven      Poe           2.50  Penguin
```

You can also use relational operators to construct conditions. GAWK has the same relational operators used in other programming languages: >, <, >=, and <=. However, unlike the C language versions, GAWK relational operators can compare strings, ranking them by alphabetic order. For example, "Aleina" is less than "Larisa". The equality and relational operators are listed in Table 5-7.

In the next example, the command lists all books that cost more than $10.00. Notice that an arithmetic constant is used for the operand.

```
$ gawk '$3 > 10.00 {print}' books
Tempest    Shakespeare  15.75  Penguin
Iliad      Homer        10.25  Random
```

An operand in a GAWK condition may also be a value returned by a function. In the next example, the **length** function is used to print out only those records whose second field has a length greater than 5.

```
$ gawk 'length($2) > 5 {print}' books
Tempest    Shakespeare  15.75  Penguin
Christmas  Dickens       3.50  Academic
```

Logical Operators

GAWK has a set of logical operators that you can use to create complex conditions. The logical operators are the same as those used in the C programming language, and they are listed in Table 5-7. The logical operator for AND is a double ampersand (**&&**), the logical operator for OR is a double bar (**||**), and the logical operator for NOT is a single exclamation point (**!**). The operands for logical operators are themselves conditions. These are each usually enclosed within parentheses.

In the next example, all books published by Penguin that cost over $10.00 are printed. This involves comparing the fourth field to "Penguin" and testing to see if the third field is greater than 10.00.

```
$ gawk '($4 == "Penguin") && ($3 > 10.00) {print}' books
Tempest    Shakespeare  15.75  Penguin
```

In the next example, the command prints books that are published either by Penguin or Academic. This involves checking to see if the fourth field is equal to either the string "Penguin" or the string "Academic".

```
$ gawk '($4 == "Penguin") || ($4 == "Academic") {print}' books
Tempest    Shakespeare  15.75  Penguin
Christmas  Dickens       3.50  Academic
Raven      Poe           2.50  Penguin
```

Pattern Search Operators

You can use two pattern matching operators, the tilde (~) and the exclamation tilde (!~), to carry out pattern searches on fields. Instead of using the equality operator to compare the entire field to a string, you can use the ~ operators to see whether a certain pattern exists within the field. When using these operators to search fields, the right operand is the pattern and the left operand is the field to be searched. In the next example, the first field is searched for "mas."

```
$ gawk '($1 ~ /mas/) {print}' books
Christmas    Dickens    3.50  Academic
```

The next example retrieves all records whose first field does not contain the pattern "mas."

```
$ gawk '($1 !~ /mas/) {print}' books
Tempest      Shakespeare 15.75  Penguin
Iliad        Homer       10.25  Random
Raven        Poe          2.50  Penguin
```

Just as you can use special characters in a general pattern search, you can also use special characters to search fields. In the next example, the user matches both uppercase and lowercase versions of "Penguin" in the fourth field. The brackets special characters ([ ]) are used to define a class for uppercase and lowercase *P*.

```
$ gawk '($4 ~ /[Pp]eng/) {print}' books
Tempest      Shakespeare 15.75  Penguin
Raven        Poe          2.50  Penguin
```

BEGIN and **END** Special Patterns

The GAWK instruction has two special patterns that allow the user to specify actions to be executed before and after processing lines in the input. The **BEGIN** pattern is a condition that specifies actions to be performed before lines are processed, and the **END** pattern specifies actions to be performed after lines are processed.

In the following example, the heading "Book List" is output before any lines are processed. After processing, the value of **NR** is printed. Since **NR** increments with each line, after processing, **NR** will hold the total count of the records in the file.

| BEGIN **condition executed** |
| **before processing** |

```
$ gawk 'BEGIN {print "Book List"} {print} END{ print "Total recs", NR}' books
Book List
Tempest    Shakespeare  15.75  Penguin
Christmas  Dickens       3.50  Academic
Iliad      Homer        10.25  Random
Raven      Poe           2.50  Penguin
Total recs 4
```

| END **condition executed** |
| **after processing** |

Range Patterns

The GAWK utility has a special comma operator that can be placed between two conditions to retrieve a range of lines. The first line in the set is the first line that matches the first condition. The last line in the set is the next line that matches the second condition.

The comma operator is particularly useful for selecting a range of lines using the **NR** special variable, which holds the current line number. The condition **NR == 4** will select the fourth line, because when line four is reached, the value of **NR** will be 4 and the condition will be true. **NR==1,NR==3** specifies a range of lines beginning with line 1 and ending with line 3. In the next example, only the first three lines are printed.

```
$ gawk 'NR == 1, NR == 3 {print}' books
Tempest    Shakespeare  15.75  Penguin
Christmas  Dickens       3.50  Academic
Iliad      Homer        10.25  Random
```

Hint

The GAWK instruction literally searches for the first condition. Once the first condition is met, it then searches exclusively for the second condition. In the process, it may pass over other matches of the first condition. In fact, there may be other matching sets, and GAWK will retrieve all of them. GAWK does not stop with the first set retrieved—it restarts its searching after the second condition is met, looking for another matched pair.

5

Arithmetic and Assignment Operations

GAWK has a full set of arithmetic operators. You can perform multiplication, division, addition, subtraction, and modulo calculations. The arithmetic operators are the same as those used in the C programming language, and they are listed in Table 5–8, along with the assignment operators, which will be discussed shortly.

Arithmetic Operators and Functions	Description
*	Multiplication
/	Division
+	Addition
–	Subtraction
%	Modulo; results in the remainder of a division
int(*num*)	Truncates a floating-point number, *num*, to its integer value
cos(*num*)	Returns the cosine of *num*
sin(*num*)	Returns the sine of *num*
log(*num*)	Returns the natural log of *num*
exp(*num*)	Returns the exponential of *num*
sqrt(*num*)	Returns the square root of *num*
rand()	Returns a random number
srand(*num*)	Uses *num* as a new seed for **rand()**
Assignment Operators	
=	Assignment
++	Increment
——	Decrement
+=	Addition and assignment; **i = i + 1** is the same as **i += 1**
–=	Subtraction and assignment; **i = i – 1** is the same as **i –= 1**
*=	Multiplication and assignment; **i = i * 1** is the same as **i *= 1**
/=	Division and assignment; **i = i / 1** is the same as **i /= 1**
%=	Modulo and assignment; **i = i % 1** is the same as **i %= 1**

Table 5-8　The GAWK Arithmetic and Assignment Operators and Functions

You can perform arithmetic calculations on numeric values represented by numeric patterns. A numeric pattern is any sequence of digits, and an arithmetic constant is an obvious numeric pattern. A field whose contents are digits is also a numeric pattern. Arithmetic constants, field variables, and user-defined variables whose values are numeric patterns all can be used as operands in arithmetic operations. There are also certain special GAWK variables that are defined as numeric, such as **NR** and **NF**. These can also be arithmetic operands.

Arithmetic operations can be used in either the action or pattern segment of the GAWK instruction. In the next example, the user outputs every even-numbered line. The percent sign (**%**) is a modulo operator that results in the remainder of a division. If 2 divides evenly into the line number with no remainder, then the line is an even-numbered line. Notice how parentheses are used to arrange the expression.

5

```
$ gawk '(NR % 2) == 0 {print NR, $0}' books
2 Christmas    Dickens   3.50    Academic
4 Raven        Poe       2.50    Penguin
```

With arithmetic operators and variables, you can easily perform calculations on a field in a database file. For example, you could sum the values of the same field in each line, just as you could sum up a column in a spreadsheet. The next example sums up the third field in the *books* file. The user-defined variable **tot** holds the sum, and the **END** condition then prints out the final value of the **tot** variable. Since variables are automatically initialized to 0, the **tot** variable begins with an initial value of 0.

```
$ gawk '{print; tot = tot + $3} END {print "Total=",tot}' books
Tempest      Shakespeare  15.75  Penguin
Christmas    Dickens       3.50  Academic
Iliad        Homer        10.25  Random
Raven        Poe           2.50  Penguin
Total= 32
```

In addition to the standard arithmetic operators, there is also a set of arithmetic assignment operators, listed in Table 5-7. These operators combine the assignment operation with an arithmetic operation. They are used as a kind of shorthand for specifying an operation that assigns a variable to the result of an expression in which that same variable is also an operand. The operation **tot = tot + 1** can be written with the arithmetic operator **+=** as **tot += 1**. You do not have to specify the **tot** variable in the arithmetic expression because the arithmetic assignment operation assumes it. The operation **i = i * 2** can be written as **i *= 2**. The following command produces the same result as the previous example using an arithmetic assignment operation.

```
$ gawk '{print; tot += $3} END {print "Total=", tot}' books
```

Ask the Expert

Question: How are increments and decrements implemented?

Answer: There are two special increment and decrement arithmetic operators. The increment operator consists of two plus signs (**++**), and the decrement operator consists of two minus signs (**--**). The increment operation is a combined addition and assignment operation.

The increment operation first adds 1 to the variable and then assigns the incremented value to that same variable. The expression **i++** is equivalent to **i=i+1**. The decrement operator performs a combined subtraction and assignment operation. The expression **I--** is equivalent to **i=i−1**.

Increment operations are very useful for progressing through an array, and they are often used in loops to update variables that control a loop. In the next example, the user uses the variable **linenum** to keep track of each line number instead of using **NR**. **linenum** is incremented by 1 at each line and is then used to output the line number.

```
$ gawk '{ linenum++; print linenum, $0 }' books
1 Tempest    Shakespeare  15.75  Penguin
2 Christmas  Dickens       3.50  Academic
3 Iliad      Homer        10.25  Random
4 Raven      Poe           2.50  Penguin
```

Arrays and Associative Arrays

A subscript enclosed in brackets and placed next to an array name references an element in the array. Like variables, the first use of a subscript in GAWK also defines the array. Unlike programming languages, arrays are not declared, and no maximum size needs to be given for an array. An array will dynamically expand as elements are referenced.

In the following example, the array **titles** is defined. Each element of **titles** is assigned the value of the first field of a line. There will be only as many elements in the array as there are values assigned. The variable **num** is used to reference each element of the array, and it is incremented after each use. At the end, the last element in the array is printed out.

```
$ gawk '{titles[num] = $1; num++} END{print titles[num - 1]}' books
Raven
```

Suppose, however, that you want to assign each field in a particular record to an array. You could do this through individual assignment operations for each field, but GAWK provides a shortcut. You can assign fields to array elements with the **split** function. The **split** function takes as its arguments a line, an array, and a field separator. The field separator is specified by a string—to use a colon as a field separator, you would specify the string **":"**. The field separator is optional, and if no field separator is entered, either a tab or a space is assumed by default.

The **split** function can also operate on any string. **split("9-10-92", date, "-")** assigns **9** to **date[1]**, **10** to **date[2]**, and **92** to **date[3]**. In the following example, each field in a line is assigned to an element of the **myrec** array. The line assigned is selected by the search pattern **/Dickens/**. The fields are then output in reverse order.

```
$ gawk '/Dickens/ {split($0, myrec); print myrec[4], myrec[3],
    myrec[2], myrec[1]}' books
Academic  3.50  Dickens    Christmas
```

GAWK also allows you to define *associative arrays*. An associative array allows strings to be array subscripts. Suppose you want to reference an author's publisher by the author's name. In the next example, and in Figure 5-2, the user assigns publishers to an array indexed by the author's name. The second field is the author name and the fourth field is the publisher name. In this case, the Dickens publisher is printed. Notice the double quotes around **"Dickens"**. When you use a string constant as a subscript in an associative array, you need to enclose the string within double quotes.

```
$ gawk '{publ[$2] = $4} END{ print publ["Dickens"]}' books
Academic
```

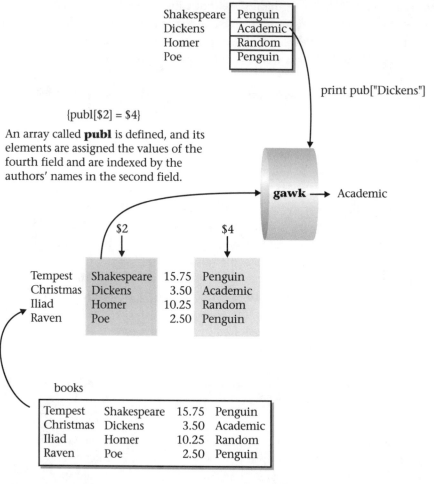

Figure 5-2   An associative array using strings to index elements

GAWK Instruction Files

As GAWK instructions become more complex, it is easier to handle them in files that can be read by GAWK. If you need to ever make any changes, you only need to modify the file. The **–f** option allows GAWK to read GAWK instructions from a file instead of from the command line. (The **–f** option was discussed in a question in the "The **gawk** Command" section at the beginning of this module.) In the next example, the GAWK instructions to list books published by Penguin are placed in a file called *findbk*. GAWK is then invoked with the **–f** option and the *findbk* file name. The GAWK instruction will be read from the file *findbk*.

```
BEGIN { print "Book List";
            count = 0;
        }

$4 ~  /Penguin/  {
          count = count + 1;
          print;
              }
END  {
   print "Total records found is ", count;
    }
```

A run of the *findbk* script follows.

```
$ gawk -f findbk  books
Book List
Tempest     Shakespeare  15.75  Penguin
Raven       Poe           2.50  Penguin
Total records found is 2
```

Tip

Notice that you do not need any single quotes around the instruction. You can also organize different parts of your instruction on separate lines, making for a more readable instruction. This feature is very helpful when using control structures.

1-Minute Drill

● **Can you use GAWK to access standard input and output on the Linux command line like Linux filters do?**

● **Can you place the entire GAWK command within an executable file, making it part of a shell script?**

Control Structures

GAWK operates like a programming language and permits you to define variables, construct expressions, and assign values. It also includes a set of control structures to provide iteration and selection capability. There are three control structures for constructing loops in GAWK: the **while**, **for**, and **for-in** loops. There is one selection control structure: the **if** structure. The GAWK control structures are listed in Table 5-9 and are described in detail in the following discussions. With the exception of the **for-in** loop, these control structures are similar to those in the C programming language.

The **while** Loop

The **while** loop consists of the keyword *while* followed by a *test expression* encased in parentheses. A GAWK action follows the *test expression*, and several GAWK actions can be combined into a block of actions with braces, each action separated by a semicolon. Placing a block of actions after the *test expression* of a **while** loop executes all those actions within the loop. Here is the syntax for a **while** loop:

```
while ( test expression )
     {
     gawk-actions;
     }
```

Most loops require three components to work properly: an initialization, a test, and an increment. All components operate on a variable that is used to control the loop.

In the *threefields* file, shown next, the first three fields of each record are printed out. The variable **i** is used to control the loop, and the

---

● Yes, GAWK can read from the standard input and write to the standard output.
● Yes, you can create shell scripts that use GAWK commands.

Control Structure Syntax	Description
{ *actions* }	A block is formed by opening and closing braces; and it is used to group actions, making them subject to a control structure—such as a loop—or enclosing the actions in the GAWK instruction proper.

if(*expression*)
   action
else
   action
	The **if** control structure executes an action if its *expression* is true. If it is false, the **else** action is executed.

while(*expression*) *action*	The **while** control structure executes an *action* as long as its *expression* is true.
for(*exp1*; *exp2*; *exp3*) *action*	The **for** control structure executes an *action* as long as *exp2* is true. The first expression, *exp1*, is executed before the loop begins. The third expression, *exp3*, is executed within the loop after the action.
for(*variable in arrayname*) *action*	The **for-in** control structure is designed for use with associative arrays. The *variable* operand is consecutively assigned the strings that index the array.
next	The **next** statement stops operations on the current record and skips to the next record.
exit	The **exit** statement ends all processing and executes the **END** command if there is one.

Table 5-9 The GAWK Control Structures

5

increment of **i** is placed within a block enclosed within braces inside the loop. The variable is then tested in a relational operation with the loop's test expression in order to determine when to stop the loop.

The value of **i** is used to reference each field in the record. The first time through the loop, the value of **i** will be 1, so **$i** will reference the first field variable for the record. As **i** is incremented, its value will change; and **$i** will consecutively reference each field variable for the line in turn, up to the third field, at which point the loop cuts off.

┤*Tip*

You can use any user-defined numeric variable, such as the **i** variable, to reference a field variable. The identification of a field variable consists of a dollar sign placed before a numeric value, and this value can be obtained from a constant or a numeric variable. If the value of the variable **i** is 2, then **$i** references the second field.

Here is the *threefields* script:

```
{
i=1;
while(i <= 3)
    {
    printf("%s\t", $i);
    i++
    }
printf("\n");
}
```

This is the run of the *threefields* script:

```
$ gawk -f threefields books
Tempest      Shakespeare   15.75
Christmas    Dickens        3.50
Iliad        Homer         10.25
Raven        Poe            2.50
```

You can easily adapt the **while** loop for use with arrays. The variable used to control a loop can also be used, inside the loop, to index an array. In the following *titlearray* script, the elements of the **title** array are assigned the value of each title. Then the contents of each element are printed out using a **for** loop. Notice that the **num** variable is used during processing to keep track of the next element to be assigned. After processing, **num** holds the count of elements in the array. **num** is used as the upper bound in the **for** loop's test expression in order to check when the loop should stop.

```
{ num++; title[num] = $1}
END{
    i=1;
    while (i <= num)
            {
            print title[i];
            i++;
            }
    }
```

The following example shows the execution of the *titlearray* script.

```
$ gawk -f titlearray books
Tempest
Christmas
Iliad
Raven
```

You can also use loops to manage elements of an array assigned with the **split** function. The **split** function copies each field in a line into consecutive elements of an array, so each element of the array will contain a field copied from the line. However, you will need to know how many fields were copied in order to know how many elements are in the array, because if you don't, you will not know when to stop the loop. The **split** function returns as its return value the number of fields it copied, so you can assign the return value of the **split** function to a variable and use that variable to test for the end of the array.

In the *fieldarray* script that follows, each field in a line is assigned to an element of the **myrec** array. The line assigned is selected by the search pattern **/Dickens/**. The number of fields copied by **split** is then assigned to the variable **fnum**, and the elements of the array are printed out using **fnum** as the upper bound.

```
/Dickens/ { fnum = split($0, myrec) }
END{
    i=1;
    while (i <= fnum)
        {
        print myrec[i];
        i++;
        }
    }
```

The following example shows a run of the *fieldarray* script.

```
$ gawk -f fieldarray books
Christmas
Dickens
3.50
Academic
```

The **for** Loop

The **for** loop performs the same tasks as the **while** loop, but it has a different format. The initialization, test, and increment components of a loop are all incorporated into the **for** loop syntax. The **for** loop has three expressions encased within parentheses and separated by semicolons.

```
for( expression1; expression2; expression3)
    {
    gawk-actions;
    }
```

The first expression is executed before the loop is actually entered. It usually consists of an initialization of a variable used to control the loop. The second expression is the test expression, such as a relational expression that controls the loop. The third expression is executed within the loop at the end. It is usually used for incrementing the variable that controls the loop. Following the expressions is the GAWK action to be executed within the loop. This action can be a block of actions encased in braces. The third expression is executed after the GAWK action.

```
for( initialization; test expression; increment)
    {
    gawk-actions;
    }
```

In the *field3for* file, the first three fields are printed out using a **for** loop. Notice how much more compact the **for** loop is than the **while** loop.

```
{
for(i=1;(i <= 3);i++)
    {
    printf("%s\t", $i);
    }
printf("\n");
}
```

The following example shows a run of the *field3for* script.

```
$ gawk -f field3for books
Tempest     Shakespeare  15.75
Christmas   Dickens       3.50
Iliad       Homer        10.25
Raven       Poe           2.50
```

As with the **while** loop, you can easily use the **for** loop to manage arrays. The variable used to control a loop can also be used inside the loop to index an array. In the *titlearrayf* file, the elements of the **title** array are assigned the value of each title. Then the contents of each element are printed out using a **for** loop. The **i** variable is used to control the loop. It is initialized to 1 in the **for**'s first expression, and incremented in the last expression—the increment will take place after the **print** action. The second expression is the test expression that controls the loop.

5

```
{ num++; title[num] = $1}
END{
    for(i=1;(i <= num);i++)  ◄────── for loop executed after
        {                            GAWK processing
        print title[i];
        }
    }
```

Here is a run of the *titlearrayf* script:

```
$ gawk -f titlearrayf books
Tempest
Christmas
Iliad
Raven
```

The **for-in** Loop

Though a numeric variable was used in previous examples to reference elements in an array, it is of no help when you need to reference elements of an associative array. Elements of an associative array are referenced by strings, not numbers. GAWK has a special **for-in** loop control structure that allows you to reference an associative array.

This loop structure also begins with the keyword *for*, but it is very different from the **for** loop. It has one specialized expression that uses the keyword *in* as its operator, which is why the loop is described as a **for-in** loop, rather than just a **for** loop.

The first operand in the **for-in** loop's expression is a variable, and the second operand is the name of the array. As the loop executes, the string that indexes each element is assigned to this variable. You can then use the contents of this variable to index an element in the array. No other type of expression is allowed. The **for-in** loop for an associative array is very restrictive in this regard. The syntax for the **for-in** loop is as follows:

```
for(variable in array-name)
    {
    gawk-actions;
    }
```

In the following *bkcount* script, each element of the **bookcnt** array is printed out after the lines have been processed. During processing, the index for the **bookcnt** array is the fourth field of the record, the name of the publisher. In the **for-in** loop, the string variable **pubname** is used for the index of the **bookcnt** array, rather than a numeric variable. Each time the loop is executed, the string that references the next element is assigned to **pubname**. The **pubname** variable is then used to index that array element. Both the index and the array element are printed.

```
{ bookcnt[$4] = bookcnt[$4] + 1 }

END {
    for(pubname in bookcnt)
        {
        print bookcnt[pubname], pubname;
        }
    }
```

Here is a run of the *bkcount* script.

```
$ gawk -f bkcount books
2  Penguin
1  Academic
1  Random
```

The **if** Control Structure

GAWK also has a selection control structure, the **if** structure, that allows you to select alternative actions. The **if** structure has a test expression encased in parentheses, and following the test is a GAWK action. If the test is true, the action is performed. If not, the action is skipped. This is the syntax for the **if** structure:

```
if(test-expression)
    {
    gawk-actions;
    }
```

The **if** structure also has an optional **else** component, which is followed by another GAWK action. If the test expression of the **if** structure is false, then the action following the **else** is executed. In this respect, the **if-else** structure can be thought of as a branching structure. If the test is true, one action is taken; if false, the other action is taken. This is the syntax for the **if-else** structure:

```
if(test-expression)
    gawk-actions
else
    gawk-actions
```

Note

Take special note, that there is no semicolon at the end of the GAWK actions that come before the **else**. The GAWK **if-else** structure is similar to the C programming language's **if-else** structure with this one exception. If you use programming languages, you may inadvertently add a semicolon, which will be considered an error because a semicolon in GAWK separates actions.

In the *markup* script that follows, the third field of the *books* file is a price. If the price is more than $10.00, then this script will raise it by 10 percent. Otherwise, it is raised by 20 percent. Notice that there is no semicolon at the end of the action before the **else**.

```
{
if($3 > 10.00)
    $3 = $3 + (0.10 * $3 )
else
    $3 = $3 + (0.20 * $3 );
print $0
}
```

A run of the *markup* script follows.

```
$ gawk -f markup books
Tempest    Shakespeare  17.325   Penguin
Christmas  Dickens       4.2     Academic
Iliad      Homer        11.275   Random
Raven      Poe           3       Penguin
```

The **next** and **exit** Statements

GAWK has two other statements, **next** and **exit**, that are often used with loops and the **if** structure. Both statements stop the processing of a record.

The **next** statement stops the processing of the current record and goes on to process the next one. In effect, **next** stops the execution of the GAWK instructions on a particular record. Then the next record is read and processing continues. The **next** statement is often used to skip a record.

The **exit** statement stops the processing of records altogether and executes the **END** instruction.

The **getline** Statement

The **getline** statement allows you to control the actual reading of input lines. Ordinarily, GAWK will read one line of input at a time and apply all commands and actions in a GAWK file to that line. **getline** allows you to read an input line within a GAWK action. You can then perform a few specific operations on the line instead of having all commands and actions applied to it.

For example, suppose you want to perform an action not on the line you are matching on, but on the line following it. You can use the powerful pattern-matching capabilities of a **gawk** command to locate the line you need to match on, and then, using **getline**, read the following line and perform whatever operation you want on it.

The **getline** command reads a line of input and places it in the **$0** variable. The first time you use **getline** in an action, it replaces the input line that has just been automatically read by GAWK. Be sure to perform any operations you need to on the GAWK-read input line before you wipe it out with your **getline** statement.

When using **getline** in a loop, you need to check for an end-of-file condition. **getline** will not automatically stop GAWK at the end of a file, but it does return a 0 if the end of the file is reached. It returns 1 if you are not at the end. You can assign this return value to a variable and then test the variable in your loop so that you can stop when you reach the end.

In the *gettables* example that follows, the script makes use of the **endfile** variable to check whether the end of the file has been reached (**endfile** is an ordinary variable). First, **endfile** is initialized to 1, and then it is checked within the **while** loop's test. In each call to **getline**, the return value of **getline** is assigned to the **endfile** variable; so if the end of the file is reached, **getline** will return a 0, which will be assigned to **endfile**, making the **while** test on **endfile** false. The initialization in this example is redundant, but it is included for emphasis.

The *gettables* script is designed to extract all table-formatted text from a UNIX troff file. You could use the same logic to extract a range of lines from any document with begin and end separators. Any range of lines beginning with **.TS** and ending with **.TE** are table-formatted text. The **gawk** command matches on the initial **.TS**, and the loop continues reading lines until the end of the file is reached or the ending **.TE** line is reached. Recall that the ^ character indicates a pattern at the beginning of a line, so **/^\.TS/** specifies a line beginning with **.TS**.

```
/^\.TS/      {
    endfile = 1;
    while( (endfile != 0)  && ( $0  !~ /^\.TE/ ) )
          {
          print $0;
          endfile = getline;
          }
      print $0;
   }
```

Tip

It is important to test for this end condition when you use loops with **getline**. Without it, **getline** will continue to try to read from your input, even when it is at the end of the file. The loop itself will continue on as an infinite loop until you forcibly kill it with an interrupt key, CTRL-C.

Using Files with GAWK

You have seen how GAWK can read data from files and send output to the standard output. The standard output can be redirected to write the output to a file. And any files that you specify as input are actually combined into one continuous data stream that is read in line by line. In effect, there is one continuous input stream and one output stream for GAWK.

Suppose, though, that you want to output different types of data to separate data files. Using the books example, suppose you wanted to output a list of publishers and a list of titles to separate files. You could write two different GAWK filters, one for each task, but you can also create one GAWK script and write to the two files directly. GAWK's input and output commands for files are listed in Table 5-10, and they are explained in the following discussions.

To write data to a file within a GAWK program, you just have to use a redirection operator with an output operation such as **print** or **printf**. To append data to a file, be sure to use the append redirection operator, **>>**. The following **gawk** command will write the contents of the third field to the file *costfile*. The file name is a string, and it is here quoted as a string constant.

```
print $3 >> "costfile";
```

To read data from a file is a simple matter of using a standard input redirection operator with the file name and a GAWK input command, such as **getline**, along with the variable you want to read the data into. The following example reads a line of data from the *publist* script and places it in the **bufferpub** variable. Notice that the file name is quoted—GAWK

Output Operations	Description
print	Outputs the current line to the standard output.
print *var*	Outputs the variable *var* to the standard output.
print *var* >> *filename*	Outputs the variable *var* to a file.
print >> *filename*	Outputs the current line to the specified file.
printf(*format, vars*)>> *filename*	Outputs the formatted output to the specified file.

Input Operations	
getline *var*	Reads the next input line and returns 0 if it is at the end of the file. If a variable, *var*, is specified, it will read the input line to it.
getline *var* << *filename*	Reads the next input line from the specified file and returns 0 if it is at the end of the file. The line is read into the specified variable, *var*.

Table 5-10   GAWK Input and Output Operations with Files

expects to use a string as the file name, and in this case, it is getting a string constant. You could assign the file name to a variable and use that instead.

```
getline bufferpub < "publist";
```

The *getat* program that we'll see shortly will check for records that have publishers listed in the *publist* file. The *publist* file was created separately and contains the set of unique publisher names, as shown here:

```
$ cat publist
Penguin
Random
```

In the *getat* program, this list of publishers in the *publist* file is used to index an associative array whose element is assigned the value 1. Any other publishers indexed in this array will have the default value of 0. Using the fourth field, the publisher field, the **pubarray** is referenced. If its value is 1, then the author field, **$2**, is written to the *authorlist* file; and the title field, **$1**, is written to the *titlelist* file. The **print** command with append redirection performs the write operation.

The *getat* program is shown here:

```
BEGIN {
        count = 0;                    Reading data from a file
        while ( (getline bufferpub < "publist") != 0)
                pubarray[bufferpub] = 1;
        }
{
   if (pubarray[$4] == 1)
        {
                                      Writing data to a file
        count += 1;
        print $1 >> "titlelist";
        print $2 >> "authorlist";
        }
   }
END {
    print "Total records found is ", count
    }
```

Here is a run of the *getat* script:

```
$ gawk -f getat  books
Total records found is 3
$ cat titlelist
Tempest
Iliad
Raven
$ cat authorlist
Shakespeare
Homer
Poe
```

field3

Project 5-1: GAWK Scripts

You can use GAWK to define your own filters by placing the whole GAWK instruction in a script file. You can then make the file executable, and the file name becomes a new Linux command.

Within the script file, GAWK instructions must be quoted. A script file literally contains a Linux command that will be executed in the shell; so within the script file, you need to write the instruction as if you were going to execute it on the command line. You can write the GAWK conditions and actions on their own lines, but any carriage returns need to be enclosed within the GAWK instruction's beginning and end quotes. This means that the first line of the GAWK operation will begin with the keyword *gawk* followed on the same line by a single quote. Then you can enter the condition and actions of the GAWK instruction on different lines. However, the end of the action needs to be terminated by a single quote, followed on the same line by any file name arguments. The syntax for such a format follows:

```
gawk  '
      pattern {
             gawk-actions;
      } ' filenames
```

Step-by-Step

1. Create a script file called *field3* in which you can place the GAWK instruction. The instruction will print out the first three fields in each line.

2. Quote the GAWK instruction, starting with a single quote before the opening brace, and ending with one after the **gawk** command.

3. Create a **for** loop that will initialize a variable called **i** and increment it three times.

4. Create **printf** statements that use the value of **i** to reference a field, starting with the first and going to the third field.

5. Create a final **printf** statement that outputs a newline character after the loop finishes.

6. On the last line, follow the closing brace with a closing single quote. Then enter the name of the file to be read by GAWK (*books*).

7. Set the execution permission for the script file, and then execute the file by simply entering the script's file name.

The contents of the *field3* script are shown here:

```
gawk '{
for(i=1;(i <= 3);i++)
        {
        printf("%s\t", $i);
        }
printf("\n");
}' books
```

Here is a run of the *field3* script:

```
$ chmod 755 field3
$ field3
Tempest     Shakespeare  15.75
Christmas   Dickens       3.50
Iliad       Homer        10.25
Raven       Poe           2.50
```

☑ *Mastery Check*

1. Can you use regular expressions in test expressions?

2. What are the differences among the symbols ~, =, and == ?

3. The **for-in** control structure is designed to work with what kind of arrays?

4. What function could you use to assign each word in a sentence to an element in an array in a single operation?

5. What special GAWK variable would you use to create a GAWK operation that would display just the fourth through the seventh lines of a file?

Module 6

Perl

The Goals of This Module

- Use single Perl commands for basic operations

- Create and execute Perl scripts

- Manage Perl input and output for files and for the standard input, output, and error

- Learn to define and control arrays using Perl array-management functions

- Use Perl control structures to implement loops and conditional tests

- Learn to use Perl functions and pattern-matching and string-manipulation features

Perl (the Practical Extraction and Report Language) is a scripting language that has all the capabilities of GAWK but with many more features. Perl was originally designed to operate on files like GAWK does, generating reports and handling very large files. However, Perl was designed as a core program to which features could be easily added. Over the years, Perl's capabilities have been greatly enhanced. It can now control network connection process interaction, and it even supports a variety of database management files. At the same time, Perl remains completely portable. A Perl script will run on any Linux system. You can find out more about Perl at **www.perl.org**.

Note

There are extensive and detailed man pages on Perl that discuss all aspects of the language with a great many examples. The man pages begin with the term **perl**; for example, **perlfunc** discusses the built-in Perl functions and **perlsyn** describes the different control structures.

Perl Command Line Operations

Perl can execute either a Perl command entered on the command line or a file of Perl commands. Files of commands are more commonly used, letting you create what are essentially Perl programs. Perl is invoked using the command **perl**. After entering the command, you need to enter an option to specify whether you are executing a Perl script or a single Perl command: **-e** for a single command and **-f** for reading commands from a file. Perl options are listed in Table 6-1.

Command Line Option	**Description**
–e	Enter one line of a Perl program
–n	Read from files listed on the command line
–p	Output any data read to standard output

Table 6-1   Perl Command Line Options

To execute a Perl single command on the shell command line, use the command **perl** with the **–e** option. The Perl command you want to execute should then be entered and quoted within single quotes. The following Perl operation prints the string "hello" using the Perl **print** command. The command ends with a semicolon.

```
perl -e 'print "hello"; '
```

┤Note

You can use Perl this way for simple operations, much as you would single-line GAWK commands. This command line use of Perl is rare. Normally, Perl commands are placed in script files that are then executed, much like shell scripts.

6

❓Ask the Expert

Question: How can Perl read from the standard input?

Answer: Perl will not read from the standard input unless you explicitly instruct it to with a **while** loop. Unlike GAWK, it does not read the standard input by default. The following example searches for the pattern "Dickens." The file *books* is first output to the standard output by the **cat** command and piped to the Perl command as standard input.

```
cat books | perl -e 'while(<STDIN>){ if(/Dickens/){ print; }}'
```

The following GAWK command is equivalent.

```
cat books | gawk '/Dickens/ {print}'
```

This is discussed in greater detail in the "Input and Output" section, later in this module.

Perl Scripts

Usually Perl commands are placed in a file that is then read and executed by the **perl** command. In effect, you are creating a shell in which your Perl commands are executed. Files containing Perl commands must have the extension **.pl**. This identifies the file as a Perl script that can be read by the **perl** command. There are two ways that you can use the **perl** command to read Perl scripts.

The first option is to enter the **perl** command on the shell command line, followed by the name of the Perl script. Perl will read and execute the commands. The following example executes a Perl script called *hello.pl*.

```
$ perl hello.pl
```

The second way is to include the invocation of the **perl** command within the Perl script file, much as you would for a shell script. **/usr/bin/perl** should be the location of the **perl** command on your system. If you place the following shell instruction on the first line of your file, it automatically invokes the Perl shell and will execute the following Perl commands in the script.

```
#!/usr/bin/perl
```

To make the script executable, you would have to set its permissions to be executable. The **chmod** command with the **755** option sets executable permissions for a file, turning it into a program that can be run on the command line. You only have to do this once per script, and you do not have to do this if you are using the **perl** command on the command line, as noted previously.

The following example sets the executable permissions for the *hello.pl* script.

```
$ chmod 755 hello.pl
```

Perl has many similarities to the C programming language and to GAWK. Like C, Perl commands end with a semicolon. As in GAWK, there is a **print** command for outputting text. Perl also uses the same escape sequence character to output newlines (**\n**) and tabs (**\t**). Comments, as in the shell and GAWK, are lines that begin with a **#**.

The following *helloprg* script is an example of a Perl script. It prints out the word "hello" and a newline. Notice the invocation of the **perl** command on the first line.

```
#!/usr/bin/perl
print "hello";
```

Here is a run of the *helloprg* script.

```
$ helloprg
hello
```

6

Ask the Expert

Question: What are some common syntax errors?

Answer: Though Perl is an interpreted language, the entire Perl script is first validated before it is executed, checking for errors ahead of time. Should there be any, they will be displayed on your screen, specifying line numbers and error messages.

Many of the error messages can be obscure. The following are some of the more common errors:

● One of the more common errors is failing to enter semicolons at the end of a line. Perl commands look a lot like shell and GAWK commands, which do not take semicolons, so it is easy to forget them.

● Control structures must have blocks; they cannot have just a single command, as is the case in C.

● Variables must always be prefixed with a dollar symbol (**$**). This is very different from GAWK and C.

Parts of a Perl program can be split into separate files and then read into a main file with the **use** command. Such files end with the extension **.pm** and are referred to as either packages or modules. Often they contain enhanced operations for tasks such as file handling or text searches. A standard set of Perl modules and packages are located in the **/usr/lib/perl5** directory. The **perlmod** man page has a detailed discussion of Perl packages and modules, including dynamically loaded modules.

The following command reads in the **find.pm** package that provides a Perl version of the shell **find** command for searching directories.

```
use /usr/lib/perl5/File/find.pm ;
```

Input and Output

A Perl script can accept input from different sources. It can read input from different files, from the standard input, and even from pipes. Because of this, you have to identify the source of your input within the program; and unlike GAWK, but like a shell program, you have to explicitly instruct a Perl script to read input. A particular source of input is identified by a *file handle*, a name used by a program to reference an input source such as a particular file. Perl already sets up a file handle for the standard input and the standard output, as well as the standard error. The file handle for the standard input is **STDIN**.

The same applies to output. Perl can output to many different destinations, whether they be files, pipes, or the standard output, and file handles are used to identify files and pipes when used for either input or output. The file handle **STDOUT** identifies the standard output, and **STDERR** is the file handle for the standard error. We shall first examine how Perl uses the standard input and output and then discuss how files are operated on. Table 6-2 lists the various input and output commands.

Using the Standard Input

The command for reading from standard input consists of the less-than symbol (**<**) and greater-than symbol (**>**). To read from a file, a file handle

**Input/Output
Command Syntax**

Description

open(*file-handle*,
  permission-with-filename)

Opens the file identified by *file-handle*.

close(file-handle)

Closes the file identified by *file-handle*.

< *filename*>

Reads from the file with name *filename*.

<STDIN>

Reads from the standard input.

<>

Reads from files whose file names are provided in the argument list when the program was invoked.

print <*file-handle*> *text*;

Writes to a file; if *file-handle* is not specified, it writes to standard output; and if no text is specified, it writes the contents of **$_**.

printf < *file-handle*> " *format-str* ", *values* ;

Writes a formatted string to a file; conversion specifiers, *format-str*, are used to format values. If *file-handle* is not specified, it writes to standard output; and if no *values* are specified, it uses the contents of **$_**.

sprintf *str-var* " *format-str* ", *values* ;

Writes formatted values to a string, using conversion specifiers, *format-str*, to format the *values*. If no values are specified, it uses the contents of **$_**.

Table 6-2	**Perl File Operations**

is placed between them, like **<MYFILE>**. To read from the standard input, you can simply use the **STDIN** file handle, like this:

```
<STDIN>
```

<STDIN> is similar to the **read** command in the BASH shell programming language.

To use the input that the **<STDIN>** command reads, you assign it to a variable. You can use a variable you define or a default variable called **$_** as shown in the next example. **$_** is the default for many commands. If the **print** command has no argument, it will print the value of **$_**. If the **chomp** command has no argument, it operates on **$_**, cutting off the

6

newline. The *myread* script that follows illustrates the use of **$_** with the standard input.

```perl
#!/usr/bin/perl

$_=<STDIN>;
print "This is what I entered: $_";
```

Here is a run of the *myread* script.

```
$ myread
larisa and aleina
This is what I entered: larisa and aleina
```

Using the Standard Output

You can use the **print** command to write data to any file or to the standard output. File handles are placed after the **print** command and before any data such as strings or variables. If no file handle is specified, then **print** outputs to the standard output. The following examples both write the "hello\n" string to the standard output. The explicit file handle for the standard output is **STDOUT**.

```perl
print STDOUT "hello\n";
print "hello\n";
```

If there is no data specified to be written, the **print** command will use the contents of **$_**. In other words, whatever the previous **<STDIN>** command reads and assigns to **$_**, **print** will write. If **print** is outputting to the standard output, the contents of **$_** are placed in the standard output. The *myecho.pl* script that follows reads in a line from the standard input, and then outputs whatever was read.

```perl
#!/usr/bin/perl
$_=<STDIN>;
print;
```

Here is a run of the *myecho.pl* script.

```
$ myecho.pl
my name is Dylan
my name is Dylan
```

Perl also has a **printf** command that operates much like the **printf** commands in GAWK and C. It takes as arguments a format list and a list of variables or values. The format list uses conversion specifiers to convert data in corresponding variables or values for output. For example, **%d** is the conversion specifier for an integer, **%s** is for a string, and **%f** is for floating-point numbers. See Module 5, "GAWK," for a complete list and a more detailed explanation of **printf**. The following example converts an integer and a string.

```
$num = 14;
$myname = "Larisa";
printf "For lunch %s ate %d apples\n", $myname, $num;
```

6

The output for this **printf** operation is as follows:

```
For lunch Larisa ate 14 apples
```

A null file handle, **<>**, is a special input operation that will read input from a file listed on the command line when the Perl script was invoked. Perl will automatically set up a file handle for it and read. If you list several files on the command line, then Perl will read the contents of all of them using the null file handle. You can think of this as a **cat** operation in which the contents of the listed files are concatenated and then read into the Perl script.

The *mycat.pl* Perl script and following GAWK command are equivalent. Notice that in Perl, a loop has to be used to explicitly read each line of input.

Here is the *mycat.pl* script:

```
#!/usr/bin/perl
    while ( <> )   ◄──────  Read from files entered as
        {                   arguments to the Perl script
        print;
        }
```

And here is the GAWK command.

```
cat report sum | gawk '{print}'
```

File Handles

You use the **open** command to create a file handle for a file or pipe. The **open** command takes two arguments: the name of the file handle and the file name string. The name of the file handle can be whatever you want, and by convention it is in uppercase. The file name string can be the name of the file or a variable that holds the name of the file. This string can also include different modes for opening a file. By default, a file is opened for reading; but you can also open a file for writing, for appending, or for both reading and writing. The syntax for **open** follows:

```
open ( file-handle, filename-string);
```

The next example opens the *reports* file, calling the file handle for it REPS.

```
open (REPS, "reports");
```

To open a file in a specific mode, such as writing or appending, you include the appropriate mode symbols in the file name string before the file name, separated by a space. Mode symbols are listed in Table 6-3.

Ask the Expert

Question: **Can I keep the file name in a variable?**

Answer: Often the file name will be held in a variable. You then use the dollar sign (**$**) with the variable name to reference the file name. In this example, the file name "reports" is held in the variable **filen**.

```
filen = "reports";
open (REPS, $filen );
```

Permission for Opening File	Description
< *filename*	Read only
> *filename*	Write only
+> *filename*	Read and write
>> *filename*	Append (written data is added to the end of the file)
command		Reads data from a pipe
	command	Sends data out through a pipe

Table 6-3 Perl File Operations

6

The greater-than symbol (**>**) opens a file for writing and the plus sign followed by the greater-than (**+>**) for both reading and writing. In the next example, the *reports* file is opened for both reading and writing.

```
open (REPS, "+> reports");
```

If you are using a variable to hold the file name, you can include the evaluated variable within the file name string, as shown here:

```
open (REPS, "+> $filen");
```

To read from a file by using that file's file handle, place the handle within the **<** and **>**. **<REPS>** reads a line of input from the *reports* file. In this *myreport* script, the *reports* file is opened and its contents are displayed.

```
#!/usr/bin/perl

    open(REPS, "< reports");  ←——— Open a file for reading
    while ( <REPS> )
        {
        print;
        }
    close REPS;
```

To read input from a pipe, you use the **open** command to create a file handle for that pipe. For the file name string, you list the command that inputs data to the pipe, followed by the **|** operator. For example, using **"cat -n reports |"** as the file name string will execute the **cat -n**

reports command that outputs each line in the *reports* file with line numbers, and then inputs them to a pipe. The output of this pipe will be the numbered lines output from the *reports* file. Using the file handle for this pipe, **PREP**, your Perl program can read these numbered lines.

```
open (PREP, "cat -n reports |");
```

You can also output data to a pipe that can then be channeled to another command. In this case, the | operator is placed before the command that the data is being piped to. In the next example, the **PTF** handle identifies a pipe that sends data to the **pr** text formatter.

```
open (PTF, "| pr");
```

The *myrepor2.pl* script shows how you would use pipe operations to read input from a pipe and output it to another pipe. Such piping operations let you take full advantage of the shell filters, such as **sort**, **cut**, **unique**, or other programs that work with the standard input and output.

```
#!/usr/bin/perl

open (PREP, "cat reports |");
open (PTF, "| pr");
while ( <PREP> )
    {
    print PTF;
    }
close PREP;
close PTF;
```

1-Minute Drill

● **What command do you use to read from the standard input?**
● **What default variable can be used for output?**
● **What operator do you use to open a file for both reading and writing?**

● <STDIN>
● $_
● +>

Text Operator: <<

Perl has a special kind of input that operates like the << operation used in the BASH shell. In Perl, the << operator reads text that has been typed directly into the Perl script. It then generates a string from that text that you can assign to a variable, print out, or even turn into a list. The syntax for this command is the << operator followed immediately by a tag and a semicolon. There is no space between the << and the tag. The tag is used to specify the end of the text to be read. Everything you enter from the << statement on will be read in as you typed it, until a line with that tag is reached. The syntax for the text operation is as follows.

```
<<TAG;
text
TAG
```

The << command can treat the text in three different ways, depending upon how the tag is quoted. The text can be treated as verbatim text that is read exactly as it was typed; or it can be treated as a quoted string in which Perl variables and special characters can be evaluated; or it can be treated as a series of commands, such as shell commands, to be executed line by line. The action taken depends on the type of quotes placed around the tag. You can apply either single quotes, double quotes, or back quotes to the entire text by placing a set of these quotes around the tag.

Single quotes placed around the tag will read in the text exactly as it is typed, with no changes, as if it were a string enclosed with single quotes.

Double quotes around the tag will cause any variables placed within the text to be evaluated. If you type in a variable reference, such as **$myname**, then the value will be read in instead of the variable name.

Back quotes around the tag cause each line in the text to be read in as a command, and they are executed just as back quotes around a shell command in a shell program execute that command.

In all of these cases, the results of the operations are placed in a string that you then use in your program.

```
'TAG'   Quote everything
"TAB"   Evaluate variables in a string
`TAB`   Execute commands
```

Single quotes are the default and are assumed if there are no quotes around the tag. Single quotes are helpful for dealing with large amounts of text without having to use either string constants or a file. Double quotes allow you more flexibility, letting you make use of all the features of double-quoted strings. The following example generates a string consisting of three lines. The **$title** and **$author** values will be substituted in.

```
$title =  "Golf and Hockey"
$author = "Dylan Christopher"
print <<"BKINFO";  ◄─────────────── Tag label
The title of this book is $title
The author is $author
The next edition is under development
BKINFO ◄─
```

When a tag label is encased in back quotes, it will expect to read executable commands. When run from the shell, a Perl script with a back quoted tag will execute shell commands. By assigning the output of the tag operation to a variable, you can, in effect, channel the standard output of a shell command into a variable in your Perl script.

In the following example, the **ls –m *.c** shell command will generate a list of C files. This list is the output of the **<<`CF`** operation that is then assigned to **$mycfiles**. The **<<`LC`** operation executes a more complicated shell command that counts all the lines in the **.c** and **.h** files, returning that number, which is then assigned to **$linescode**. Though only one shell command is used in each of these examples, you can have as many as you want. Instead of assigning the output to a variable, you could use the **print** command to just display them. However, context is important. If you invoke the Perl script from a TCSH shell, it will expect to execute TCSH commands, some of which are slightly different.

```
$mycfiles = <<`CF`;
ls -m *.c
CF

$linescode = <<`LC`;
cat *.c *.h | wc -l
```

```
LC

chomp $linescode;
print "List of C files: $mycfiles\n";
print "Program has $linescode lines of code\n"
```

Hint

The text operation is used extensively in CGI programming. In such programs, the text input often consists of HTML commands that will be executed by the browser. In this case, since the Perl script was called from the Web browser, HTML commands can be executed. Values of Perl variables can be substituted into various parts of the HTML commands. Their results can be directly assigned to a Perl variable.

6

Variables and Expressions

Perl variables can be numeric or string variables. Their type is determined by context—the way they are used. You do not have to declare them. A variable that is assigned a numeric value and is used in arithmetic operations is a numeric variable, and all others are treated as strings. To reference a variable in your program, you precede the variable name with a dollar sign ($), just as you would for a shell variable.

You can use the same set of operators with Perl variables as with C variables, with the exception of the operators for strings. Strings use the same special comparison terms as are used in the BASH shell; the standard comparison operators are reserved for numeric variables. However, other operators, such as assignment operators, work on both string and numeric variables. Arithmetic operators and arithmetic assignment operators work on numeric values. The various Perl operators are listed in Table 6-4.

In the next example, the variable **myname** is assigned the string "Aleina". The assignment operator is the equal symbol (=).

```
$myname = "Aleina";
```

Arithmetic Operators	Function
*	Multiplication
/	Division
+	Addition
–	Subtraction
%	Modulo; results in the remainder of a division
**	Power (exponentiation)

Numeric Comparison Operators	
>	Greater than
<	Less than
>=	Greater than or equal to
<=	Less than or equal to
==	Equal in **let**
!=	Not equal to

String Comparison Operators	Description
gt	Greater than
lt	Less than
ge	Greater than or equal to
le	Less than or equal to
eq	Equal to
ne	Not equal to

Increment Operators	
++	Increment variable by one
– –	Decrement variable by one

Arithmetic Assignment Operators	
+=	Increment by specified value
–=	Decrement by specified value
/=	Variable is equal to itself divided by specified value
*=	Variable is equal to itself multiplied by specified value
%=	Variable is equal to itself remaindered by specified value

Assignment Operator	
=	Assign a value to a variable

Table 6-4 Perl Operators

You can assign either an integer or a floating-point value to a numeric variable. Perl treats all floating-point values as double precision.

```
$mynum = 45;
$price = 54.72;
```

Perl also supports arithmetic expressions, and expressions can be nested using parentheses. All the standard arithmetic operators found in other programming languages are used in Perl. Operands can be numeric constants, numeric variables, or other numeric expressions. In the following examples, **$mynum** is assigned the result of an addition expression. Its value is then used in a complex arithmetic expression whose result is assigned to **$price**.

```
$mynum = 3 + 6;
$price = ( 5 * ($num / 3);
```

Perl supports the full range of assignment operators found in GAWK and C. The **++** and **−−** operators increment or decrement a variable. The **+=** and **−=** operators and their variations will perform the equivalent of updating a variable. For example, **i++** is the same as **i = i + 1**, and **i += 5** is the same as **i = i + 5**. Increment operations such as **i++** are used extensively with loops.

You can easily include the value of a variable within a string by simply placing the variable within it. Given the earlier assignment for the variable **$myname**, in the following example, the value of **$nameinfo** would be the string "My name is Aleina \n".

```
$nameinfo = "My name is $myname \n"
```

To assign data that is read from a file to a variable, just assign the result of the **read** operation to the variable. In the next example, data read from the standard input is assigned to the variable **$mydata**.

```
$mydata = <STDIN>;
```

In the *myread2* script that follows, the *myread* script has been modified to use the variable **$myinput**. Whatever the user types in is assigned to

$myinput. Then the contents of that variable are printed as part of a string, using the **print** command.

```
#!/usr/bin/perl

$myinput = <STDIN>;
print "This is what I entered: $myinput \n";
```

The run of the *myread2.pl* script is shown here.

```
$ myread2.pl
larisa and aleina
This is what I entered: larisa and aleina
```

When reading data from the keyboard into a variable, the carriage return character will be included with the input string. You may not want to have this carriage return remain a part of the value of the variable. To remove it, you can use the **chomp** command. **chomp** removes the last character of any string; and with data input from the keyboard, this happens to be the carriage return.

```
chomp $myinput;
```

In the *readname.pl* script that follows, the user inputs his or her name, and it is assigned to the **myname** variable. The contents of **myname** are then printed as part of a string. **chomp** is used to remove the carriage return from the end of the **$myname** string before it is used as part of the output string.

```
#!/usr/bin/perl
$myname = <STDIN>;
chomp $myname;

print "$myname just ran this program\n";
```

The run of the *readname.pl* script follows:

```
$ readname.pl
Justin Petersen
Justin Petersen just ran this program
```

Perl also supports aliases and references. An alias is another name for a variable, array, or function. You can set up a general alias using the asterisk (*) by putting it in front of the name of the object you are aliasing, and then assigning it to the alias name, which is also preceded with an asterisk. For example, the following assignment creates an alias called **count** for the variable **num**.

```
*count = *num;
```

count is now another name for **num**.

This is called a *glob* operation because it actually aliases all variables, arrays, or functions that have the same name. So, based on the preceding example, if there were an array **@num**, it would now also have an alias called **@count**; and if there were a function named **num**, there would also be an alias for it called **count**.

To alias just a specific variable or array, you use a *reference*. A reference is a variable, array, or function name preceded by a backslash. The following example creates **cost** as a reference only to the variable **$mycost**, not to any array or function of that name.

```
*cost = \$mycost
```

Tip
References are used extensively for call-by-reference operations for array arguments used in function calls.

Arrays and Lists

In Perl, you create an array by assigning it a list of values. A list in Perl consists of a set of values encased in parentheses and separated by colons. The following is a list of four values.

```
(23, 41, 92, 7)
```

You assign this list to the array you wish to create, preceding the array name with an at (**@**) symbol. This assignment will initialize the array, sequentially beginning with the first value in the list. Each value will be assigned in turn to a corresponding element, starting from the first element.

```
@mynums = (23, 41, 92, 7);
```

Once the array has been created, you can reference its individual elements. The elements start from 0, not 1; thus, the **mynums** array has four elements, numbered from 0 to 3. You can reference individual elements using an index number encased within brackets. **[0]** references the first element, and **[2]** references the third element. The following example prints out the first element and then the fourth element.

Note

Notice that you use a dollar sign (**$**), not an at symbol (**@**), preceding an individual array element. The **@** is used to reference the entire array and is used when you are assigning whole lists of values to it. The **$** references a particular element, which is essentially a variable.

```
print $mynums[0] ;
print $mynums[3] ;
```

You can change the value of any element in the array by assigning it a new value, as in the following example.

```
$mynums[2] = 40;
```

There is no limit to the number of elements in the array. You can add more by simply referencing a new element and assigning it a value. The following assignment will add a fifth element to the **mynums** array.

```
$mynums[4] = 63;
```

Each array will have a special variable that consists of a number (or pound) sign (**#**) and the name of the array. This variable is the number of elements currently in the array. For example, **#mynums** holds the number of elements in the **mynums** array. The following example prints out the number of elements in the **mynums** array. Notice the preceding **$**.

```
print "$#mynums";
```

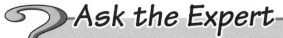

Ask the Expert

Question: Do I need to assign the same types of values to an array?

Answer: When assigning a list to an array, the values in the list do not have to be of the same type. You can have numbers, strings, and even values of variables in a list. Similarly, elements of the array do not have to be of the same type. In the next example, a list with varied elements is assigned to the **myvar** array.

```
@myvar = ( "aleina", 11, 4.5, "a new car");
```

You can reference the entire set of elements in an array as just one list of values. To do this, you use the array name prefixed by **@**. The following example will print all the values in the **mynums** array.

```
print @mynums;
```

The **@** is used here instead of the **$** because the array name is not itself a variable. It is considered a list of values. Only the individual elements are variables.

This syntax also applies when you want to assign one array to another. In the next example, the values of each element in **mynums** are assigned to corresponding elements in **newnums**. Notice the **@** used for **mynums**. You can think of **@mynums** as evaluating to a list of the values in the **mynums** array, and this list is then assigned to **newnums**.

```
@newnums = @mynums;
```

The list of values referenced by an array name can be used in a string, just as the value of a variable can. In the next example, the values of the elements in the **mynums** array are incorporated into a string, which is then assigned to the **myreport** variable. Notice the use of the **@** as a prefix to the array name, **mynums**.

```
$myreport = "Here are the numbers I have: @mynums \n";
print $myreport;
```

6

As mentioned before, though, individual elements of an array are variables, and they need to be referenced using an index and the **$**. The following example uses the value of the third element in the **mynums** array.

```
$myelement= "Value of the 3rd element is $mynums[2] \n";
print $myelement;
```

Tip

Arrays that use sequential numbers to identify the various array elements, such as those we have looked at so far, are referred to as *scalar arrays*. Later we will look at *associative arrays,* which use strings to index the elements instead of numbers.

Array Subsets: Slices

Perl allows you to reference a subset of elements in an array, using them in assignment operations or as lists of values. Such subsets are called *slices*. They can be any subset of elements or even a range of elements in the array. Slices are referenced by a **@** placed before the array name, not a **$**. Slices are not considered to be variables, but rather lists.

To reference a slice of an array, you list the index numbers of the elements you want within brackets separated by commas. **[0,2,4]** references the first, third, and fifth elements in an array. The following example prints out those elements. Notice the **@** prefixing the array name, **mynums**.

```
print @mynums[0, 2, 4] ;
```

You can also specify a range of elements for a slice. A set of two periods indicates a range. A range of elements is specified by the first number in the range, followed by two periods, and then the last number in the range. **[1..3]** references the range of elements beginning with the second element, 1, and ending with the fourth element, 3 (remember that elements are numbered from 0). The next example prints out the second, third, and fourth elements in the **mynums** array.

```
print "@mynums[1..3]" ;
```

You can use these kind of indexes in assignment operations, either specifying particular elements that you want to have new values, or specifying a range of elements. In the next example, the first element of the **mynum** array is assigned the value 1700, and the fourth element is assigned the value 34.

```
@mynums[0, 3] = (1700, 34);
```

Using a range of elements, you can assign a set of values to a range of the array. In the next example, the third, fourth, and fifth elements of the **mynums** array are assigned new values. These elements are referenced with the range **[2..4]**.

```
@mynums[2..4] = (92, 55, 8);
```

Note

If there are more values in the list than the number of referenced array elements, then the remaining values are ignored. If there are more referenced array elements than values in the list, the remaining array elements are assigned a null string.

Ask the Expert

Question: Can I assign several elements at once from one array to another?

Answer: You can use slices to assign part of one array to another, or particular elements in an array to elements in another array. The next example assigns the values of the third, fourth, and fifth elements of the **mynums** array to the **newnums** array. Then the first and third elements of the **mynums** array are assigned to the **partnums** array.

```
@newnums = @mynums[2..4];
@partnums = @mynums[0, 2];
```

Slices can be used for both the array elements being assigned and the array to which they are assigned. In the next example, the third and fifth elements of the **mynums** array are assigned to the second and fourth elements of the **newnums** array. Then the second, fourth, and fifth elements of the **mynums** array, **[1, 3, 4]**, are assigned to the third, fourth, and fifth elements of the **partnums** array, **[2..4]**.

```
@newnums[1,3] = @mynums[2,4];
@partnums[2..4] = @mynums[1, 3, 4];
```

Scalar Array Management Functions: List Operations

Perl has a set of functions designed to help you easily manage scalar arrays. With simple commands you can perform common array operations, such as listing the contents of an array, sorting an array, or sequentially referencing each element one by one. In this respect, you can think of an array as a list, and these functions as performing list operations. The scalar array operations are listed in Table 6-5, and they are explained in the following discussion.

Both **push** and **pop** operate on the end of an array, adding or removing the last element. You can think of them as adding or removing an element at the end of a list. **push** adds a new element to the end

Scalar Array Operations	Description
push(*array,value-list*)	Adds elements listed in *value-list* to the end of *array*
pop(*array*)	Removes the last element from the end of *array*
shift(*array,value-list*)	Adds the element in *value-list* to the beginning of *array*
unshift(*array*)	Removes an element from the beginning of *array*
sort(*array*)	Sorts *array* in ascending order (alphabetic)
reverse(*array*)	Sorts *array* in descending order (alphabetic)
split(*delim, str*)	Splits a string, *str*, into an array of elements. *delimiter* can be either a pattern or a string, and it is used as the delimiter to separate the string into element values.
join(*delim, array*)	Combines the elements in *array* into one string
grep(*array, pattern*)	Searches the elements in *array* for *pattern*

Table 6-5 Perl Scalar Array Operations

of the array, and it takes as its arguments the array, followed by a list of values that you want added as elements to the array. It can add several new elements at a time. The **pop** operation removes an element from the beginning of the array.

The **shift** and **unshift** operators work on the beginning of a list. **shift** will remove the first element in a list, making the next element the first one. The **unshift** operation adds a new element to the beginning of the list. **shift** takes as its argument an array and returns the value of the first element it removes. **unshift** takes as its argument an array followed by the value of the element you want to add. It then returns the total number of elements now in the array.

The **sort** operations will sort the elements in an array according to the system's character set, usually the ASCII character set. **sort** will arrange elements in ascending order and returns the list of sorted values. You can then assign this to another array, and this array would then be the sorted version of the original. **sort** does not change the original array. In the next example, **sort** generates a sorted list using the elements of the **mylist** array. This list is then assigned to the **mysort** array, which then becomes the sorted version of **mylist**.

```
@mysort = sort(@mylist);
```

The **reverse** operation also performs a sort, but in descending order rather than ascending order. As with **sort**, **reverse** generates a sorted list that you can then assign to an array, providing a sorted version in descending order.

```
@mydecend = reverse(@mylist);
```

The **split** operation is used to create an array and assign it values derived from a string. The values are determined by a specified delimiter that is used to segment the string, forming the different values that will be assigned to elements in the array. **split** is often used with lines of input data that are already arranged into fields that are separated by a delimiter such as a comma or colon. **split** will automatically parse the line of data using the delimiter, detecting each field and assigning it to the next element in the array.

split takes as its argument a delimiter and string. The delimiter can be indicated by either a string or a pattern, and it is the delimiter that will be used to parse the string into elements. As a pattern, the delimiter can be any regular expression, allowing you to specify several different delimiters or even delimiters consisting of whole words.

In the next example, the split operation separates the string in **$myline** into fields using the comma as the delimiter. The resulting list is then assigned to the **linelist** array. Notice the use of the literal string designators ('') in specifying the comma delimiter.

```
@linelist = split(',', $myline);
```

You can use the **grep** function to search an array or any list. **grep** operates much like the UNIX utility **grep**. It takes as its arguments a pattern and a list, usually an array, and you can use regular expressions in the pattern to match more than one element. **grep** will return a list of all the elements it has matched. Any pattern can be used in the Perl version of **grep**, as shown in the next example, which searches for lines beginning with the letter *d*.

```
@myres = grep( /^d/, @mylist);
```

Associative Arrays

An associative array uses strings to index elements in an array, instead of numbers. You can think of the index string as a keyword that you can use to find an element. In Perl, an associative array is defined with a percent symbol (%) prefixing the array name. The list of values that it is assigned consists of pairs of index strings and element values. An index string is followed by the element value, which is then followed by the next index string and element value, and so on. In the next example, the associative array **city** is defined with four elements, each having an integer value, and each indexed with the name of a city.

```
%city = ('Sacramento', 4,
         'Fallon', 86,
         'Napa', 7,
         'Alameda', 53 ) ;
```

Index string

Element value

You reference an element in an associative array using its index string. The index string is encased in single quotes and braces (not parentheses).

```
print  $city{'Fallon'};
```

To add a new element in an associative array, you need to provide both the string to be used as the index for this element and the element's value.

```
$city{'LA'} = 45;
```

To reference the list of values for an associative array, you use **%** with the array name. The following example prints out all values of the **city** array.

```
print %city ;
```

Perl also has a set of list operations designed to work on associative arrays. With these operations you can generate lists of keys or values. They are helpful for easily iterating through an associative array. The operations are listed in Table 6-6, and they are explained in the following discussion.

In a scalar array, you know that the index always starts at 0 and runs consecutively to the last element; but in an associative array, the strings used to index elements may be any arbitrary strings. To print out an associative array, you would need to know what these index strings are to reference the array elements. The **keys** operation allows you to generate a list of just the index strings in an associative array. It takes as its argument an associative array and returns a list of all the index strings used to reference the elements in that array. Having obtained the index strings, you can then use them for referencing the elements in the array.

Associative Array Operations	Description
keys(%*assoc-array*)	Generates a list of all the index strings in an associative array
values(%*assoc-array*)	Generates a list of all the values of the elements in an associative array
each(%*assoc-array*)	Returns both the value and index string of the next element of an associative array
delete(%*assoc-array, index-string*)	Deletes the element with the specified *index-string* from an associative array

Table 6-6   Perl Associative Array Operations

The **each** operation works much like the **keys** operation. However, it returns both the index string for an element and the value of the element. **each** takes as its argument an array, and each time it is called it returns the next element of the array and its index string. You can use **each** in a loop to reference each element in the array.

The **values** operation returns a list of all the values in an associative array. You can use this to easily print out the elements in an associative array, dispensing with the need for index strings.

You use the **delete** operation to remove an element from an associative array. **delete** takes as its argument the index string of the element you want to remove. It will then return the contents of that element. In the next example, **delete** is used to remove the element with the index string "Sacramento".

```
delete(%myarr,"Sacramento");
```

Note

To remove the entire array, you use the **undef** operation. **undef** works on either scalar or associative arrays. It eliminates the array completely, releasing its memory.

1-Minute Drill

● **Can you assign values to different elements of an array at the same time?**

● **What kind of array can be indexed using words?**

Control Structures

Perl has a set of control structures similar to those used in GAWK, C-shell, and C programming languages. Perl has loops with which you can repeat commands, and conditions that allow you to choose among specified commands. There are two different sets of operators for the test

---

● **Yes; just specify the elements separated by commas, as in** @mynums[4,9,17].
● **An associative array.**

expressions, for use with strings and numeric values. You can also use pattern operations that allow the use of regular expressions.

Test Expressions

Perl has different sets or operators for numeric and string comparisons. You have to be careful not to mix up the different operators. The string operators are two-letter codes similar to those used in the BASH shell. For example, the **eq** operator tests for the equality of two strings and the **gt** operator tests to see if one is greater than the other. Numeric comparisons, on the other hand, use symbols similar to those found in programming languages as operators. For example, **>** stands for greater than, and **==** tests for equality, and these are essentially the same comparison operators used for the C programming language. These operators were all listed earlier in the module in Table 6-4. There are two important exceptions: string patterns and patterns.

The string–pattern operator, **=~**, tests for a pattern in a string variable. The right-hand operand is the pattern and the left-hand operand is the string. The pattern can be any regular expression, making this a very flexible and powerful operation.

Patterns perform pattern matching on either a string or the contents of the **_$** special variable. The pattern operator consists of two slashes that enclose the pattern searched for, **/pattern/**. The pattern can be any regular expression.

There are also a number of tests that you can perform on a file to check its status. For example, you can use the **−e** text to make sure a file exists or use a **−s** to check whether it is empty (see Table 6-7).

The Logical Commands: &&, ||, !

Perl supports the AND (**&&**), OR (**||**), and NOT (**!**) logical operations. They take as their operands expressions, just as they do in the C programming language. Their syntax is as follows:

```
(expression) && (expression)
(expression) || (expression)
!(expression)
```

6

File Tests	Description
–e	File exists
–f	File exists and is a regular file
–s	File is not empty
–z	File is empty, zero size
–r	File is readable
–w	File can be written to and modified
–x	File is executable
–d	File name is a directory name
–b	File is a binary file
–t	File is a text file

Table 6-7   File Test Operations

The evaluation of these logical commands is summarized in Table 6–8. You can extend these commands with added **&&** or | | commands, creating complex AND and OR operations. The logical commands allow you to use logical operations as your test command in control structures, and you can also use them independently.

Logical Operation Syntax	Evaluation
expression && *expression* *expression* and *expression*	The logical AND condition returns a true (0) value if both expressions return a true (0) value; if one returns a nonzero value, then the AND condition is false and it also returns a nonzero value. Execution stops at the first false expression. The **and** operation is the same as **&&** but has a lower precedence.
expression || *expression* *expression* or *expression*	The logical OR operation returns a true (0) value if one or the other expression returns a true (0) value; if both expressions return a nonzero value, then the OR condition is false and it also returns a nonzero value. Evaluation stops at the first true expression. The **or** operation is the same as || but has a lower precedence.
! *expression* not *expression*	The logical NOT condition inverts the true or false value of the expression. The **not** operation is the same as **!** but has a lower precedence.

Table 6-8   Evaluation of Perl Logical Commands

The other implementation of the logical operators, **and**, **or**, and **not**, supports list processing. They perform the same tests on expressions, and their evaluation is the same as the other logical operators (as summarized in Table 6-8), but they can also have lists as their operands. They have a lower precedence than the standard logical operators. Their syntax is as follows:

```
(list/expr) and (list/expr)
(list/expr) or (list/expr)
not(list/expr)
```

The logical operators are usually used in test expressions for control structures such as **while** and **if**. However, they can also be used independently as their own statements. In effect, they provide a simple way to write a conditional operation. In Perl scripts, you may often see an **or** operation used with a file **open** command. For example, in an **or** operation, if the first expression fails, then the second one is checked. If that second one is the **die** command to end the program, then this is an operation to end the program if the file **open** operation fails.

```
open (REPS, "+> $filen") or die "Can't open $filen";
```

The **and** operation works similarly, except that if the first expression is true, then the second one is checked. The following example looks for an empty line; and, if it finds one, it prints the message.

```
/^$/ && print "Found empty line";
```

Loops

Perl loops include **while**, **do-until**, **for**, and **foreach** loops. The **while** loop is the more general-purpose loop, whereas the **for** and **foreach** loops provide special capabilities. The **foreach** loop is similar to its counterpart in the C-shell and is particularly helpful in processing lists and arrays. The **while**, **do-until**, and **for** loops operate much like their counterparts in the C programming language. The **for** loop, in particular, has the same three expression formats as the C **for** loop. Table 6-9 summarizes the Perl loop structures.

Loop-Control Structures	Description

while(*expression*) {
   statements;
}
	while executes statements as long as its test expression is true.

for(*init-expr; test-expr; incr-expr*)
{
   statements;
}
	The **for** control structure executes statements as long as *test-expr* is true. The first expression, *init-expr*, is executed before the loop begins. The third expression, *incr-expr*, is executed within the loop after the *statements*.

foreach *variable* (*list-values*)
{
   statements;
}
	foreach is designed for use with lists of values, such as those generated by an array; the *variable* operand is consecutively assigned the values in the *list-values* list.

do{ *statements;* } until(*expression*)	**do-until** executes statements as long as its test expression is false.
next	Skips the remainder of the loop and starts the next iteration. **next** is like the C **continue** command; it will execute any **continue** block.
continue { *statements;*}	Executes a **continue** block as the last statements in a loop. The block is executed even if a **next** statement starts the next iteration.

Table 6-9   Perl Loop–Control Structures

while Loop

In Perl, the **while** loop begins with the keyword **while**, which is followed by an expression enclosed in parentheses. A block follows the expression, usually on the next line. This block can hold several statements and ends with a semicolon. A block is a set of statements encased in a set of braces.

You can easily adapt the **while** loop for use with arrays. The variable used to control a loop can also be used, inside the loop, to index an array. In the *titlearr.pl* script that follows, the elements of the title array are assigned the values of the titles. Then, the contents of each element are printed out using a **while** loop. Notice that **$#title** holds the count of elements in the array. **$#title** is used as the upper bound in the **while** loop's test expression in order to check when the loop should stop.

```perl
#!/usr/bin/perl
@title = ("Tempest", "Iliad", "Raven");
$i = 0;
while($i <= $#title)
    {
    print "$title[$i] \n";
    $i++
    }
```

Here is a run of the *titelarr.pl* script.

```
$ titlearr.pl
Tempest
Iliad
Raven
```

for Loops

The **for** loop consists of three expressions followed by a block of statements. The three expressions are placed within parentheses and separated by semicolons, and the block to be executed within the **for** loop is placed after the expressions.

The three expressions correspond to those used to manage a **while** loop: the initialization, test, and update expressions. The first expression is executed once, before the loop begins. It is often used to initialize variables used in the test expression. The second expression is the test expression for the loop. When it evaluates to false, the loop stops. The last expression is an update expression. It is executed as if it were the last statement within the loop and is usually used to update variables in the test expression. Here is the syntax for the **for** loop.

```
for (initialization; test-expression; update-expression)
{
statements;
}
```

A **for** loop is often used to implement simple counting loops. In the following example, the **for** loop implements a counting loop using the **i** variable. In the initialization expression, **i** is assigned the value 0. This expression is executed once, before entry into the loop. Then the test expression checks to see whether the value of **i** is less than 3. When **i** is greater than or equal to 3, then the test is false and the **for** loop ends.

In each iteration of the loop, the block following the **for** expression is executed, and in this case, the **print** statement is executed. After this statement, the update expression is executed, which here is an increment of the **i** variable. This increment is performed at the end of each iteration— you should think of the update expression as the last statement in the loop. Whereas the initialization expression is executed only once before the loop, the update expression is executed with each iteration as the last statement within the loop. In this example, the update expression will increment the variable **i** by 1 with each iteration. On the third iteration, **i** will be set to 3, making the test expression false and ending the **for** loop.

```
for($i = 1; $i <= 3; $i++)
    {
    print "This is the $i iteration\n";
    }
```

Hint

The **for** loop has the same flexibility as a **while** loop. In fact, you can think of the **for** loop as just another way of writing a **while** loop. To replace a **for** loop with a **while** loop, change the initialization expression to be a statement located just before the **while** statement. The update expression would be an expression statement located at the end of the **while** block, and the test expression would be the **while** loop's test expression.

foreach Loops

The **foreach** loop is designed to sequentially reference a list of values. It is very similar to the C-shell's **for-in** structure. The **foreach** loop takes two operands: a variable and a list of values enclosed in parentheses. Each time through the loop, the next value in the list is assigned to the variable in the **foreach** loop. When the end of the list is reached, the loop stops. Like

 Ask the Expert

Question: What kind of expressions does a for loop take?

Answer: The **for** loop does not in any way require that the first expression actually be an initialization. Nor does it require that the last expression be an update or increment operation. The expressions can be any valid expressions. The **for** loop simply places these expressions in a loop structure. The first expression is placed before the loop, where an initialization is likely to occur. The last expression is placed at the end of the loop, where an update is likely to occur. The **for** loop does not even require that there actually be a first or last expression. The following example is a simple way to write a **for** loop to read from the standard input. It is equivalent to **while(<STDIN>)**.

```
for (;<STDIN>;){
}
```

Question: What if the for loop has no test expression?

Answer: Though the first and last expressions in a **for** loop may be any kind of expression, the middle expression is special in that it must be a test expression. Its result will determine whether execution of the loop continues. You can, however, leave the test expression empty. An empty test expression evaluates to true, which will give you an infinite loop. In fact, should you need an infinite loop in your program, an easy way to write one is to use a **for** statement with empty expressions.

```
for( ; ; )
```

the **while** loop, the expression is followed by a block of statements. The syntax for the **foreach** loop follows.

```
foreach variable ( list-of-values )
        {
        statements;
        }
```

The **foreach** loop is useful for managing arrays. You can use the array name to generate a list of all the element values in the array, and then use this list as the list referenced by the **foreach** loop. You can also specify a range of array elements, using only those specified values for the list, or you can use a set of individual elements.

In the *mynumlist.pl* script that follows, the array name **@mylist** is used to generate a list of its values, which the **foreach** loop then operates on, assigning each one to **$mynum** in turn.

```perl
#!/usr/bin/perl

@mylist = (34, 21, 96, 85);

foreach $mynum ( @mylist )
        {
        print "$mynum \n";
        }
```

Here is a run of the *mynumlist.pl* script.

```
$ mynumlist.pl
34
21
96
85
```

The **@ARGV** array is a special array that holds the arguments that a user enters on the command line. Using the **@ARGV** array, you can specify the command line arguments as a list of values. The arguments specified on the command line when the program was invoked become a list of values referenced by the **foreach** loop. The variable used in the **foreach** loop is automatically set to each argument value in sequence: the first time through the loop, the variable is set to the value of the first argument; the second time, it is set to the value of the second argument; and so on.

The number of arguments that a user actually enters on the command line can vary, and the value of the **#ARGV** special variable will always be the number of elements that are in the **ARGV** array. You can use **#ARGV** to determine when you have referenced all the elements in the **ARGV** array using their indexes. For example, to use the **foreach** loop to reference each element in the **ARGV** array, you would use the **..** operator to generate a list of indexes: **0.. $#ARGV** generates a list of numbers beginning with 0 and running through to the value of **$#ARGV**.

In the *pbackuparg.pl* script that follows, a list of C program files is entered on the command line when the shell file *cbackuparg* is invoked. In the **foreach** loop, **0.. $#ARGV** generates a list of numbers. For three arguments, **$#ARGV** would have the value 3, and the list would be (1, 2, 3). Each number is consecutively assigned to the **i** variable, which is then used to index the **ARGV** array.

```perl
#!/usr/bin/perl

foreach $i (0 .. $#ARGV)
        {
        print "Copying $ARGV[$i]\n";
                open(SFILE, "< $ARGV[$i]");
                open(BFILE, "> sourcebak/$ARGV[$i]");
                while(<SFILE>) {
                    print BFILE ;
                    }
                close(SFILE);
                close(BFILE);
        }
```

A run of the *pbackuparg.pl* script is shown here.

```
$ pbackuparg.pl  main.c  lib.c  io.c
Copying main.c
main.c
Copying lib.c
lib.c
Copying io.c
io.c
```

Loop and Block Controls

Perl has a set of special commands designed to give you refined control over loops and blocks. These correspond to similar commands used in the C language. These commands need to make use of labels; so if you use the commands within a loop, you need to label that loop. When one of these commands is used, it references that loop.

The **last** command corresponds to the C **break** command. It stops
execution of a loop. It can also be used to break out of a block. **last** is used
with blocks to simulate switch structures. The following **last** command
will break out of a loop if the user enters a *q* on a line by itself. The regular
expression **/^q$/** uses the caret (**^**) to indicate the beginning of a line and
the dollar sign (**$**) to indicate the end of the line. The loop is labeled with
the **MLB:** label that is then referenced by the **last** command. The label
can be any name you want.

```
MLB: while (<STDIN>)
     {
      if ( /^q$/) {last MLB;}
     print $_;
     }
```

The **next** command skips over the remaining statements in the loop.
It is similar to the C **continue** command. **next** is designed to work with
the continue block. A continue block consists of the command **continue**
followed by a block. This block is executed at the end of the loop. Even if
a **next** command skips over the remaining statements, the **continue** block
is always executed. You can use **next** to ensure that operations such as
increments are performed. The **redo** command will re-execute a loop,
even if its test proves false. It has no corresponding C command. Both
the **redo** and the **last** commands will ignore any **continue** block.

Conditions: **if, elsif, unless,** and **switch**

Perl supports **if-else** operations much as they are used in other
programming languages. The **if** structure with its **else** and **elsif** components
allows you to select alternative actions. You can use just the **if** command to
choose one alternative, or combine that with **else** and **elsif** components to
choose among several alternatives. These condition-control structures are
summarized in Table 6-10.

The **if** structure has a test expression encased in parentheses, followed
by a block of statements. If the test is true, the statements in the block
are performed. If not, the block is skipped. Unlike other programming
languages, only a block can follow the test; and any statements, even just
one, must be encased within it.

Condition-Control Structures	Description

if(*expression*) {
    statements;
    }
	if executes statements if its test expression is true. The *statements* must be included within a block.

if(*expression*) {
    statements;
    }
 else(*expression*) {
    statements;
    }
	if-else executes the **if** statements if the test expression is true; if it is false, the **else** statements are executed.

if(*expression*) {
    statements;
    }
 elsif(*expression*) {
    statements;
    }
 else(*expression*) {
    statements;
    }
	elsif allows you to nest **if** structures, enabling selection among several alternatives; at the first true **if** expression, its statements are executed and control leaves the entire **elsif** structure.

unless(*expression*) {
    statements;
    }
	unless executes statements if its test expression is false.

LABEL:{
if(*expr*){*statements*;last *LABEL*};
}
	This structure simulates a switch structure by using listed **if** statements within a block, with the last statement referencing a label for the block.

Table 6-10   Perl Condition–Control Structures

6

An **if-else** combination allows you to make alternative choices, taking either one action or the other. If the test expression of the **if** structure is false, the block of statements following the **else** is executed. The following example tests to see if an open operation on a file was successful. If not, it will execute a **die** command to end the program. The NOT operator (!) will make the test true if **open** fails, thereby executing the **die** command.

```
if (!(open (REPS, "< $filen"))) {
    die "Can't open $filen";
}
else  {
        print "Opened $filen successfully";
        }
```

The **elsif** structure allows you to nest **if-else** operations. With **elsif**, you can choose between several alternatives. The first alternative is specified with the **if** structure, and it is followed by other alternatives, each specified by its own **elsif** structure. The alternative to the last **elsif** structure is specified with an **else**. If the test for the first **if** structure fails, control will be passed to the next **elsif** structure, and its test will be executed. If it fails, control is passed to the next **elsif** and its test will be checked. This continues until a test is true, at which point that **elsif** has its commands executed and control passes out of the **if** structure to the next command.

The following example illustrates the use of nested **if-else** operations. Notice that each **if**, **else**, and **elsif** structure has its own block, even though there is only one statement in them. The **system** function is used here to execute a shell command.

```
if ($option eq "s") {
        system("ls -s");
        }
        elsif ($option eq "l") {
            system("ls -l");
            }
        elsif ($option eq "d") {
                system("ls -F");
                }
        else {
                print "Invalid Option\n";
                }
```

unless

The **unless** command performs the opposite test of an **if** command. If the **unless** command's test is false, its statements are executed; if the test is true, the statements are not executed. The syntax is the same as that of the **if** command. **unless** is often used for tests in which you want to check for a failed operations. You will often see it used with the **open** command to test for a failed file open operation, as shown next:

```
unless(open (REPS, "+> $filen") {
    die "Can't open $filen";
}
```

switch

There is no switch control structure in Perl, although it can be simulated. In a classic switch structure, a choice is made by comparing a value with several possible patterns, and each possible value is associated with a set of operations. If a match is found, the associated operations are performed.

You can simulate a switch in Perl using a block and a **last** command. Blocks are valid control structures in their own right. You can list a block by itself, and its statements will be executed consecutively. The statements within a block are considered to be a group. The **last** command exits a block or loop and skips a **continue** block if there is one. **last** is like the C **break** statement. When used in a statement within a block, the **last** command will immediately exit the block.

In the next example, the final statement is never executed because the **last** command forces an exit from the block.

```
{
print "The first statement\n";
print "the second statement\n";
last;
print "The third statement\n";
}
```

There are several ways to construct the statements in a block to simulate a switch control structure. The easiest is to have a series of **if** structures followed by a block of statements ending with a **last** statement. The block would be given a label that the **last** statement would reference, thereby exiting the labeled block. The final statement in the block would be a default operation, executed if all the **if** tests fail. The syntax for this structure would look like the following:

```
LABEL:{
if(expr){statements;last LABEL};
}
```

6

The following example simulates a switch using a block of **if** structures. The block is labeled with **MYSW:** placed before the opening brace. Each **if** structure tests the same variable's values, **num**. If a test is true, then its block of statements is executed. The last statement in each **if** is a **last** command, which will exit the outer block.

```
MYSW: {
if ($num == 1) { print "The first choice"; last MYSW;};
if ($num == 2) { print "The second choice"; last MYSW;};
if ($num == 3) { print "The third choice"; last MYSW;};
print "Invalid Option";
}
```

Directories

Perl also has a full set of built-in commands used for handling directories, which operate much like the file commands, such **open** and **close**. The **opendir** command opens a directory, much like a file is opened. A *directory handle*, much like a file handle, is assigned to the directory. The following example will open a directory called **reports** and assign it to the variable **repdir**, which then becomes the directory handle.

```
opendir(repdir, "reports");
```

The **readdir** command will read the first item in a directory. However, when used in a list context, the command will return a list of all the file and directory names in that directory. For example, a **foreach** statement will operate on a list instead of an expression. Used in a **foreach** statement, **readdir** will return an entire list of files and subdirectories. In the next example, the **readdir** command is used in a **foreach** structure to generate a list of file names and subdirectories in the directory referenced by **repdir**. Each file name and subdirectory, in turn, is assigned to the **filen** variable.

```
foreach $filen (  (readdir($repdir)) )
```

closedir closes the directory, **chdir** changes directories, **mkdir** creates directories, and **rmdir** remove directories. The following example closes the reports directory as referenced by the **repdir** directory handle:

```
closedir ($repdir)
```

1-Minute Drill

● **How many expressions does a** for **loop have?**

● **What control structure can you use to easily read script arguments?**

● **What command do you use to simulate a switch structure?**

myht.pl

Project 6-1: Indexing with Perl

The following programming example implements the **myindex** program described in Module 3, the BASH shell programming module.

This program will first detect any directories in the current directory and then check to see if there are any Web pages in them. Web pages are any files that have an **.html** or **.htm** extension. The names of these files are placed in strings that consist of HTML **href** commands to select and display the files. The HTML references are organized into a list with the **<ul>** and **</ul>** tags, with each item being preceded with a **<li>** tag. Directory names are used as headings with the **<h1>** tag.

6

Step-by-Step

1. The program should first generate the HTML code to set the title to "My Index" and the heading to "Index of HTML Files." The Perl **print** command can be used to output the characters to the standard output.

2. The **opendir** command should then open the current working directory (**.**) using the handle **CDIR**.

3. The **foreach** command can be used to read the list of files and directories in the working directory generated by the **readdir** command. Place them one by one in the **dirname** variable with every iteration.

4. If a subdirectory is found and it is not the working directory, the directory name should be printed as the subheading.

● **Three: initialization, test, and increment.**
● **Use** foreach **to reference the** ARGV **array.**
● **last.**

5. The subdirectory should then be searched for any HTML files in an inner **foreach** loop. Generate the list of files and directories for the subdirectory with the **readdir** command, and place them one by one in the **filen** variable.

6. Check each file name to determine whether it is a file and that it has the extension **.html** or **.htm**, an HTML file.

7. For each valid HTML file, search the file for a title and use that as the link text in the index. To do so, open the file with the handle **HFILE**; use a **while** loop to read this file line by line, and use **grep** to search for the occurrence of a **<TITLE>** pattern. Set the **found** flag to 1 if the title is found.

8. If **grep** does not find a **<TITLE>** line, assign the file name to **ntitle**. Use the **substr** function to remove the extension.

9. If **grep** finds a **<TITLE>** pattern, use the **rindex** and **substr** functions to strip the preceding and tailing **<TITLE>** and **</TITLE>** tags, along with any other characters in the line. The title text itself will remain. Assign it to the **ntitle** variable.

10. After text is assigned for **ntitle**, use the **ntitle** value as the link text in the **href** HTML line. This line begins with a **<li>** tag indicating it is a list item.

11. End the program by outputting an end **BODY** tag and then closing the current directory, **CDIR**.

The completed *myht.pl* program is shown here:

```perl
#!/usr/bin/perl

print "<HTML>\n<HEAD>\n<TITLE>My Index</TITLE>\n</HEAD>\n<BODY>\n";
print "<H1>Index of HTML Files</H1>\n";
opendir(CDIR, ".");

foreach $dirname ( readdir(CDIR) )
    {
#select only directories, but not . or .. directories
    if ( -d $dirname && !( $dirname =~ /^\./))
        {
        print "<h2>$dirname</h2>\n";
        print '<ul>';
            opendir(HDIR, "$dirname");

        foreach $filen (  (readdir(HDIR)) )
            {
```

```
                    if ( -f  "$dirname/$filen" &&  ( $filen =~ /.html?$/) )
                        {
                unless(open(HFILE, "< $dirname/$filen")) {
                            die "Count no open file $dirname/$filen";
                        }
        $found = 0;
    while ( ($hline = <HFILE>) && $found == 0)
        {
        if($hline =~ /TITLE/) {
            $tline = $hline;
            $found = 1;
            }
        }
    close(HFILE);
            if ( $found == 0 )
                {
            $ntitle = substr($filen, 0, index($filen, ".") );
                }
                else  {
            $lpos = index($tline, "TITLE>") + length("TITLE>");
                $rpos = rindex($tline, "</TITLE");
                $ntitle = substr($tline, $lpos, $rpos - $lpos);
                }
            print "<li><a href=$dirname/$filen>$ntitle</a>\n";
            }
        }
        print "</ul>\n";
closedir(HDIR);
    }
}
print "</BODY>\n</HTML>\n";
closedir(CDIR);
```

6

String Functions

Perl provides several functions and operators for manipulating strings, and they are summarized in Table 6-11.

The **length**, **index**, and **substr** functions perform standard string operations, such as obtaining the length of a string or copying a substring from a string. **split** performs a special task. It generates an array from a string, cutting the string into array element values (see the earlier section "Scalar Array Management Functions: List Operations"). The **dot** operator concatenates strings, and the **x** operator generates strings consisting of repeated characters. The **chomp** function will cut a trailing newline, space, or tab that may be at the end of a string. It is helpful for removing the newline character appended to strings read from the standard input, **<STDIN>** (text the user enters interactively on a Perl program).

String Operation	Description
str . str	The dot operator (.) concatenates strings
str x *num*	The **x** operator repeats a string or character, *str*, *num* number of times

String Function	
chomp(*str*)	Removes a trailing newline
substr(*str, start-pos, length*)	Returns a substring of the specified string, *str*, beginning at the *start-pos* starting position for the *length* specified
substr(*str, start-pos, length*) = *string*	Replaces the specified section of the string, *str*, beginning at the *start-pos* starting position for the *length* specified, with the assigned *string*
length(*str*)	Finds the length of a string, *str*
index(*str, pattern*)	Finds the position of the specified *pattern* in a string, *str*
rindex(*str, pattern*)	Finds the last position of a specified *pattern* in a string, *str*

Table 6-11   String Operations and Functions

You use the dot operator (.) to concatenate two strings. The following example adds a .dat suffix to a root file name. If the content of **$curfile** is "myaddress", **$newfile** would be "myaddress.dat".

```
$newfilename = $curfile . ".dat" ;
```

With the repetition operator (**x**) you can repeat a string any number of times. You precede the **x** operator with the string to be repeated and then follow the **x** operator with the number of times you want to repeat the string. The string can be one or more characters. The following example repeats "hi" four times.

```
"hi " x 4
```

The **length** function obtains the length of a string. It can be applied to any string variable including field variables. The function call **length("Christopher")** returns 11 because it contains 11 characters.

The **length** function can be applied to any variable. **length($filename)** returns the length of the file name string held in the **$filename** variable. When used without an argument, the **length** function returns the length of the string in the **$_** variable, which is usually the number of characters in an input line.

The **index** function finds the first position of a pattern within a string, and the **rindex** function finds the last position of a pattern in a string. You can think of the **rindex** as the right index, searching from the right end of the string. The position of the pattern "en" in Dickens is 5, as returned by **index**.

The **substr** function is used either to copy a substring of a given string, or to replace a substring of a specified string. The **substr** function takes three arguments. The first is the string that **substr** operates on, the second is the position where the substring begins, and the third is the number of characters from the beginning position (the length of the substring). The **substr** function normally operates as a copy operation. The one exception is when it is used on the left side of an assignment operation, in which case **substr** becomes a replacement operation.

Pattern Matching

Like GAWK, Perl can search for patterns. The syntax for the different searches are listed in Table 6-12.

To search for a pattern on a given line, the search pattern is indicated by enclosing slashes. **/Dickens/** searches for the pattern "Dickens" in a line. By default, a pattern search operates on the contents of the _$ special variable, which usually holds the contents of the most recently read line of input, wherever that came from. If the most recent input command

Pattern Matching Syntax	Description
/reg-expr/	Matches a pattern using a regular expression
var =~ /reg-expr/	Finds the occurrence of the regular expression in a string variable, var
var !~ /reg-expr/	Checks whether the regular expression does not occur in a string variable, var

Table 6-12 Perl Pattern Matching

was **<STDIN>**, **_$** will hold a line read from the standard input, and any following pattern search that doesn't specify another target will search that line. The next example reads a line from the standard input and then searches for the pattern **/Dickens/** in it.

```
$_ = <STDIN>;
/Dickens/;
```

Unlike GAWK, Perl does not automatically read all lines from an input source. To read all the lines from the standard input, you have to explicitly issue a **read** command for each line. Therefore, to search each line in the standard input, you have to explicitly read each line with the **<STDIN>** command and then search it with a pattern search operation. You can do this easily with a **while** loop.

In the following example, the **while** loop reads each line of input from the standard input, and searches for the pattern /Dickens/. An **if** condition is used with the search pattern, **/Dickens/**, and the **print** command, so that only those lines with the pattern are printed.

```
while ( <STDIN> )
    {
    if ( /Dickens/ )
        {
        print;
        }
    }
```

Pattern Matching on Variables: =~

To search the contents of a variable for a pattern, you can use the **=~** operator with the pattern search operation. You use the variable name as the left operand and the pattern search operation as the right operand. The following example looks for the pattern "Christmas" in the **$title** variable.

```
$title =~ /Christmas/
```

If you were to read data from an input source into a variable, you could search that data by using the matching operator, **=~**, and a pattern search on that variable. The next example reads in data from the standard input to the variable **$title**. Then the pattern search operation is used to check for the pattern "Christmas."

```
$title = <STDIN>;
$title =~ /Christmas/ ;
```

You can use such a technique to search files line by line. Suppose there is a file of titles called **newtitles** in which each line is the title of a book. The following program will search for all titles with the pattern "Christmas." reading the titles one by one (a line at a time) and assigning them to the **$title** variable which is then searched.

```
open ( NTITLES,  "< books");
while ( $title = <NTITLES> )
    {
    if ( $title =~  /Christmas/ )
                {
         print $title;
                }
    }
close(NTITLES);
```

The pattern-matching operation has a set of options with which you can qualify your search, and these options are listed in Table 6-13.

Options are placed after the closing slash of the pattern–matching operation. For example, the **i** option placed after the closing slash instructs the pattern-matching operation to ignore the case of characters.

Pattern-Matching Option	Description
i	Does case-insensitive pattern matching
m	Treats a string as multiple lines
s	Treats a string as a single line
x	Extends your pattern's legibility with white space and comments

Table 6-13   Perl Pattern–Matching Options

The following example searches for both lowercase and uppercase versions of "Christmas."

```
/Christmas/i
```

Perl supports the full range of regular expressions in its pattern matching, including extended special characters. The *****, **+**, **?**, **{}**, **.**, **^**, **$**, and **[ ]** special characters can all be used to construct complex search operations.

1-Minute Drill

● **What two pieces of information do you need to obtain a substring of a string?**

● **What control structure can you use to easily read script arguments?**

Functions: **sub**

In your Perl script, you can define subroutines, permitting you to better organize your program. Instead of one long series of statements, you can define separate subroutines for specific tasks. Tasks you wish to perform more than once do not have to have their code repeated in the program—you can just define a subroutine for that task and call that subroutine as many times as you need to.

Subroutines are defined with the **sub** command, followed by the subroutine name and a block of statements. Within the block of statements, you can have any Perl statements you wish. Subroutines operate like functions do in C programs, and like procedures in other programming languages. They can take arguments and have parameters with predetermined names.

Perl functions and related commands are shown in Table 6-14.

● **The start position within the string and the number of characters in the substring.**

● foreach.

Function or Command	Description
sub *function-name* ;	Declares a function

sub *function-name* {
    statements;
}
	Defines a function with the name *function-name*

& *function-name*(*arg-list*)	Calls a function with arguments specified in *arg-list*
@_	Holds the values of arguments passed to the current function; **$_** and an index number references an argument, so that **$_[0]** is the first argument
$#_	Returns the number of arguments passed to the current function
\@*array-name*	Array reference (used in argument list to maintain the integrity of an array)
my(*object-list*)	Define local variable restricted to a subroutine or block

Table 6-14   Perl Functions and Related Commands

6

The following example defines a subroutine called *dispfile*.

```
sub dispfile

    {
    print "Please enter in name of file to be displayed: ";
    chomp($filename = <STDIN>);
    system("cat $filename");
}
```

You can define Perl subroutines before or after the main statements in your script, and it is helpful to place the main statements in a block of their own. However, if subroutines are called in statements that occur before the subroutine's definition, then you should place forward declarations of the subroutines in the code before the subroutine calls. Subroutine declarations operate like C function declarations. They consist of the **sub** command and the subroutine name, followed by a semicolon, with no block of code. Usually, you would place subroutine declarations at the beginning of the Perl script, followed by the main block of statements and then by your subroutine definitions. The following example is a subroutine declaration for *dispfile*.

```
sub dispfile;
```

In Perl there are several ways to call subroutines. Traditionally, a subroutine is called with the subroutine name preceded by an ampersand (**&**). For example, **&dispfile** would call the *dispfile* subroutine. You can also use parentheses instead of the preceding **&**. If you have a preceding subroutine declaration, you can just use the subroutine name itself. The following subroutine calls are equivalent, but using the name alone requires a subroutine declaration.

```
dispfile;
&dispfile;
dispfile();
```

Subroutines can have arguments passed to them and can return values back to the calling statement. These arguments and return values are passed as lists. Arguments specified in a subroutine call are placed in a list and assigned to the **@_** array that is then passed to the subroutine. The **@_** array will hold the arguments for the subroutine currently being called. To access a particular argument, you use array or list operations to reference elements of the **@_** array. The **@_** array is used in every subroutine to access that subroutine's arguments.

Arguments are arranged in the **@_** array counting from 0, and they are referenced as are elements of any scalar array. The first argument is referenced with **$_[0]**, the second with **$_[1]**, and so on. The following subroutine example, *dispfilearg*, is designed to receive as its argument the name of a file. It uses **$_[0]** to access a file name passed to it in the **@_** array.

```
sub dispfilearg
    {
    system("cat $_[0]");
}
```

The subroutine calls could be either of the following:

```
dispfilearg ("myfile");
&dispfilearg  "myfile";
```

For constants, the **@_** list holds only values. However, if you use a variable or array as an argument, then **@_** will reference those objects. In effect, with variables and arrays, call-by-reference is implemented. This means that references to elements of the **@_** array reference the original objects. Changes made by referencing these objects through the **@_** array will change the original objects in the calling function. Therefore, if a string variable is used as an argument to a function, and that argument is referenced through **@_** and is assigned a new value in the subroutine, then the value of that variable is changed in the calling function, too.

Return values can be specified by the **return** statement. Any values listed with it are placed in a list and returned to the calling statement. If there is no **return** statement, then the value of the last statement in the subroutine is used as the returned value. Since the return value is a list, this means that a Perl subroutine can return more than one value. These values can be returned and assigned to a list of variables.

Scoping

Scoping allows you to define variables that exist only within a subroutine or file. Those familiar with scoping in other programming languages will find some differences in Perl. With the **my** operation, you can define a local variable known only to a subroutine.

The **my** operation restricts the scope of a variable to the function or block within which it was defined. A variable defined with **my** is technically a static variable though within a subroutine, and it operates like a C auto variable. However, if you define a variable with the **my** operation outside of any subroutine at the top of the file, then it operates like a C static variable. Such a variable is known to all subroutines within that Perl script, but not to any other Perl scripts that may make up the Perl program.

The **my** operation works within blocks as well as within subroutines. You can define a block by itself, without making it part of a function definition or control structure. Any variables you define in it with the **my** operation will only be known within it. Should you define a variable with the **my** operation within a block and then follow it with a subroutine also defined within that block, then the variable will be visible to the subroutine.

myhtsub.pl

Project 6-2: Using Subroutines

The *myhtsub.pl* program reorganizes the **myht.pl** program, created earlier, into subroutines.

Step-by-Step

1. Create a subroutine called **search_file** that performs a search of a text file for a specified string, in this case, **<TITLE>**.

2. **select_title** that decides whether to take the title from the file name or from the **<TITLE>** line.

3. If **select_title** takes the title from the **<TITLE>** line, it should call the **get_title** subroutine to parse out the title using index and substring operations.

4. Notice that **search_file** returns two values. The first is a 0 or 1 value indicating the pattern was found, and the other is the line containing the pattern.

5. **select_title** is passed three arguments, all of which are assigned to local variables (**found**, **filename**, and **titleline**), assigning the **@_** array values to that list of local variables. **search_file** uses individual assignments for its arguments and local variables, but it just as easily could use a variable list and the **@_** array. For example,

```perl
my ($hfile, $searchstr) = @_;
```

Here is the *myhtsub.pl* script.

```perl
#!/usr/bin/perl
sub search_file;
sub select_title;
sub get_title;

print "<HTML>\n<HEAD>\n<TITLE>My Index</TITLE>\n</HEAD>\n<BODY>\n";
print "<H1>Index of HTML Files</H1>\n";

opendir(CDIR, ".");
foreach $dirname ( readdir(CDIR) )
    {
    if ( -d $dirname && !( $dirname =~ /^\./))
        {
        print "<h2>$dirname</h2>\n<ul>\n";
                opendir(HDIR, "$dirname");
            foreach $filen ( (readdir(HDIR)) )
```

```perl
                    {
                    if ( -f "$dirname/$filen" && ( $filen =~ /.html?$/) )
                        {
                    ($found, $tline) = search_file("$dirname/$filen", "TITLE");
                        $ntitle = select_title( $found, $filen, $tline );
                         print "<li><a href=$dirname/$filen>$ntitle</a>\n";
                         }
            }
         print "</ul>\n";
        closedir(HDIR);
    }
}
print "</BODY>\n</HTML>\n";
closedir(CDIR);


sub search_file
  {
my $hfile = $_[0];
my $searchstr = $_[1];
my ($hline, $found) = ("", 0);
      unless(open(HFILE, "< $hfile")) {
             die "Count no open file $hfile";
             }
    while (($found == 0) && ($hline = <HFILE>) )
        {
        if($hline =~ /$searchstr/) {
               $found = 1;
               }
        }
    close(HFILE);
    return ($found, "$hline");
    }

sub select_title
  {
  my ($found, $filename, $titleline) = @_;

             if ( $found == 0 )
                   {
                 return( substr($filename, 0, index($filename, ".") ));
                   }
                    else {
                        return( get_title( $titleline ));
                        }
      }

sub get_title
   {
   my $tline = $_[0];
   my $lpos = index($tline, "TITLE>") + length("TITLE>");
   my $rpos = rindex($tline, "</TITLE");
   return (substr($tline, $lpos, $rpos - $lpos) );
   }
```

6

☑ Mastery Check

1. What symbols do you use to read input from a file?

2. If a **print** command has no argument, does it output anything?

3. How do you assign a list of values to an array?

4. Can you delete elements in an associative array?

5. How can you find out what strings are used to index an associative array?

6. If a script attempts but fails to open a file, how can you end the program at that point?

Module 7

Tool Command Language (Tcl)

The Goals of This Module

- Define Tcl variables and create complex expressions

- Manage arrays, associative arrays, arguments, and lists

- Control Tcl input and output operations, managing files and pipes

- Develop complex Tcl programs using loop and condition structures

- Use procedures to organize your program

- Define, search, and format strings

- Create Expect scripts to run interactive programs automatically

- Use Expect to run FTP tasks automatically

Tcl is a general-purpose command language developed by John Ousterhout in 1987 at the University of California, Berkeley. Originally designed to customize applications, it has become a fully functional language in its own right. As with Perl and GAWK, you can write Tcl scripts to develop your own Tcl programs. Tcl is a very simple language to use.

Tk and *Expect* are Tcl applications that extend the capabilities of the language. The Tk application allows easy development of graphical interactive applications. You can create your own windows and dialog boxes with buttons and text boxes of your choosing. The Expect application provides easy communication with interactive programs such as ftp and telnet.

Tk is often used in conjunction with Tcl to create graphical applications. Tk is used to create the graphical elements such as windows, and Tcl performs the programming actions such as managing user input. Like Java, Tcl and Tk are cross-platform applications. A Tcl/Tk program will run on any platform that has the Tcl/Tk interpreter installed. Currently, Tcl/Tk versions for Windows, Macintosh, and UNIX systems, including Linux, are available. You can write a Tcl application on Linux and run the same code on Windows or on a Mac. The new versions of Tcl and Tk 8.0 even support local look and feel for graphical user interface (GUI) widgets using Mac-like windows on the Mac and Windows-like windows on Windows.

Note

The Tcl and Tk languages are organized according to different types of graphical objects such as windows, buttons, menus, and scroll bars. Such objects are referred to as *widgets*. For even more about widgets, see Module 8.

Tcl is an interpreted language that operates, like Perl, within its own shell. The command for invoking the Tcl shell is **tclsh**. Within this shell, you can execute Tcl commands. You can also create files within which you can invoke the Tcl shell and list Tcl commands (list commands are explained in the section "Lists," later in this module), effectively creating a Tcl program. A significant advantage to the Tcl language and its applications is the fact that it is fully compatible with the C programming language, and Tcl libraries can be incorporated directly into C programs. In effect, this allows you to create very fast compiled versions of Tcl programs.

When you install Tk and Tcl on your system, *man pages* for Tcl/Tk commands are also installed. The man pages are the pages displayed by the Linux online manual, which is accessed with the **man** command. Use the

man command with the name of the Tcl or Tk command to bring up detailed information about that command. For example, the **man switch** command displays the manual page for the Tcl **switch** command, and **man button** displays information on the Tk **button** widget. Once you have installed Tk, you can run a demo program called *widget* that shows you all the Tk widgets available. The *widget* program uses Tcl/Tk sample programs and can display the source code for each. You can find the *widget* program by changing to the Tk *demos* directory as shown here:

```
cd /usr/lib/tk*/demos
```

(The **tk*** in this code matches the directory name consisting of **tk** and its version number, such as **tk8.3** for version 8.3.)

From the Xterm window on the GNOME desktop, enter the command **widget** to launch the demo program. You can also examine the individual demo files and modify them as you wish. If you have installed a version of Tk yourself into the */usr/local/bin* directory rather than */usr/bin,* the *demos* directory will be located in */usr/local/lib/tk**.

7

Tcl/Tk Extensions and Applications

Currently, both Tcl and Tk are being developed and supported by Scriptics, a company founded in 1997 by John Ousterhout. The current release (at time of printing) of both Tcl and Tk is 8.3. Current versions of Tcl and Tk are available free of charge from the ScripticsTcl/Tk Web site at **http://dev.scriptics.com**. Also available on this site is extensive documentation for each product in PostScript, Adobe PDF, and HTML formats. The HTML documentation can be viewed online. RPM packaged versions can also be found at the Red Hat distribution site at **ftp.redhat.com**. You will need both the Tcl and Tk RPM packages as well as the development packages for each.

Tcl/Tk has been enhanced by extensions that increase the capabilities of the language. Several commonly used extensions are TclX, incr Tcl, and Oratcl. These extensions are available though links on the Scriptics Web site. Access the Tcl Resources page, and from there go to the Tcl Software page. From there, you can access the Tcl Extensions page, which lists those extensions currently available (*dev.scriptics.com/resources/software/ extensions*)—most of which you can download and install for free.

- **TclX** extends capabilities such as file access and time and date manipulation, many of which have been incorporated into recent Tcl releases.

- **[incr Tcl]** supports the easy implementation of higher level widgets, using an object-oriented programming structure.

- **BLT** adds graph and bar widgets to Tk.

- **Sybtcl** and **Oratcl** implement database interfaces to the Sybase and Oracle databases.

- **TclDP** provides support for distributed programming across a network.

- The **TrfCrypt** extension adds encryption that was removed from the standard Tcl/Tk release to make it exportable.

Note

Numerous Tcl/Tk applications, development tools, and utilities are freely available for download from various Internet sites. You can link to most of these sites through the Tcl software panel on the Scriptics site.

The **tclsh** Shell and Scripts

Within the Tcl shell, you can execute Tcl commands interactively, entering commands at a Tcl shell prompt and executing them one by one; or you can place the commands in a script file and execute them all at once. Enter the command **tclsh** to start up the Tcl shell with the **%** prompt. You can then enter single Tcl commands and have them evaluated when you press ENTER. You leave the Tcl shell by entering either an **exit** command or by pressing CTRL-D.

```
$ tclsh
% set age 11
% puts $age
11
% exit
$
```

The **tclsh** command is implemented as a link to the actual *tclsh* program. This program's name consists of the *tclsh* with the version number attached, such as *tclsh8.3* for version 8.3. If your system does not implement a tclsh link, you will have to use the **tclsh** command or implement a link yourself.

You can run a Tcl script either as a stand-alone program or as a file explicitly read by the Tcl shell command **tclsh**. A Tcl script has the extension **.tcl**. For example, the *myread.tcl* Tcl script would be read and executed by the following command:

```
$ tclsh myread.tcl
```

To create a stand-alone script that operates more like a command, you need to invoke the **tclsh** command within the script. You can do this by placing an explicit path name for the **tclsh** command as the first line of the script, as shown here:

```
#!/usr/bin/tclsh
```

Tcl Commands

The Tcl programming language is simple to use. Its statements consist of a command followed by arguments; it also has a complete set of control structures, including while and for loops. Commands can be terminated either by a semicolon (;) or by a newline character. You can think of a Tcl command as a function call, where the command name operates like a function name, followed by arguments to the function. However, unlike the function call, no parentheses or commas enclose the arguments. You simply enter the command name and its arguments, separated only by spaces. A newline character entered after the last argument will end the statement.

You can see the features in this format clearly in the Tcl assignment command **set**. To assign a value to a variable, you first enter the assignment command **set**. Then enter the name of the variable followed by the value to be assigned. The command name, variable, and value are separated only by spaces. The newline at the end of the line ends the statement. The following statement assigns a string "Dylan" to the variable **myname**, and the next statement assigns the integer value 5 to the variable **age**.

```
set myname  "Dylan"
set age 5
```

Hint

As in GAWK and Perl, variable types are determined by their use. A variable assigned an integer will be considered an integer, and one assigned a string will be a character array. For those readers who are familiar with Lisp, this command name format will look familiar.

You can use a number of Tcl commands to perform system tasks, such as stopping a script (**exit**), changing a working directory (**cd**), or trapping errors (**catch**). These are listed in Table 7-1.

Expressions

Expressions are also handled as commands in Tcl. The command **expr** evaluates as an expression and returns its resulting value as a string. It takes as its arguments the operands and operators of an expression. Tcl supports all the standard arithmetic, comparison, and logical operators. The result of an arithmetic expression will be the same form as its operands; so, for example, if the operands are real numbers, the result will be a real number. You can mix operands of different types, and Tcl will convert one to match the other. In the case of real and integer operands, the integer will be converted to a real automatically. In the first statement that follows, the addition of 4 and 3 is evaluated by the **expr** command. The next statement multiplies 25 by 2.

Tcl Command	Action
catch	Traps errors
cd	Changes the working directory
clock	Returns the time and format date strings
error	Raises an error
eval	Evaluates as a command a list of arguments
exec	Executes a Linux command
exit	Ends the program and exit
pwd	Returns the current working directory
info	Queries the state of the Tcl interpreter
trace	Checks values of variables

Table 7-1   Tcl System Commands

```
expr 4 + 3
expr 25 * 2
```

You can create complex expressions using parentheses. The most deeply nested expressions are evaluated first. In the following example, 25 * 2 is evaluated; and the result, 50, has 20 subtracted from it.

```
expr (25 * 2) - 20
```

Hint

The resulting value returned by any Tcl command is always a string. In the case of arithmetic operations, the arithmetic value is converted first to a string, which is then returned by the **expr** command.

7

Ask the Expert

Question: Can I embed Tcl commands?

Answer: Yes. You can combine commands by embedding one within the other. Embedding is commonly used for assigning the result of an expression to a variable. This involves two commands: the **set** command to perform the assignment, and the **expr** command to evaluate an expression. You embed commands using brackets (**[** and **]**). An embedded command is another Tcl command whose result is used as an argument in the outer Tcl command. The embedded command is executed first, and its result is used as the argument to the outer command.

The following statement assigns the result of the arithmetic operation **25 * 2** to the variable **num**. The **expr 25 * 2** command is embedded within the **set** command. First, the embedded command is executed; and its result, 50, is assigned to the variable **num**.

```
set num [expr 25 * 2]
```

Embedded expression

> **Question:** Can I execute Linux commands from within a Tcl script?
>
> **Answer:** With the **exec** command you can execute any Linux command within a Tcl program. The **exec** command will execute a Linux command, waiting for it to finish before continuing with your program. The result of the Linux command will be returned by **exec** to your program. In the following example, the **exec** command executes the Linux **date** command. The returned date is assigned to the variable **mydate**. Then the **ls –l** command will be output by the **puts** command to the standard output (the screen).
>
> ```
> set mydate [ exec date ]
> puts [exec ls -l]
> ```

Variables

Tcl supports numeric and string variables, as well as arrays, including *associative arrays*, which are discussed in the next section. All variables hold a string as their content. However, although the content of a variable is a string, that string can be used as an integer or real value in an arithmetic expression, provided that the string consists of numbers. Whenever such a variable is used as an operand in an arithmetic expression, its contents are first to be converted to an integer or real value. The operation is performed, and then the arithmetic values and the result returned by **expr** are converted back to a string. This means that you do not have to worry about declaring the type of variable or even defining a variable. All variables are automatically defined when they are first used in a statement.

As we have seen, variables can be assigned values using the **set** command, which takes as its argument the variable name and the value assigned. A variable's name can be any set of alphabetic or numeric characters plus the underscore character (_). Punctuation and other characters are not allowed.

When you need to use the value of a variable within a statement, you first need to evaluate it. Evaluating a variable substitutes its name with its value. Placing a **$** in front of a variable name performs such an evaluation. To use a variable's value as an operand in an expression, you need to evaluate the variable by preceding its name with the **$**. In the next example, the value 5 is assigned to the **mynum** variable. Then **mynum** is evaluated in an expression, **$mynum**, providing its value, 5, as an operand in that expression.

```
set mynum 5            ┌─Evaluate a variable
expr  10 * $mynum  ◄───┘
```

Should you want to make the value of a variable part of a string, you need only to evaluate it within that string. The value of the variable becomes part of the string. In the following statement, the value of the variable **myname** is used as part of a string. In this case, the string will be "My name is Larisa".

```
set myname "Larisa"
set mystr "My name is $myname"
```

Certain commands are designed to operate on variables. For example, the **append** command concatenates a string to a variable. The **incr** command will increment an integer. And the **unset** command will undefine a variable. The different commands that operate on variables are listed in Table 7-2.

Command	Description
set	Assigns a value to a variable
global	Declares global variables
incr	Increments a variable by an integer value
unset	Deletes variables
upvar	References a variable in a different scope
variable	Declares namespace variables
array	Specifies array access operations such as searches
expr	Executes math expressions

Table 7-2   Assignment and Variable Operations

1-Minute Drill

- **What type of value does a numeric expression return?**
- **Can you combine assignment and arithmetic operations?**

Arrays

Array elements are defined and assigned values using the **set** command with an added argument for the index. The following example assigns the number *23* to the first element of the **mynum** array.

```
set mynum(1)  23  Array index
```

You can then reference individual elements as you would a variable, preceding the element with a **$**, as shown here:

```
$mynum(1)
```

Tcl also supports associative arrays, which use strings as indexes. Associative array elements are defined and assigned values using the **set** command with an added argument for the index string. The index string is encased in parentheses and is placed immediately following the array name and preceding the value. The following statements add two elements to the **city** array with the index strings Napa and Alameda.

```
set city(Napa) 34  Associative array index
set city(Alameda) 17
```

- A string.
- Yes; use the arithmetic assignment operators, such as =+.

The elements of an associative array are referenced using a preceding **$** and the index string enclosed in parentheses:

```
$city(Napa)
```

You can then use the **array** command to manipulate an array, checking certain features such as its size and its indexes, and whether it exists. You can even use **array** to assign all an array's elements at once using a list. The **array** command takes several options that specify the action you want to take. With the **exists** option, you can see if an array is defined, and the **size** option displays the number of elements in the array.

```
% array exists city
1
% array size city          array command option
2
```

The **get** and **names** options let you access element and index values. These options can take an added argument specifying a pattern that you can use to retrieve element values or indexes. The **get** option will display both element values and indexes, whereas the **names** option will display only indexes. Without an argument, all element or index values are shown.

```
% array get city
Napa 34 Alameda 17
% array names city
Napa Alameda
% array names mynum
1
```

Note

You can search array elements one by one using the **startsearch**, **nextelement**, and **anymore** options, with the **donesearch** option ending your search.

Special Variables and Arrays: **argv** and **env**

Every time you run a Tcl script, several special arrays and variables are set up for your use in the program. Tcl sets up an **argv** variable that holds the arguments you used on the UNIX command line when you invoked your program. The special variable **argc** holds the count of the number of arguments. And **argv0** holds the name of your program.

Tcl also sets up a special associative array called **env** that holds all the environmental variables from your Linux shell. You can reference the value of any of these Linux environmental variables by using the name to index the **env** array. For example, **$env(HOME)** gives you the value of the **HOME** environmental variable. **$env(PATH)** provides the paths used in command lookups.

Lists

Tcl supports a type of object not found in most programming languages: the *list*. A list is a set of words, strings, or numbers encased in braces ({ }). Tcl includes a set of flexible list commands that you can use to manipulate lists, by combining them, separating them, or adding and deleting elements from them. Table 7–3 shows several of the commonly used list commands.

Command	Description
set *list values*	Creates a list and assigns values to it
lsearch *list pattern*	Searches for a pattern in elements of a list
lindex *list index*	Returns the value of the indexed element in a list
llength *list*	Returns the number of elements in a list
lrange *list first last*	Returns a subrange of the list specified by *first* and *last*
linsert *list index value-list*	Inserts a new element into a list after the index
lreplace *list index value-list*	Replaces the element indexed with a new value
lappend *list-name value-list*	Appends new values to the list
concat *lists*	Combines elements of several lists into one list

Table 7-3   Tcl List Operations

Command	Description
list *lists*	Combines lists into a larger list whose elements are the respective lists
split *str delim*	Splits a string into a list using a delimiter to separate values
join *list*	Joins elements of a list into a string
lsort *list*	Sorts the list alphabetically or numerically

Table 7-3   Tcl List Operations *(continued)*

To define a list, place a set of words, numbers, or strings within a set of curly braces. You can assign this list to a variable or use it with commands that operate on lists. The following example creates a list of three words and assigns them to the variable **weather**. Notice that only spaces separate the components of a list.

Tcl list

```
set weather {sun rain wind}
```

To access and operate on the list, you use a set of list commands. Many of these commands can reference a particular element according to its place in the list. The elements are indexed beginning with 0 for the first element; 1 would reference the second element, and so on. In the weather list, the index for **sun** is 0, for **rain** is 1, and for **wind** is 2.

The **lindex** command returns an element from a list using its index. It takes two arguments, the list and the index for the element you want. In the following statement, **rain** is obtained from the weather list. The next statement uses a list explicitly defined. It obtains the third element (index of 2) of the list, **yellow**.

```
lindex $weather 1
lindex {red blue yellow} 2
```

7

The **lrange** command obtains a subset of a list. **lrange** takes as its arguments a list and the first and last element of the range, like so:

```
% lrange $weather 1 2
rain wind
```

The **lsearch** command searches elements of a list for a specified pattern. It returns the index of the first element it finds that matches the pattern. It takes two arguments: the list to search and the pattern. The following statement searches for the pattern **wind** in the weather list, **{sun rain wind}**. This command will return a 2, the index of the third element, which is **wind**.

```
lsearch $weather wind
```

The **llength** command returns the number of elements in the list. The following statement returns 3:

```
% llength {red blue yellow}
3
```

The **linsert** command inserts one or more new elements into a list at a specified position. It takes three arguments: the list, the index where the first new element is to be placed, and the new elements to be inserted. The following statement inserts the word *orange* into a list as the second element (index of 1). It will return the list **{red orange blue yellow}**.

```
% linsert {red blue yellow} 1 orange
```

You can insert several elements at a time by entering those elements as arguments to **linsert**. The new elements are added starting from the index specified. The next statement adds two new elements to the **weather** list starting from the third element (index of 2). The statement returns the list **{sun rain storm hail wind}**.

```
linsert $weather 2 storm hail
```

The **lreplace** command will replace elements of a list at a specified position with new elements. **lreplace** takes as its arguments the list, a beginning index, an ending index, and the new elements. The following statement replaces the second element, **blue**, with **green** (starting index of 1, and ending index of 1). This statement will return the list **{red green yellow}**:

```
% lreplace {red blue yellow} 1 1 green
```

The **lreplace** command can replace several elements at once. If the number of elements is larger than the remainder of the list, the list is simply expanded to include the new elements. The next statement returns the list **{red purple aqua tan}**:

```
% lreplace {red blue yellow} 1 2 purple aqua tan
red purple aqua tan
```

The **lappend** command appends new elements to the end of a list. It takes as its arguments the name of the list and the elements to be added. To add more elements, just specify the list name and the new elements. In the following statement, the elements are added to the list, with the **lappend** command returning the list **{red blue yellow purple aqua tan}**:

```
% echo mylist
red blue yellow
%lappend mylist purple aqua tan
red blue yellow purple aqua tan
```

concat combines several lists into one. It takes as its arguments any number of lists. It then returns a list that is the combination of all these lists. In the following statement, **concat** will return a combination of the two lists specified as arguments, **{red blue aqua tan}**:

```
% concat {red blue} {aqua tan}
red blue aqua tan
```

The **list** command also combines lists, but it preserves the original lists within the new list. You can nest lists, having a list whose elements are themselves lists. Such a list can be created by the following **list** command.

Bear in mind that it creates a list of only two elements, whereas in the previous example, the **concat** command created a list of four elements.

```
% list {red blue} {aqua tan}
% echo $list
{red blue} {aqua tan}
```

The **lsort** command sorts a list either alphabetically or numerically. By default, it performs an alphabetic search. With the **–integer** option, it performs a numeric search. The following statement returns the list **{aqua blue red tan}**. The next statement performs a numeric sort, returning the list **{45 67 89 100}**.

```
% lsort {red blue aqua tan}
% lsort -integer {89 15 100 67}
```

The **split** and **join** commands make use of delimiters to split apart or join elements of a list. The delimiter can be any regular separator, such as a colon (:). The **split** command generates elements by splitting apart a word containing delimiters. The delimiters are replaced by spaces, creating new elements. The **split** command takes as its arguments the word to be split and the delimiter. In the next example, *sun:rain:storm* is split into a list with three elements **{sun rain storm}**:

```
split sun:rain:storm :
```

The **join** command takes a list and replaces the spaces with a specified delimiter, effectively joining the elements into one element. The **join** command takes as its arguments the list to be joined and the delimiter. In the next example, the list *{25 50 100}* is joined into one element, with the former elements separated by colons **(25:50:100)**:

```
% join {25 50 100} :
```

1-Minute Drill

● **Can you index an array using ordinary names?**

● **Could a list of items contain as one of its items another list or an operation that generates a list?**

Tcl Input and Output: **gets** and **puts**

Tcl can read input from the standard input or a file using the **gets** command and output to the standard output with the **puts** command. To read input from your keyboard, use the **gets** command. To read from the keyboard, you must specify **stdin** (standard input, which is the kind of input read from your keyboard) as the **gets** command's first argument. To place the input in a variable, specify the variable name as the second argument. The following command reads a line from the standard input, **stdin**, and places the input in the variable **line**:

```
gets stdin $line
```

The **puts** command outputs a string to the standard output or to a file. It takes as its argument the string to be output. In the following examples, **puts** first outputs the string "Hello" and then outputs the string that is the contents of the **line** variable:

```
puts "Hello"
puts $line
```

● **Yes; these are called associative arrays.**
● **Yes.**

If you want to use a single **puts** operation to output the contents of several variables, you need to make the variables part of a single string. You can do this by placing the variables within a pair of double quotes. The following example makes the contents of **firstname** and **lastname** part of a single string that can then be output by **puts**:

```
puts "$firstname  $lastname"
```

gets reads a line into the variable specified as its argument. You can then use this variable to manipulate whatever has been read. For example, in the following *mygets* script, you can use **line** in a **puts** command to display what was input.

```
#!/usr/bin/tclsh
gets stdin line
puts  "This is what I entered: $line"
```

The run of the *mygets* script follows:

```
$ mygets
larisa and aleina
This is what I entered: larisa and aleina
```

You can use the **puts** command to write data to any file or to the standard output. File handle names are placed after the **puts** command and before any data, such as strings or variables. A file handle references a file (file handles are explained later in the chapter in the section "Tcl File Handles"). If no file handle is specified, **puts** outputs to the standard output. The following examples both write the "hello" string to the standard output. The explicit file handle for the standard output is **STDOUT**.

```
puts  "hello"
puts STDOUT "hello"
```

To output formatted values, you can use the results of a format command as the argument of a **puts** command. The **format** command performs a **sprintf** operation on a set of values, formatting them according to conversion specifiers in a format string, like so:

```
puts [format "%s" $myname]
```

If you want to output more than one string or value in the same **puts** operation, you can use the **format** command to first transform the values into a single string. The **puts** command will output only a single string. In the following example, the contents of the **$firstname** and **$lastname** variables are output as a single string by first using the **format** command with two string specifiers, **"%s %s"**, to make them one string:

```
puts [format "%s %s" $firstname  $lastname]
```

Pipes

You can also use the **open** command to create pipes that transfer output from one command to the input of another command, rather than accessing the actual files. Then use the **puts** or **gets** command to output to or input from a pipe. To specify the name of a pipe, use the | symbol encased in braces, like so: { | }. You can also include any Linux commands that you want data to be piped into or out of. The file mode for a pipe can be write or read: write is used for pipes that you would use **puts** to write to, and read would be for pipes that you would use **gets** to read from. For example, to pipe data to the printer, you would specify a pipe name with the **lpr** command, like so: { |**lpr**}. The file mode would be **w** for write. Once the pipe is established, you can use **puts** to write data to the printer using the file handle for this pipe. Here's an example:

7

Pipe to lpr **printer command**

```
set printhandle [ open { | lpr } w ]
puts $printhandle  "Hello world "
```

Control Structures

Tcl has a set of control structures similar to those used in Perl, GAWK, TCSH, and C programming languages. Tcl has *loops* with which you can repeat commands and *conditions* that allow you to choose among specified commands. Table 7-4 lists the Tcl control structures.

Control Structures	Description
if	Conditional test that selects commands and extends with **else** and **elseif** blocks
switch	Switches selection structure
while	Repeats commands
for	Like the C for loop, repeats commands
foreach	Loops through a list, or lists, of values
break	Forces loop exit
continue	Skips remainder of block and continues with next loop iteration

Table 7-4   Tcl Control Structures

Control structures will perform tests using test expressions. A test expression is enclosed in braces. For example, to test whether the value of the variable **mynum** is less than 3, you would use the following test:

```
{ $mynum < 3}
```

Tcl supports the standard comparison operators found in other languages, such as **<** for less than, **>** for greater than, and **<=** for less than or equal to. The operator for equality is the double equal sign (**==**) (as in Perl and C), not the single equal sign (**=**). To test whether **mynum** is equal to 5, you would use this:

```
{ $mynum == 5}
```

If you need to execute a command as part of a test expression, you can use brackets to embed it. For example, to embed a **gets** command in a **while** expression, you would use the following test:

```
while {[gets $shandle line]} {
```

Make sure that you always follow the test with the opening brace of the control structures block, as shown above. Control structures in Tcl often make use of a block of Tcl commands. A block of commands consists of Tcl commands enclosed in braces. The opening brace must begin on the same line as that of the control structure that uses it. On following lines, several Tcl commands can be listed—each on its own line. The block ends with a closing brace on a line by itself. A block is literally an argument to a Tcl command. The block is passed to a control structure command and the control structure will execute the commands in that block. Following is a simple block used for a **while** command:

```
while {$i <= 3} {
    puts "Your name is $myname"
    incr i 1
}
```

The **if** and **else** Control Structures

The **if** control structure allows you to select alternative actions. The **if** command takes two arguments: a test expression and a Tcl command or block of commands—both commands are encased in their own set of braces. The test expression is used to determine whether the Tcl commands will be executed. If the test expression is true, the commands are performed. If false, the commands are skipped. Below is the syntax for the **if** structure:

```
if {test-expression} {
    Tcl commands
    }
```

The *ifls* script below allows you to list files by size. If you enter an **s** at the prompt, each file in the current directory is listed, followed by the number of blocks it uses. If you enter any other character, the **if** test fails and the script does nothing. Notice that the opening brace for the **if** structure's block is located after the **if** test expression on the same line:

```
#!/usr/bin/tclsh
    puts  "Please enter option: "
    gets stdin option

if { $option == "s"} {
        puts  "Listing files by size"
        puts [exec ls -s]
}
```

The run of the *ifls* script follows:

```
$ ifls
  Please enter option: s
  Listing files by size
  total 2
         1 monday      2 today
```

The **if** structure is often used to check whether you entered the appropriate number of arguments for a shell script. The special shell variable **ARGC** contains the number of arguments the user entered.

Using **$ARGC** in a test operation allows you to check whether the user entered the correct number of arguments. If an incorrect number of arguments has been entered, you may need to end the shell script. You can do this with the **exit** command. The **exit** command ends the shell script returning an exit condition. **exit** takes a number argument: 0 indicates that the shell script ended successfully; any other argument, such as 1, indicates that an error occurred.

In the next example, the *ifarg* script takes only one argument. If the user fails to enter an argument or enters more than one argument, the **if** test will be true and the error message printed out and the script will exit with an error value.

```
if {$argc != 1} {
        puts "Invalid number of arguments "
        exit 1
}
puts  $1
```

The **if** command also has an **else** component. Often, you need to choose between two alternatives based on whether or not a test expression is successful. The **else** command allows an **if** structure two alternatives. Tcl commands follow the **else** command. If the test expression of the **if** structure is false, the commands following the **else** are executed. In this respect, the **if-else** structure can be thought of as a *branch* structure—that is, if the test is true, one branch of action is taken; if false, the other branch of action is taken. Keep in mind that the *else* keyword must be placed on the same line as the closing brace of the previous block, and that same *else* must be followed by the open brace for its own block.

```
} else {
```

Below is the syntax for the **if-else** structure:

if {*test-expression*} {
        Tcl commands
} else {
        Tcl commands
}

The *elsels* script below executes the **ls** command to list files with two possible options: either by size or with all file information. If the user enters an **s**, files are listed by size; otherwise, all file information is listed.

```
#!/usr/bin/tclsh

    puts -nonewline "Enter s to list file sizes, "
    puts "otherwise all file information is listed."
    puts "Please enter option: "
    gets stdin choice

if {$choice == "s"} {
        puts [exec ls -s]
}
else {
        puts [exec ls -l]
}
puts  Goodbye
```

Here is the run of the *elsels* script:

```
$ elsels
Enter s to list file sizes, otherwise all file information is listed.
Please enter option:
s
total 2
1 monday     2 today
```

The **elseif** Structure

The **elseif** structure allows you to nest if-then-else operations. The **elseif** structure stands for "else if." Using **elseif** lets the shell choose between several alternatives. The first alternative is specified with the **if** structure followed by other alternatives, each specified by its own **elseif** structure. The alternative to the last **elseif** structure is specified with an **else**. If the test for the first **if** structure fails, control will be passed to the next **elseif** structure. Its test will be executed. If it fails, control is passed to the next **elseif** and its test checked. This continues until a test returns true. The **elseif** that tests true has its commands executed and control passes out of the **if** structure to the next command after the *fi* keyword. Shown next is the syntax for the **elseif** structure. Keep in mind that the *elseif* keyword must be on the same line as the closing brace of the previous block, as in **} elseif {*test–expression*} {** .

```
if {test expression} {
        Tcl Commands
} elseif {test expression} {
        Tcl Commands
} else {
        Tcl Commands
}
```

In the *elseifls* script, two possible ways of listing files are presented. The last **else** is reserved for detecting invalid input, in this case an invalid choice.

```
#!/usr/bin/tclsh
    puts  "s. List Sizes"
    puts  "l. List All Information"
    puts "Please enter option: "
    gets stdin choice

if {$choice == "s"} {
        puts [exec ls -s]
{
elseif {$choice = "l"} {
        puts [exec ls -l]
}
else {
        puts  "Invalid Option"
}
    puts  "Goodbye"
```

Here is a run of the *elseifls* script:

```
$ ./elseifls
s. List Sizes
l. List All File Information
Please enter option:
l
total 2
-rw-rw-r-x  1  chris weather 568  Feb 14  10:30  today
-rw-rw-r--  1  chris weather 308  Feb 17  12:40  Monday
```

The **switch** Structure

The **switch** structure chooses among several possible alternatives. The choice is made by comparing a string value with several possible patterns. Each pattern has its own block of Tcl commands. If a match is found, the associated block is executed. The default keyword indicates a pattern that matches anything. If all the other matches fail, the block associated with the default keyword is executed. The **switch** structure begins with the keyword *switch*, then options prefixed with –, and then the string pattern to be matched followed by a block containing all the patterns with their blocks. The syntax for the case structure is describe here:

```
switch –options string-pattern {
    pattern {
        Tcl commands
        }
    pattern {
        Tcl commands
        }
    default {
        Tcl commands
        }
    }
```

Options specify the pattern-matching capabilities. The following options are supported.

Option	Description
−exact	Use exact matching when comparing a string to a pattern. This is the default.
−glob	When matching a string to the patterns, use glob style matching.
−regexp	When matching a string to the patterns, use regular expression matching (i.e., the same as implemented by the **regexp** command).
− −	Marks the end of options. The argument following this one will be treated as a string, even if it starts with a −.

The **−regexp** option lets you match any regular expression, whereas **−glob** lets you use the shell file name matching methods. With **−glob**, the shell special characters *****, **[ ]**, and **?** let you easily match on part of a string. With the **−regexp** option, you can match on complex alternative strings, specifying multiple instances of characters, beginning or end of a string, and classes of characters.

A **switch** structure is often used to implement menus. In the program *lschoice*, the user is asked to enter a choice for listing files in different ways. Notice the default option that warns of invalid input:

```
#!/usr/bin/tclsh

# Program to allow the user to select different ways of
#    listing files

    puts " s. List Sizes"
    puts " l. List All File Information"
    puts " c. List C Files"

    puts "Please enter choice: "
    gets stdin choice

    switch $choice {
        s {
        puts [exec ls -s]
            }
        l {
        puts [exec ls -l]
            }
        c {
        puts [exec ls *.c]
            }
            default {
              puts "Invalid Option"
                }
    }
```

Here is a run of the *lschoice* program:

```
$ lschoice
s. List Sizes
l. List All File Information
c. List C Files
Please enter choice:
c
main.c   lib.c   file.c
```

Ask the Expert

Question: In a switch **structure, can I specify several patterns for the same body?**

Answer: If the hyphen (–) is used as the body for a **switch** entry, a match on its pattern will execute the block for the next pattern. If the next pattern also has a hyphen for its body, the body after that is used, and so on. Using hyphens in **switch** entry bodies makes it possible for you to share a single body among several preceding patterns. This way you can easily specify alternative patterns for a given block—for example, uppercase and lowercase instances of a character. In the following example, a match on an uppercase *S* will execute the block for the following lowercase *s*.

```
S  -
s {
    ls -S
  }
```

The – will fall through to the next body

Question: **Can I use the regular expressions in switch tests?**

Answer: Using regular expressions in patterns can give you a great deal more flexibility than simple patterns. If you use the | special character in the pattern, it will allow you to specify more than one possible match. For example, using **c | C** will match on both an uppercase *C* and a lowercase *c*. In the next example, **c | C** will match both uppercase and lowercase versions:

```
c|C {
     ls -l
   }
```

7

Note that an alternative format for the **switch** command lets you enter an entire sequence on one line as a single command. In this format, no block encases the pattern-block pairs. This format is useful for small **switch** operations. Here's an example:

```
switch string-pattern pattern {Tcl commands} pattern {Tcl commands}

switch $choice l { ls -l } s { ls -S }
```

The **while** Loop

Tcl loops are the **while**, **for**, and **foreach** loops. The **while** loop is the more general-purpose loop, whereas the **for** and **foreach** loops are much more restrictive. The **while** loop repeats commands. In Tcl, the **while** loop begins with the **while** command and takes two arguments: an expression and either a single Tcl command or a block of Tcl commands. The expression is enclosed in braces. A block of Tcl commands begins with an opening brace on the same line as the **while** command. Then, following lines contain the Tcl commands that will be repeated in the loop. The block ends with a closing brace, usually on a line by itself. The syntax for the **while** loop with a single statement is shown here:

```
while {expression } {
    Tcl command
    Tcl command
}
```

Most loops require three components to work properly: an initialization, a test, and an increment. All operate on a variable used to control the loop. In the next example, the *tclmyloop* program prompts the user for a name and then prints it out three times. The variable **i** is used to control the loop. The variable is first initialized before entering the loop. The variable is then tested in a relational operation with the loop's test expression to determine when to stop the loop. The variable is then incremented each time the loop is executed. When **i** is incremented to 4, the loop's test expression is false and the loop stops.

```
#!/usr/bin/tclsh
puts "Please enter your name: "
  gets stdin myname
set i 1
while {$i <= 3} {
    puts  "Your name is $myname "
    incr i 1
}
```

The run of the *tclmyloop* program follows:

```
$ tclmyloop
Please enter your name:
Aleina Petersen
Your name is Aleina Petersen
Your name is Aleina Petersen
Your name is Aleina Petersen
```

You can easily adapt the **while** loop for use with arrays. The variable used to control a loop can also be used inside the loop to index an array. In the following *tcltitlearray* script, the elements of the **title** array are assigned the value of each title. Then the contents of each element are printed out using a **for** loop. Notice that the **num** variable is used during processing to keep track of the next element to be assigned. **num** holds the count of elements in the array, and it is used as the upper bound in the **for** loop test expression to check when the loop should stop.

```
#!/usr/bin/tclsh
array set title  {1 Tempest 2 Iliad 3 Raven}
set num 3
set i 1
while {$i <= $num} {
    puts  $title($i)
    incr i 1
}
```

The run of the *tcltitlearray* follows:

```
$ tcltitlearray
Tempest
Iliad
Raven
```

The **for** Loop

The **for** loop performs the same tasks as the **while** loop. However, it has a different format. The **for** loop takes four arguments, the first three of which are expressions and the last is a block of Tcl commands. The first three arguments are expressions that incorporate the initialization, test, and increment components of a loop. These expressions are each enclosed in braces. The last argument, the block of Tcl commands, begins with an opening brace and then continues with Tcl commands on the following lines, ending with a closing brace. Here's the syntax:

```
for {expression1} {expression2} {expression3} {
    Tcl commands
    }
```

The first expression is usually reserved for an initialization of a variable used to control the loop. This expression is executed before the loop is actually entered. The second expression is the test expression, such as a relational expression that controls the loop. The third expression is executed within and at the end of the loop. It is usually used for incrementing the variable used to control the loop. Following the expressions is the block of Tcl commands to be executed within the loop. The third expression is executed after the block of commands.

```
for {initialization} {test expression} {increment} {
    Tcl commands
    }
```

The following example shows a simple **for** loop. Notice how much more compact the **for** loop is than the **while** loop.

```
for {set i 1} {$i <= 3} {incr i 1} {
    puts $i
    }
```

As with the **while** loop, you can easily use the **for** loop to manage arrays. The variable used to control a loop can also be used, inside the loop, to index an array. In the *tcltitlearray* script that follows, the elements of the title array are assigned the value of each title. Then the contents of each element are printed out using a **for** loop. The **i** variable is used to control the loop. It is initialized to 1 in the **for**'s first expression and incremented in the last expression. The increment will take place after the print action. The second expression is the test expression that controls the loop.

```
#!/usr/bin/tclsh
array set title {1 Tempest 2 Iliad 3 Raven}
set num 3
for {set i 1} {$i <= $num} {incr i} {
    puts $title($i)
}
```

The **foreach** Structure

The **foreach** structure is designed to sequentially reference a list of values. It is similar to the C shell's **for-in** structure. The **foreach** structure takes three arguments: a variable, a list, and a block of Tcl commands. Each value in the list is assigned to the variable in the **foreach** structure. Like the **while** structure, the **foreach** structure is a loop. Each time through the loop, the next value in the list is assigned to the variable. When the end of the list is reached, the loop stops. Like the **while** loop, the block of Tcl commands is enclosed in braces. The syntax for the **foreach** loop is described here:

```
foreach variable-list  value-list variable-list  value-list .. .. {
Tcl commands
   }
```

In the *booklist* script, the user simply outputs a list of titles. The list of titles make up the list of values read by the **foreach** loop. Each title is consecutively assigned to the variable **booktitle**.

```
#!/usr/bin/tclsh
foreach booktitle [list Tempest  Iliad  Raven] {
    puts $booktitle
    }
```

The Tcl **foreach** loop differs from **foreach** loops in other languages in that Tcl **foreach** can support several variables and their corresponding lists

7

at once. For example, you could have two variables with two lists of values, one list for each variable. The first variable will take on the values of the first list, in turn, and the second variable will take on the values of the second list. If one list is longer than the other, the variable for the shorter list is assigned a null value for the extra iterations. The next example uses two variables, **title** and **author**, to reference values in two different lists:

```
#!/usr/bin/tclsh
 foreach title {Tempest Iliad Raven} author {Shakespeare Homer Poe} {
    puts "$title $author"
    }
```

The **break** and **continue** Commands

The **break** and **continue** commands are designed to work with loops. The **break** command will break out of a loop, continuing on to the **next** command. The **continue** loop will skip over the rest of the block of commands that are executed within the loop and begin at the next iteration. Usually, these command are part of an **if** command. Only rarely will you use **break** statements in a **while** or **for** loop. The **break** is *nonstructured* in that it provides an exit condition other than that of the statement's test expression. For example, in the next program, the **break** will force an exit from the loop when **i** is equal to 3:

```
    set i 1
     while {i >= 1} {
           if {i == 3} {
           break
       }
       puts "This is $i iteration"
       incr i 1
    }
```

The **continue** statement is uniquely designed to work with loops. The **continue** statement skips over the rest of the statements in a loop and begins the next iteration. You can think of the **continue** as a statement that jumps over the rest of the statements in the loop and continues with the next execution of the loop. The following example prints out the iteration only when **i** is an odd number. On even iterations, **continue** skips over the **printf** statement.

```
set i 0
while {i < 10} {
    incr i 1
    if {i % 2 == 0} {
        continue
    }
    puts "This is an odd iteration $i"
}
```

Tcl File Handles

With Tcl you can access and manage files easily. See Table 7-5 for a list of Tcl file access commands.

The **open** and **close** commands will open and close files for access. You use the **open** command to create a file handle for a file or pipe (|). The **open** command takes two arguments: the file name string and the file

File Access Commands	Description
file	Obtains file information
open	Opens a file
close	Closes a file
eof	Checks for end of file
fcopy	Copies from one file to another
flush	Flushes output from a file's internal buffers
glob	Matches file names using glob pattern characters
read	Reads blocks of characters from a file
seek	Sets the seek offset of a file
tell	Returns the current offset of a file
socket	Opens a TCP/IP network connection
Input/Output Commands	**Description**
format	Formats a string with conversion specifiers, like sprintf in C
scan	Reads and converts elements in a string using conversion specifiers, like **scanf** in C
gets	Reads a line of input
puts	Writes a string to output

Table 7-5   Tcl File Access and Input/Output Commands

mode, and returns a file handle that can be used to access the file. The *file name string* can be the name of the file or a variable that holds the name of the file. The *file mode* is the group of permissions you are using to open the file. This can be **r** for read only, **w** for write only, or **a** for append only. To obtain both read and write permission for overwriting and updating a file, you attach **a+** to the file mode. Attaching **r+** gives you read and write permission. The syntax for **open** follows:

open *filename-string file-mode*

You usually use the **open** command in a **set** command so that you can assign the file handle returned by **open** to a variable. You can then use that file handle in the variable in other file commands to access the file. In the next example, the user opens the file reports with a file mode for reading, **r**, and assigns the returned file handle to the **myfile** variable.

```
set myfile [open  "reports" r]
```

Often the file name will be held in a variable. You then use the **$** with the variable name to reference the file name. In this example, the file name "reports" is held in the variable **filen**:

```
set filen="reports"
set myfile [open  $filen r]
```

After you have finished using the file, you close it with the **close** command. The **close** command takes as its argument the file handle of the file you want to close.

```
close $myfile
```

Using the **gets** and **puts** commands, you can use a file handle to read and write from a specific file. The **gets** command takes two arguments: a file handle and a variable. It will read a line from the file referenced by the file handle and place it as a string in the variable. If no file handle is specified, **gets** reads from the standard input. The following command reads a line from a file using the file handle in the **myfile** variable. The line is read into the **line** variable.

> The variable input data is placed

```
gets $myfile line
```

The **puts** command also takes two arguments: a file handle and a string. It will write the string to the file referenced by the file handle. If no file handle is specified, **puts** will write to the standard output. In the following example, **puts** writes the string held in the line variable to the file referenced by the file handle held in **myfile**. Notice the **$** that appears before **line** in the **puts** command, but not in the previous **gets** command. The **puts** command operates on a string, whereas **gets** operates on a variable.

> Data written to a file

```
puts $myfile $line
```

The following script opens a file called *reports* and displays it on the screen:

```
#!/usr/bin/tclsh
    set reps [open "reports" r]
  while {[gets $reps line]}
        {
        puts $line
        }
    close $reps
```

You can use the **file** command to check certain features of files, such as whether they exist or whether they are executable. You can also check for directories. The **file** command takes several options, depending on the action you want to take. The **exist** option checks whether a file exists and the **size** option tells you its size. The **isdirectory** option determines whether the file is a directory and the **isfile** checks to see whether it is a file. With the executable, readable, and writeable options, you can detect whether a file is executable, can be read, or can be written to. The **dirname** option displays the full path name of the file, and the **extension** and **root name** options show the extension or root name of the file, respectively. The **atime**, **mtime**, and **owned** options display the last access time and the modification time, and whether it is owned by the user.

```
file exits reps
file isfile reps
file size reps
file executable myreport
```

Often file names will be used as arguments to Tcl programs. In this case, you can use the **argv** list to obtain the file names. The **argv** command lists all arguments entered on the command line when the Tcl script was invoked. You use the **lindex** command to extract a particular argument from the **argv** list. Many programs use file names as their arguments. Many also specify options. Remember that the **lindex** command indexes a list from 0. So the first argument in the **argv** list would be obtained by the following (be sure to precede **argv** with the **$**):

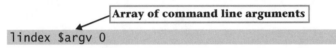
Array of command line arguments

```
lindex $argv 0
```

You can, if you wish, reference an argument in the **argv** list within the **open** command. Here, the **lindex** operation is enclosed in braces, in place of the file name. The **lindex** command will return the file name from the **argv** list.

```
set shandle [ open {lindex $argv 0}  r ]
```

mycp

Project 7-1: File Copy

The *mycp* program is a simple version of the Linux **cp** command that copies one file to another.

Step-by-Step

1. Detect whether the user has entered two arguments: the first will be the name of the source file and the second the name of the copy (the destination file). Use the **argc** variable to detect the number of elements. If the number of elements is wrong, output an error message and use the **exit** command to end the program.

2. Assign the first argument to the **sourcefile** variable and the second to the **destfile** variable.

3. Open the source file (**sourcefile** variable) for reading, and assign its file handle to the **shandle** variable.

4. Open the destination file (**destfile** variable) for writing, and assign its file handle to the **dhandle** variable.

5. In a **while** loop, use the **gets** command to read a line of the source file in the **line** variable with each iteration. Then use the **puts** command to write the line from the **line** variable to the destination file.

6. Output a simple message stating that the file has been copied.

7. Close both the destination (**dhandle**) and source (**shandle**) files.

The contents of the *mycp* program follows:

```
#!/usr/bin/tclsh

    if {$argc != 2} {
        puts  "Please enter two filenames\n"
         exit 1
    }

    set sourcefile [ lindex $argv 0 ]
    set destfile [ lindex $argv 1 ]
    set shandle [ open $sourcefile r ]
    set dhandle [open $destfile w ]

    while {[gets $shandle line]} {
        puts  $dhandle $line
        }
    puts  "$sourcefile copied to $destfile "
    close $dhandle
    close $shandle
```

Tcl Procedures: **proc**

The **proc** command allows you to create your own Tcl commands for use within a program. In effect, you use this command to create new procedures, much like you create procedures or functions in other programming languages. You can think of a **proc** command as defining a Tcl command, much like you would define a function in C. Table 7-6 lists the Tcl procedure commands.

The **proc** command takes three arguments: the name of the new procedure, the arguments that the procedure will take, and a block of commands that the procedure will execute. The arguments are variables that will receive the values passed to them when the procedure is used. The arguments are placed after the procedure name within braces. An opening brace then begins the block of Tcl commands for this procedure. The syntax for the **proc** command follows:

```
proc procedure-name { arguments } {
    TCL commands
    }
```

The following example implements the **lsearch** command described earlier in this chapter:

```
proc mysearch { mylist pat } {
    set i 0
    set len [length $mylist]
    while { $i < $len } {
        if { [lindex $mylist $i] == $pat)
            return $i
    }
    }
```

Command	Definition
proc	Defines a Tcl procedure
return	Returns a value from a procedure
source	Reads and executes Tcl commands in another file
uplevel	Executes a command in a different scope

Table 7-6   Tcl Procedure Commands

Tcl **string** Command

The Tcl **string** command is used to perform different operations on strings. It takes various options, depending on the task you want to perform. You can search, substring, or obtain the length of a string. The option is entered as a word following the **string** command. Arguments will vary according to the option you choose. Table 7-7 shows the Tcl string commands.

With the **string match** command, you can perform basic search operations on a string, although regular expressions are not supported by this command. It does support *****, **?**, and **[ ]** special characters for simple pattern matching, as used in the shell for file name matching. **string match** takes two arguments: the pattern to match and the string to search, as shown in this example:

```
string match report* $fname
```

The **string range** command returns a substring of a specified string. It takes three arguments: the string, and beginning and end indexes. The count starts from 0. The term **end** used for the end index will automatically copy the remainder of the string, as shown in the following example. The first example returns "ave" and the second returns "ven".

```
string range 4 9
string range 3 end
```

7

Command	Description
binary	Converts between strings and binary data
regexp	Matches on a string using regular expressions
regsub	Performs substitutions using patterns with regular expressions
split	Splits a string into list elements
string	Operates on strings
subst	Performs substitutions on a string

Table 7-7   Tcl String Operations

The **string index** command returns a single character from a string at a specified index. It takes two arguments: the string and index of the character to be returned. The following example returns the fifth character from the **mystring** variable:

```
string index $mystring 5
```

The **string length** command returns the length of a string:

```
string length $mystring
```

Regular expression pattern matching on strings is implemented with the **regexp** command. **regexp** has full extended regular expression matching capabilities, similar to **egrep**. It takes two arguments: the regular expression pattern and the string to be searched. It returns a 1 if the pattern is found in the string and 0 if it isn't. The following looks for any numbers in **mystring**:

```
regexp [0-9]+ $mystring
```

The **regsub** command is the Tcl substitute command. It matches a regular expression like **regsub**, but it then replaces the matched string with a specified replacement string, placing the entire modified string in a new variable. The **regsub** command takes four arguments. The first two are the same as **regexp**—the regular expression pattern and the string to be searched. The third argument is the replacement string, and the fourth is the variable where the modified string will placed. The syntax is shown here:

regsub *pattern string replacement-string variable*

If the pattern is not found in the string, it returns a 0:

```
regsub milk $mystring yogurt newstring
```

fileops

Project 7-2: File Operations

The *fileops* program displays a menu of three choices for operations on a file: copying a file, erasing a file, and replacing a file.

Step-by-Step

1. Define three procedures, one for each operation. For simplicity, Linux commands are used to perform the actual operation. For example the **cp** command is used to copy a file. Recall that the **exec** command allows you to execute a Linux command within a Tcl script:

```
exec cp $sourcefile $destfile
```

2. Define a **copyfile** procedure where the user is prompted for a source file and then a destination file. Use the **gets** command to read the user's response. Use the **cp** command to copy the file.

3. Define an **erasefile** procedure to prompt for a file that the user wants deleted. Use the **rm** command to remove the file.

4. Define a **renamefile** procedure to prompt for the original name of a file and then the new name that the user wants to give. Use the **mv** command to change the file's name.

5. In the main part of the program, create a menu listing the three file operations. The user's selection is read into the choice variable, which is then used in a **switch** operation to detect the option. Invoke corresponding procedures accordingly. If the user selects the fourth option (Quit), the **exit** command will end the program.

The contents of the *fileops* program follows:

```
#!/usr/bin/tclsh

# Function to copy a file
proc copyfile {} {
    puts "File to Copy: "
```

7

```
        gets stdin sourcefile
        puts "Name of file: "
        gets stdin destfile
        exec cp $sourcefile $destfile
        }


# Function to erase a file
proc erasefile {} {
        puts "File to Erase: "
        gets stdin efile
        exec rm efile
    }

# The Rename function
proc renamefile {} {
        puts "File to Copy: "
        gets stdin origname
        puts "Name of file: "
        gets stdin newname

        exec mv $ origname $ newname
}

# Main menu
puts "File Management Operations\n\n"
puts "1. Copy a file.\n"
puts "2. Erase a file.\n"
puts "3. Rename a file.\n"
puts "4. Quit.\n\n"

puts -nonewline "Please enter choice: " ; flush stdout
gets stdin choice
switch $choice {
    1 {
            copyfile
        }
    2 {
            erasefile
    }
    3 {
            renamefile
```

```
        }
    4 {
        exit
    }
      default {
        puts "Invalid Option"
          }
}
```

Expect

The Expect application adds several commands to Tcl scripts that you can use to automatically interact with any Linux program, plus a utility that prompts you for responses. For example, the login procedure for different systems using ftp or telnet can be automatically programmed with a Tcl script using Expect commands. You can find out more about Expect at **www.expect.nist.gov**. Expect commands are designed to work with any interactive program. The commands wait for a response from a program and then send the response specified in the Tcl script. You can drop out of the script with a simple CTRL-D command and interact with the program directly.

Three basic Expect commands added to Tcl scripts are the **send**, **expect**, and **interact** commands. The **expect** command will wait to receive a string or value from the application you are interacting with. The **send** command will send a string to that application. The **interact** command places you into direct interaction with the application, ending the Expect/Tcl script. In the following script, **expect** is used to perform an anonymous login with the *ftp* program. The **spawn** command starts up the *ftp* program. The internet address of the FTP site is assumed to be an argument to this script, and as such, will be held in the **argv** list.

```
#!/usr/bin/expect
spawn ftp
send "open $argv\r"
 expect "login:"
send "anonymous\r"
expect "word:"
send "richlp@turtle.mytrek.com"
interact
```

To run Expect commands, you must first enter the Expect shell. In the preceding script, the Expect shell in invoked with the command **#!/usr/bin/expect**.

The **expect** command can take two arguments: the pattern to expect and an action to take if the pattern is matched. The **expect** command can also take as its argument a block of pattern/action arguments. In this case, **expect** can match on alternative patterns, executing the action only for the pattern it receives. For example, the **ftp** command may return a "connection refused" string instead of a "name" string. In that case, you would want to issue this message and exit the Expect script. If you want more than one action taken for a pattern, you can enclose the actions in braces, separated by semicolons. An example of such an **expect** command follows:

```
send "open $argv"
expect {
    "connection refused"  {puts "Failed to connect"; exit}
    "name" puts "connection successful"
}
```

Another useful Expect command is **timeout**. You can set the **timeout** command to a number of seconds, and then have **expect** check for the timeout. To set the number of seconds for a timeout, you use **set** to assign the number to the **timeout** variable. To have the **expect** command detect a timeout, use the word *timeout* as the **expect** command's pattern. With the timeout, you can add an action for the shell to take. In the following example, a timeout has been added to the Tcl script:

```
set timeout 20
send "open $argv"
expect {
    timeout {puts "Connection timed out"; exit }
    "connection refused"  {puts "Failed to connect"; exit}
    "name" puts "connection successful"
}
```

✓ *Mastery Check*

1. How do you sort a list of numbers?

2. What operation would you use to read a record consisting of a line that has fields separated by a colon delimiter?

3. How do you open a file for both reading and writing?

4. What control structure reads items in several lists at once, assigning each to a variable in turn?

5. Could you design a script that would automatically download files from an FTP site?

7

Module 8

Tk

The Goals of This Module

- Learn to create graphical user interfaces with Tk
- Define objects such as buttons, scroll bars, and list boxes
- Organize and position objects on Tk windows
- Create Tk scripts using Tcl commands
- Associate an action with a particular event that takes place on an object
- Implement menus and references using Tk tags

The Tk application extends Tcl with commands for creating and managing graphical objects such as windows, icons, buttons, and text fields. Tk commands create graphical objects using the X Window System—which is an easier way to program X Windows objects than using the X11 toolkit directly. With Tk, you can easily create sophisticated window-based user interfaces for your programs.

Tk operates under the X Window System. Within the X Window System, Tk uses its own shell, called the *wish shell*, to execute Tk commands. To run Tk programs,

1. Start up your X Window System.

2. Start up the wish shell with the command **wish**. This will open a window in which you can then run Tk commands.

If you are using a graphical user interface, such as Open Look or Motif, X Windows is automatically started. Note that you can also enter the **wish** command from an Xterm window.

The Tk language is organized according to different types of graphical objects such as windows, buttons, menus, and scroll bars. Such objects are referred to as *widgets*.

Instead of explicitly programming Tk code to create a graphical user interface (GUI), you can use a Tcl/Tk *GUI builder*. A GUI builder generates the Tcl/Tk code for a user interface that you can then use in a Tcl/Tk program. This GUI builder X Windows program has its own GUI with windows, menus, and icons that you can use to easily create GUI widgets with simple menu selections or mouse operations. Using a GUI builder, creating and configuring a widget is as simple as clicking its icon in the palette and dragging it to a grid, or choosing the options you want from a toolbar.

Note

Several currently available Tcl/Tk GUI builders are available for free, such as Visual Tcl, SpecTcl, VisualGIPSY, and XF. These are downloadable from their respective Web sites. You can finds links to these sites on the Scriptics Web site's GUI Builder's page, which is located through the Tcl Resources page.

The wish Shell and Scripts

Within the wish shell, you can interactively enter commands and execute them one by one, or you can place the commands in a script file and execute them all at once. Usually, Tk commands are placed in a script that is run with the invocation of the **wish** command. Like Tcl scripts, Tk scripts usually have the extension **.tcl**. For example, a Tk script called *mydir.tcl* would be read and executed by the following command entered in an Xterm window:

```
$ wish mydir.tcl
```

To create a stand-alone script that operates more like a command, you need to invoke the **wish** command within the script. Ordinarily, the **wish** command will open an interactive Tk shell window whenever executed. To avoid this, you invoke **wish** with the **–f** option, like so:

```
#!/usr/bin/wish -f
```

─┤Note ───────────────────

When creating a stand-alone script, be sure to change its permissions with the **chmod** command to allow execution. You can then enter the name of the script to run the program. To read more about the **chmod** command, refer to Module 2.

```
$ chmod 755 mydir1
$ mydir1
```

Tk Widgets

A *type* of widget is considered a *class*, and each widget class has its own *class command* to create it. The corresponding command will create a particular instance of that widget class—that is, a particular widget of that type. For example, you can create a button with the **button** command or a window with the **window** command. Graphical objects, such as buttons and frames (discussed later in the module in the section "Frames and Tags") are also often referred to as widgets. Table 8-1 lists the widgets available in Tk.

Widget	Purpose
Button	A clickable button
Canvas	A window for drawing objects
checkbutton	A check button
Entry	An input box
Frame	A simple widget whose primary purpose is to act as a space or container for complex window layouts
Image	An image object for displaying pictures
Label	A label
Listbox	A list box with a selectable list of items
Menu	A menu bar
menubutton	A menu button to access the menu
Message	A message area used to create and manipulate message widgets
radiobutton	A radio button
Scrollbar	A scroll bar
Text	An editable text box
Scale	A scale

Table 8-1   Standard Tk Widgets

In Tk programs, the **class** command takes as its arguments the name of the widget followed by configuration options with their values. Table 8-2 lists several of the commonly used Tk commands.

Event Operations	Description
bind	Associates Tcl scripts with X events
bindtags	Binds commands to tags
selection	Allows object or text to be selected by a mouse
Window Operations	
destroy	Closes a Tk window
toplevel	Selects a top-level window
wm	Sets window features
up level	Moves up to the previous window level

Table 8-2   Tk Commands

Tk commands use a format similar to those used in Tcl. You enter a Tk class command on a line followed by its arguments. Tk commands are more complicated than Tcl commands, however. Graphical interface commands require a significant amount of information about a widget to set it up correctly. For example, a button requires a name, the text it will display, and the action it will take. Many Tk commands can take various options that indicate different features of a widget. With these options you can display images in widgets (**-image**), set background and foreground colors for widgets, and determine where information is displayed on a widget (anchor). Table 8-3 lists several options commonly used for Tk widgets.

Tk Command Options	Description
–activebackground	Specifies background color to use when drawing active elements
–activeborderwidth	Specifies width of the 3-D border around active elements
–activeforeground	Specifies foreground color to use when drawing active elements
–anchor	Specifies how information is displayed in the widget; must be one of the values n, ne, e, se, s, sw, w, nw, or center
–background	Indicates the normal background color to use when displaying the widget
–bitmap	Selects the bitmap to display in the widget
–borderwidth	Sets the width of the 3-D border around the perimeter of the widget
–cursor	Sets the mouse cursor to be used for the widget
–disabledforeground	Specifies the foreground color to use when drawing a disabled element
–font	Sets the font to use when drawing text inside the widget
–foreground	Specifies the normal foreground color to use when displaying the widget
–geometry	Specifies the desired geometry for the widget's window
–highlightbackground	Indicates the color to display in the traversal highlight region when the widget does not have the input focus

Table 8-3   Tk Standard Options

Tk Command Options	Description
–highlightcolor	Indicates the color to use for the traversal highlight rectangle that appears around the widget when it has the input focus
–highlightthickness	Indicates the width of the highlight rectangle to draw around the perimeter of the widget when it has the input focus
–image	Specifies an image to display in the widget
–insertbackground	Sets the color to use as background in the area covered by the insertion cursor
–insertborderwidth	Sets the width of the 3-D border around the insertion cursor
-insertofftime	Indicates the number of milliseconds the insertion cursor should remain "off" in each blink cycle
–insertontime	Inserts the number of milliseconds the insertion cursor should remain "on" in each blink cycle
–insertwidth	Inserts a value indicating the total width of the insertion cursor
–jump	Creates a slider that can be dragged to adjust a value
–justify	Justifies multiple lines of text displayed in a widget
–orient	Orients widgets that can position themselves, such as scroll bars
–padx	Specifies how much extra space to request for the widget in the X direction
–pady	Specifies how much extra space to request for the widget in the Y direction
–relief	Specifies the 3-D effect desired for the widget
–repeatdelay	Specifies the number of milliseconds a button or key must be held down before it begins to auto-repeat
–repeatinterval	Determines the number of milliseconds between auto-repeats
–selectbackground	Specifies the background color to use when displaying selected items
–selectborderwidth	Specifies width of the 3-D border
–selectforeground	Sets the foreground color
–text	Identifies string to be displayed inside the widget
–troughcolor	Sets the color to use for the rectangular trough areas in widgets, such as in scrollbars and scales

Table 8-3   Tk Standard Options *(continued)*

Tk Command Options	Description
–underline	Specifies the integer index of a character to underline in the widget
–wraplength	Sets the maximum line length for word wrapping
–xscrollcommand	Communicates with horizontal scrollbars
–yscrollcommand	Communicates with vertical scrollbars
Button Options	
–command	Specifies a Tcl command to associate with the button
–selectimage	Indicates the image to display when the check button is selected
–height	Sets the button height
–selectcolor	Sets the background color to use when the button is selected
–state	Specifies one of three states for the radio button: normal, active, or disabled
–variable	Global variable indicates whether this button is selected
–width	Sets button width

Table 8-3   Tk Standard Options *(continued)*

8

In the following example, a button is created using the **button** command. The **button** command takes as its first argument the name of the button widget. Then options define various features. The **–text** option is followed by a string that will be the text displayed by the button. The **–command** option is followed by the command that the button executes when it is clicked. This **button** command will display a button containing the text "Click Me". When you click the button, the Tk shell will exit.

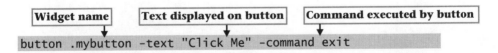

```
button .mybutton -text "Click Me" -command exit
```

To set up a working interface, you need to define all the widgets that are needed to perform a given task. Some widgets are designed to manage other widgets—for example, scrollbars are designed to manage windows. Other widgets, such as text input fields, may interact with a Tcl program. A menu choice may cause part of a Tcl program to run.

Widgets are organized hierarchically. For example, if you want to set up a window for data input, you may need to create a frame, within which may be text field widgets as well as buttons. Widget names reflect this hierarchy. So the widget (text field) contained within another widget (the frame) is prefixed with the outermost widget's name. In this example, then, if the name of the frame is **report** and you want to call the text input field **monday**, the text input field will have the name **report.monday**. A period separates each level in the hierarchy. Similarly, a button that you want to call **ok** that is within the **report** frame would be named **report.ok**.

Once you have created your widgets, you need to define their geometry. The geometry determines the size of each widget in relation to the others, their shape, and their location in the window. Tk has three geometry managers: **pack**, **place**, and **grid**.

Geometry Manager	Description
pack	Packs widgets next to each other
place	Places widgets in positions in frame
grid	Places widgets in a grid of rows and columns

Your widgets cannot be displayed until their geometry is determined. The following example determines the geometry of the **.mybutton** widget using the **pack** command.

```
pack .mybutton
```

Hint

A line of Tk code can be very long. You may want to split it up into two or more lines in your script to make it easier to read. However, to break a single code line into two you must place a backslash at the end of the first broken line of the script. For example, the following single line of code has been broken into two script lines by placing a \ at the end of the first line:

```
listbox .list -yscroll ".scroll set"  -relief sunken \
                    -width 15 -height 15 -setgrid yes
```

Many of the long lines of code in the examples and programs in this chapter are split into two or more lines in the script, even though they are interpreted by Tk as only one line. Any line ending with a \ is really part of a single code line that is continued on the next script line.

1-Minute Drill

● **What are the different geometry managers for Tk?**

● **What is the command you use to invoke Tk?**

Ask the Expert

Question: How do the geometry commands differ?

Answer: The **pack** geometry command simply packs in different widgets next to each other, taking up only the amount of space in a frame or window needed to fit in the widgets. You can add padding to space them out more if necessary. The **place** geometry command lets you position a widget at a particular place in the frame. The **grid** geometry command lets you set up a cell-like grid, in which you can position widgets.

Question: When would I use a grid?

Answer: A grid is helpful for arranging widgets in a particular format, such as in a form. For example, if you want to set up a form with entry boxes and buttons, you can use a grid to place the widgets at different parts of the form. To reference a particular cell in the grid, you would specify its row and column.

Question: How do you use the place command?

Answer: The **place** geometry command comes in handy when you want to position a widget at a particular point on the window or frame that is further away from other widgets. While the **pack** and **grid** commands place widgets next to each other, you can use **place** to put the widget anywhere by specifying x and y coordinates. For example, you could use **place** to put an OK button widget in a corner away from a text widget that appears in the middle of the screen.

8

● pack, place, **and** grid
● wish

Figure 8-1 Tk list box and scrollbar for mydir1

mydir1

Project 8-1: Display a Directory

The following *mydir1* program is a simple Tcl/Tk program that displays a list of file and directory names in a Tk list box object with an attached scrollbar. Figure 8-1 shows this list box. A list box object lets you display a list of items that can be easily scrolled through and selected using the mouse. You can attach a scrollbar to accommodate items should there be more items than fit in the designated list box size.

Step-by-Step

1. Define the scroll bar using the **scrollbar** command: name it **.scroll** and bind it with the command **.list yview**. This instructs the scrollbar to be attached vertically to the list box on the y axis.

```
scrollbar .scroll -command ".list yview"
```

2. Define the list box with the **listbox** command, name it **.list**, and provide a y axis scroll capability with the **.scroll** widget. The list box will appear "sunken," with the specified width and height.

```
listbox .list -yscroll ".scroll set" -relief sunken -width 15 -height 15 -setgrid yes
```

3. Create the two objects (the scrollbar and the list box) with the **pack** command, and position them in the window. The scrollbar and list box are placed on the left side of the window and will expand to fill the window. Their anchor is on the west side of the window, as indicated by **w** in the code that follows. The list box, **.list**, is placed first, followed by the scrollbar, **.scroll**.

```
pack .list .scroll -side left -fill both -expand yes -anchor w
```

4. Run a Tcl **if** test to determine whether the user has entered an argument when the program was invoked. The **if** test checks to determine whether a first element appears in the **argv** list, where any arguments are held. If no arguments are detected, the current directory is used, as represented by the period. This chosen directory is assigned to the **dir** variable.

5. Fill the list box using a Tcl **foreach** operation. Use the shell **ls** command, as executed with the **exec** command, to obtain the list of files and directories.

6. Place the list of files and directories in the list box with the Tk **insert** operation for the **.list** object. The **insert** command takes a position and a value. Here the value is a file name held in **$i**, which is placed at the end of the list:

```
.list insert end $i
```

7. Bind the CTRL-C character to the **exit** command to allow the user to easily close the window.

The *mydir1* script is shown here:

8

```
#!/usr/bin/wish -f

# Create a scrollbar and listbox
scrollbar .scroll -command ".list yview"
listbox .list -yscroll ".scroll set"  -relief sunken -width 15 -height 15 -setgrid yes
pack .list .scroll   -side left  -fill both -expand yes -anchor w

# If user enters a directory argument use that, otherwise use current directory
if {$argc > 0} then {
    set dir [lindex $argv 0]
    } else {
        set dir "."
        }

# Fill the listbox (.list) with the list of files and directories obtained from ls
 cd $dir
 foreach i [exec ls -a ] {
    if [file isfile $i] {
    .list insert end $i
    }
    }

# Set up bindings for the file manager.  Control-c closes the window.
bind all <Control-c> {destroy .}
```

Events and Bindings

A Tk program is event driven, which means that as it runs it waits for an event, such as a mouse event or a keyboard event, to take an action. A mouse event can be a mouse click, a double-click, or even a mouse down or up. A keyboard event can be a pressed control key or meta-key, or it can be the pressing of the ENTER key at the end of input data. When the program detects a particular event, it takes an action. The action may be another graphical operation, such as displaying another menu, or it may be a Tcl, Perl, or shell program execution.

Actions are explicitly bound to given events using the **bind** command. The **bind** command takes as its arguments the name of an object or class, the event to bind, and the action to bind to that event. Whenever the event takes place within that object, the specified action is executed. Following is an example of a bind entry. The event of pressing the CTRL-C key will perform the action of destroying all widgets, ending the program.

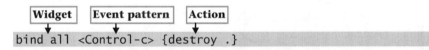

```
bind all <Control-c> {destroy .}
```

You use the **bind** command to connect events in a Tk object with a Tcl command you want executed. In a sense, you are dividing your Tcl program into segments, each of which is connected to an event in a Tk object. When an event takes place in a Tk object, its associated set of Tcl commands is executed. Other Tk commands, as well as Tcl commands, can be associated with an event bound to a Tk object. This means that you can nest objects and their events. The Tcl commands executed by one Tk event may, in turn, include other Tk commands and objects with events bound to yet other Tcl commands.

An event can be either a keyboard event triggered by pressing a key on a keyboard, or a mouse event triggered by a click of the mouse button. An event is represented in Tk code as an *event pattern*. For example, pressing the BACKSPACE key is an event represented by the event pattern **<CTRL-H>**. Event patterns are enclosed in **<>** symbols. A mouse button click is represented as **<Button-1>**. To portray a sequence of events, such as a double-click, you enter a modifier before the event. For example, the event pattern for double-click is **<Double-Button-1>**, where **Double** is the modifier for the event **Button-1**. See Table 8-4 for a listing of Tk event patterns.

Bindings are the key operational components of a Tk program. Bindings detect the events that drive a Tk program. You can think of a Tk program as an infinite loop that continually scans for the occurrence of specified events (bindings). When it detects an event, such as a mouse click or a control key

Hint

You can think of bindings as having multiple entry points, where different parts of the program begin. Bindings do not use exactly the same structure used by a traditional hierarchical, sequential program. A binding starts its own sequence of commands, or its own program of sorts. This means that to trace the flow of control for a Tk program, you start with the bindings. Each binding has its own path, or its own flow of control.

Event Patterns Sequence	Description
<Keypress>	Any keyboard key
<modifier-modifier-type-detail>	Sequence of events, such as a CTRL key or mouse click

Event Patterns Modifiers	
Control	CTRL key
Shift	SHIFT key
Lock	CAPS LOCK keyk KEY
Alt	ALT key
Meta, M	Meta-key
Button1, B1	First mouse button
Button2, B2	Second mouse button
Button3, B3	Third mouse button
Button4, B4	Fourth mouse button
Button5, B5	Fifth mouse button
Mod1, M1	Modifier 1
Mod2, M2	Modifier 2
Mod3, M3	Modifier 3
Mod4, M4	Modifier 4
Double	Double-repeated events, such as double mouse clicks

Table 8-4 Event Patterns for bind **Command**

Event Patterns Sequence	Description
Triple	Triple-repeated events, such as triple mouse clicks
Event Types	
ButtonPress, Button	Press a mouse button; default for Button modifier
ButtonRelease	Release a mouse button
Destroy	Destroy a widget
Enter	Enter a widget
KeyPress, Key	Press a key
KeyRelease	Release a key
Leave	Leave a widget
Motion	Move over a widget
Event Details	
For Buttons 1 2 3 4 5	The number of the button; if no number is given, all buttons match If type is omitted, default type of ButtonPress is used Button-1 is the same as Button-ButtonPress-1
Keypress	Key symbol representation of keyboard characters—for example, A, COMMA, SHIFT-R

Table 8-4　Event Patterns for bind Command *(continued)*

press, the program executes the actions bound to that event. These actions can be any Tcl/Tk command or a series of commands. Usually these commands call functions that can perform complex operations. When it finishes executing these commands, the program resumes its scanning for other bound events. This scanning continues indefinitely until it is forcibly broken by an **exit** or **destroy** command, as is done with the CTRL-C binding.

The *mydir2* program, shown in Figure 8-2, illustrates functions and object bindings. Here, the *mydir1* program is enhanced with the capability to display two list boxes: one for directories and one for files. Each list box has its own scrollbar. The directory list box is named **.listdir**, and its scrollbar is named **.scrolldir**. Each list box and scrollbar is defined and then created, **.listdir** and **.scrolldir** first so that they will appear on the left side of the window.

The Tcl function **listdirsfunc** is then defined to fill both the list boxes. This function takes as its argument a directory. The **cd** command will

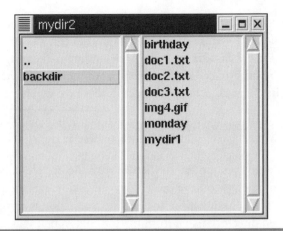

Figure 8-2   Directory and file list boxes for mydir2

change to that directory, providing the capability of listing different directories. Then a **isdirectory** test checks for directories, placing them in the **.listdir** list box.

```
proc listdirsfunc dir {
    .listdir delete 0  end
    .list delete  0 end
    cd $dir
    foreach i [exec ls -a ] {
        if [file isdirectory $i] {
            .listdir insert end $i
            } else {
                .list insert end $i
                }
        }
    }
```

Following the definition of this function is a function call. The **listdirsfuncs** function needs to be called once to fill the list boxes with the contents of the current directory.

```
# Display directories and files the first time
listdirsfunc $dir
```

There is now a *binding* for the **.listdir** object. A double-click of the left mouse button, **Double-Button-1**, is bound to a call of the **listdirfuncs** function for the **.listdir** list box. This binding makes any double-click on the **.listdir** list box call the **listdirsfuncs** function. As there is no binding for the **.list** list box, a double-click on that box will have no effect.

```
bind .listdir <Double-Button-1> {set i [selection get]
                              listdirsfunc  $i}
```

Two actions are bound to **.listdir** with the double-click. These are encased in braces—to have more than one action executed with a binding, you must place them within braces. The first action is an operation to obtain the selected directory name from the list box. When you click an item in a list box, you select it. The **[selection get]** operation will return the selected item—in this case, a directory name. The directory name is assigned to the variable **i**. This variable is used as an argument in the function call of **listdirsfunc**, the second action. These two actions illustrate how you can obtain values and pass them as arguments to a function, all within a binding. First you obtain the values, assigning them to variables, and then you use the contents of these variables as arguments in the function call.

The contents of the *mydir2* script follows:

```
#!/usr/bin/wish -f

# Create scroll bar and list box for directories
scrollbar .scrolldir -command ".listdir yview"
listbox .listdir -yscroll " .scrolldir set"  -relief sunken -width 15 -height 15 \
    -setgrid yes
pack .listdir .scrolldir  -side left  -fill both -expand yes -anchor w

# Create scroll bar and list box for files
scrollbar .scroll -command ".list yview"
listbox .list -yscroll ".scroll set"  -relief sunken -width 15 -height 15 -setgrid yes
pack .list .scroll   -side left  -fill both -expand yes -anchor w

# Check to see if an argument was entered
if $argc>0 {set dir [lindex $argv 0]} else {set dir "."}

# Function to list separate and list directories and files.
#Current entries are first deleted
proc listdirsfunc dir {
    .listdir delete 0 end
    .list delete  0 end
    cd $dir
    foreach i [exec ls -a ] {
       if [file isdirectory $i] {
```

```
           .listdir insert end $i
       } else {
              .list insert end $i
              }
      }
   }

# Display directories and files the first time
listdirsfunc $dir

# Set up bindings for the browser. Directories are bound to the Mouse double-click
bind all <Control-c> {destroy .}
bind .listdir <Double-Button-1>
           {set i [selection get] listdirsfunc  $i}
```

1-Minute Drill

- **Are Tk programs event driven?**
- **How are tasks executed?**

Windows

One of the basic components of a Tk program is the *window*. You can create as many windows as you want in a program—opening and closing them, as well as adding widgets to them such as menus, toolbars, and scrollbars. With the **wm** command you can set different window features, such as its title, size, and icon name.

The *mydir3* program shows you how to create another window with its own widgets, as well as how to access files (see Figure 8-3). The **dispfile** function creates a separate window to display the text of a file.

First, the window variable **w** is defined with the name **.dispf**, like so:

```
set w .dispf
```

Then the close box is enabled for closing the window. The **toplevel** command gives the window its own memory, creating the window. The **wm** command is used to define the window **title** (Display File) and **iconname** (DisplayFile).

- **Yes.**
- **Actions are bound to events with** bind **operations.**

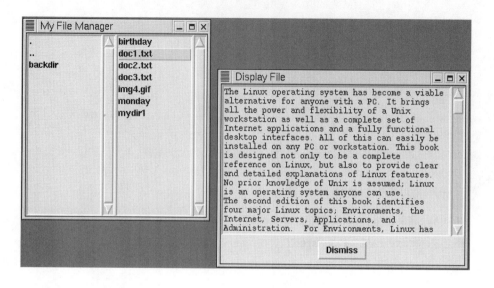

Figure 8-3 | Tk windows

```
catch {destroy $w}
toplevel $w
wm title $w "Display File"
wm iconname $w "DisplayFile"
```

A frame called **.buttons** is defined within this window. The **button**
command defines the button **dismiss** as part of this frame: **.button.dismiss**.
The text displayed within the button is "Dismiss." The command that is
executed when the button is clicked is **destroy $w**, which will destroy the
window. The frame that holds the button is placed at the bottom of the
window and centered.

```
button $w.buttons.dismiss -text Dismiss -command "destroy $w"
```

A scrollbar is defined for the text. Then the **text** command defines a
text box for the text—called **.dispf.disptext**, **.dispf** being the contents of
$w. A text box is usually editable. Various options set up a border, attach
the scrollbar, and enable word wrapping.

```
text $w.disptext -relief sunken -bd 2 -yscrollcommand
     "$w.scroll set" -setgrid 1 -height 30  -wrap word -width 80
```

Then the **LoadFileText** function is called to read the specified file into the text box. **LoadFileText** takes two arguments: the window and the file name. Notice that because there are two arguments, they must be enclosed in braces. The file is opened with the **[open $filename]** operation, returning a file ID that is assigned to the **fid** variable with the **set** command. A while loop testing for the end-of-file **![eof $fid]** reads in text to the **$w.disptext** text box. This **read** command reads text in blocks of 10,000 characters at a time. The **insert** operation places the text in **$w.disptext** object, displaying it in the window. The **$fid** command then closes the file.

```
$win.disptext insert end [read $fid 10000]
```

Following the code for the **dispfile** function is the code for defining and creating widgets for the main window. In Tcl/Tk, functions must be defined before they can be referenced in the program. For this reason, function definitions are placed at the beginning of the program and the main part of the program comes at the end.

The title and icon name are then defined for the main window. The main window is referenced by a period. When defining a feature of the main window, then, the period (.) represents the window name.

```
wm title . "My File Manager"
wm iconname .  "MFileManager"
```

After the list boxes and scrollbars for the main window are defined and created, the **selectfile** function is defined. This function receives as its argument a file name and tests to make sure it is a readable file. The function then calls the **dispfile** function to create a window to display the file. At the end of the program, another binding is added, this time for the **.list** list box for files. This **.list** binding calls the **selectfile** function that, in turn, calls the **dispfile** function. The **[selection get]** operation obtains the selected file name from the list box and assigns it to **$i**, which is then passed to **selectfile**. When the user double-clicks a file name in the file text box, a window will open and display the file name. However, when the user double-clicks a directory name, the contents of that directory are displayed in the respective list boxes. Notice how the same event, the double-click, is bound to two very different operations—the result is determined by what object the event occurs on.

The content of the *mydir3* script is shown here:

```
#!/usr/bin/wish -f

# Function to load a file into a window's textbox
proc LoadFileText {win filename} {
    set fid [open $filename]          ◄——— Open the file
    while {![eof $fid]} {
      $win.disptext insert end [read $fid 10000]  ◄——— Insert read
      }                                                   text to
    close $fid                                            .disptext
}                                                         text box

# Function to Display a file.  A window with its own
# textbox, scrollbar, and buttons
proc dispfile file  {
# Create display window, window title, and icon name.
set w .dispf  ◄——— Top level window created with the name .dispf
catch {destroy $w}
toplevel $w
wm title $w "Display File"
wm iconname $w "DisplayFile"

# Create display window buttons        Frame in the top level window created,
frame $w.buttons  ◄———                 called .buttons, w.buttons
pack $w.buttons -side bottom -fill x -pady 2m
button $w.buttons.dismiss -text Dismiss -command "destroy $w"
pack $w.buttons.dismiss -side left -expand 1
                                       Button called .dismiss
                                       is created in the
                                       w.buttons frame
# Create scrollbar for text of file
scrollbar $w.scroll -command "$w.disptext yview"
pack $w.scroll -side right -fill y ◄——— Scrollbar defined

# Create textbox to display text
text $w.disptext -relief sunken -bd 2 -yscrollcommand \  ◄———
    "$w.scroll set" -setgrid 1 -height 30  -wrap word -width 80
pack $w.disptext -expand yes -fill both
                                       Note this is a
                                       broken line
# Open the file and read in the text
LoadFileText $w $file  ◄——— Read specified file into the text box
}
```

```
# Create window title for main window.
# Main window is referenced with a period.
# Also create icon name for main window
wm title . "My File Manager"
wm iconname .  "MFileManager"
```

Title and icon name for main window

```
# Create directory listbox and scrollbar
scrollbar .scrolldir -command ".listdir yview"
listbox .listdir -yscroll " .scrolldir set"  -relief sunken \
                -width 15 -height 15 -setgrid yes
pack .listdir .scrolldir  -side left  -fill both \
                -expand yes -anchor w

# Create file listbox and scrollbar
scrollbar .scroll -command ".list yview"
listbox .list -yscroll ".scroll set"  -relief sunken \
                -width 15 -height 15 -setgrid yes
pack .list .scroll   -side left  -fill both \
                -expand yes -anchor w
wm minsize . 1 1

# Function to select a file for display
proc selectfile {dir file} {
        if {[file isfile $file]} then {
            dispfile $file
            } else {
                puts stdout \
"\"$file\" isn't a directory or regular file"
                }
        }
```

Check whether file exists

Call dispfile **to display the file**

```
if $argc>0 {set dir [lindex $argv 0]} else {set dir "."}

#Function to display files and directories
proc listdirsfunc dir {
    .listdir delete 0  end
    .list delete  0 end
    cd $dir
    set ndir [exec pwd]
    foreach i [exec ls -a ] {
        if [file isdirectory $i] {
            .listdir insert end $i
        } else {
            .list insert end $i
            }
        }
```

8

```
    }

listdirsfunc $dir
# Set up bindings for the directories and files.
bind all <Control-c> {destroy .}
bind .list <Double-Button-1> {set i [selection get] \
                                selectfile $dir $i}
bind .listdir <Double-Button-1> {set i [selection get] \
                                 listdirsfunc  $i}
```

> **Bind double-click to** selectfile **to display a file**

> **Bind double-click to** listdirsfunc **to display a directory**

Frames and Tags

Instead of creating different windows for different operations, you can use *frames* that can be displayed in a single window. When a new operation is chosen, it replaces the operation currently displayed. In effect, each operation has its own frame that, when chosen, is displayed at the bottom of the window. When finished with the operation, the frame disappears, shrinking the main window accordingly. Figure 8-4 shows an example of some frames in a window.

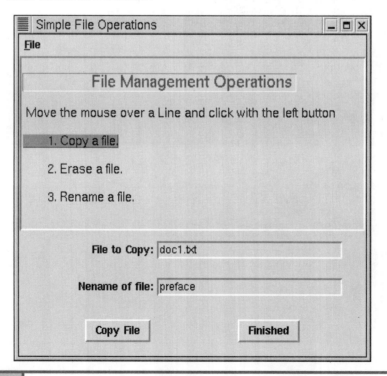

Figure 8-4   Tk frames

Tags allow you to select items displayed in a window by just clicking on them with your mouse. Tags let you create simple menu selections using any object displayed in your window. In Figure 8-4, the main menu is just a set of three text lines, beginning with the numbers 1, 2, and 3. Passing the mouse over one of these lines changes the line's background color. Clicking a line selects and executes its associated action. The text lines operate like a menu because of tags. Any text in a text box can be tagged. A tag can define features of the text itself, such as its font, size, color, or background; and a tag can also be bound to actions, just like keyboard events. With tags, text in a Tk program can operate like a hyperlink in a Web page: when you click certain text, it can execute a function.

1-Minute Drill

● **What command do you use to set a window's features?**

● **What command defines a text box?**

● **What feature would you use to implement a menu in Tk?**

myfilemgr

Project 8-2: Create a File Manager

8

The *myfilemgr* script is a more complete application that illustrates how a Tcl/Tk program can be organized into separate script files. This is handy for extra large application files; it lets you distributed a large application among several smaller files, each a Tcl/Tk script. The *myfilemgr* program is divided into three separate files: *myfilemgr*, *dispfile*, and *dispimage*. The *dispfile* script is a Tcl/Tk version of the *dispfile* function in the *mydir3* program and displays a text file. The *dispimage* script displays a graphics file, which shows you how to define, label, and create an image object for display in a window. Each script creates its own separate window. Figure 8-5 shows how the *myfilemgr* program can display images and text.

● **The** wm **command.**
● **The** text **command.**
● **Tags are used to implement a menu.**

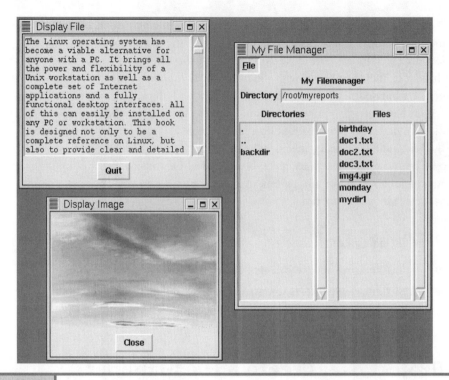

Figure 8-5 The File Manager program

Step-by-Step

1. Create a main window with a menu bar with which a user can choose a quit option to quit the program. First, define a menu bar frame called **.menuBAR** and position it at the top of the window.

2. Then define a menu button for the File menu called **.menuBAR.file** using the **menubutton** command.

3. Define a menu called **.menuBAR.file.m** for this button. Use the **menu** command. Be sure to add the Quit command to this menu.

```
frame .menuBAR
pack .menuBAR  -side top -fill x
menubutton .menuBAR.file -text File -menu .menuBAR.file.m -underline 0 -relief sunken
menu .menuBAR.file.m
.menuBAR.file.m add command -label "Quit" -command "exit" -underline 0
pack .menuBAR.file -side left
```

4. In the main window, create a text entry box to display the current directory and to allow a user to enter another one there. Use the **entry** command to define the text entry box. With the **–textvariable dir** option, tie the **dir** variable to the text box, placing the **dir** variable's contents in it. Use the **label** command to define a label to be placed next to the **dir** variable's contents.

```
label .topframe.dirlabel -text "Directory"
entry  .topframe.dirname -width 30 -textvariable dir
```

5. The introduction of a text entry box and labels to be placed above the list boxes complicate the organization of the main window. To correctly position the text boxes in the window below the labels, as well as position the entry box and labels at the top of the window, define three frames for each list box: **.files** for files, **.dirs** for directories, and **.topframe** for the entry box and labels. The file list box is now named **.files.list**, and the directory list box is **.dirs.listdir**. Each of the list box frames also has its own label positioned on top of it.

6. In the **selectfile** function, call the *dispname* and *dispimage* scripts. Use an **if** operation with the **regexp** command to check the extension of a file to determine whether it is an image file or a readable file. Then call the appropriate scripts. The **source** command executes a Tcl/Tk script file. Scripts will usually reside at a predetermined directory. Define the **progdir** variable in this program to hold the full path name of that predetermined directory. In the source operation, use the **file** command with the **join** operation to combine that path name with the script name, informing the source where the script is located. The following example is the source operations for *dispimage*:

```
source [file join $progdir dispimage ]
```

The contents of the *myfilemgr* script are shown here:

```
#!/usr/bin/wish -f

# This script generates a directory file browser, which lists
# the working directory and allows you to open files or
# subdirectories by double-clicking, including gif pictures.
#
# The script calls two separate scripts called dispfile and
```

```
# dispimage. A menu bar is added to quit the application.
# The listboxes and scrollbars have been placed in their own
 # frame to position them with a higher directory name frame.
#

# Create main window title and icon name
wm title . "My File Manager"
wm iconname . "MFileManager"

# Create menubar for File and Quit
frame .menuBAR
pack .menuBAR  -side top -fill x
menubutton .menuBAR.file -text File -menu .menuBAR.file.m \
            -underline 0 -relief sunken
menu .menuBAR.file.m
.menuBAR.file.m add command -label "Quit" \
            -command "exit" -underline 0
pack .menuBAR.file -side left


# Create title and directory textbox for path name
frame .topframe
pack  .topframe  -side top
label .topframe.title  -text "My Filemanager"
label .topframe.dirlabel -text "Directory"
entry .topframe.dirname -width 30 -textvariable dir
pack .topframe.title  -side top
pack .topframe.dirlabel .topframe.dirname -side left

# Create a scrollbar and listbox for Directories
# in their own frame, .dirs

frame .dirs
pack .dirs  -side left -fill x -pady 2m
label .dirs.dirns -text "Directories"
scrollbar .dirs.scrolldir -command ".dirs.listdir yview"
listbox .dirs.listdir -yscroll " .dirs.scrolldir set" \
        -relief sunken -width 15 -height 15 -setgrid yes
```

```
pack .dirs.dirns -side top
pack .dirs.scrolldir .dirs.listdir -side right \
            -fill both -expand yes -anchor  w

# Create a scrollbar and listbox for Files
# in their own frame, .files

frame .files
pack .files  -side right -fill x -pady 2m
label .files.filens  -text "Files"
scrollbar .files.scroll -command ".files.list yview"
listbox .files.list -yscroll ".files.scroll set" \
          -relief sunken -width 15 -height 15 -setgrid yes
pack .files.filens   -side top
pack .files.list .files.scroll   -side left \
            -fill both -expand yes -anchor w

wm minsize . 1 1


# Display a text file using dispfile and display a graphic
# file using dispimage. Call the separate dispfile and
# dispimage scripts with the source command. progdir needs to
# hold the full path name for these two scripts.

proc selectfile {dir file} {
    global progdir
    if { \
    [regexp (\.gif$|\.tiff$|\.bmp$|\.ppm|\.jpg$|\.jpeg$) \
        $file ] == 1} \
      then
        source [file join $progdir dispimage ]
          } elseif {[file isfile $file]} then {
        source [file join $progdir dispfile ]
      } else {
          puts stdout \
        "\"$file\" isn't a directory or regular file"
      }
    }

#Set dir when program first starts
if $argc>0 {set dir [lindex $argv 0]} else {set dir "."}
```

8

```
# Fill the directory listbox with directory name and the File
# listbox with file name.  The listboxes are deleted before
# being filled. ndir holds the complete path name of the
# current directory and is used to fill the .topframe.dirname
# textbox

proc listdirs dir {
    .dirs.listdir delete 0  end
    .files.list delete  0 end
    cd $dir
    foreach i [exec ls -a ] {
        if [file isdirectory $i] {
            .dirs.listdir insert end $i
            } else {
                .files.list insert end $i
                }
            }
    set ndir [exec pwd]
    .topframe.dirname delete 0 end
    .topframe.dirname insert 0   $ndir
    }

# if a user enters in a directory in the .topframe.dirname
# textbox, this command will call listdirs for it
proc getdir {} {
    set dir [.topframe.dirname get]
    listdirs $dir
    }

#Initialy filling of the directory and file listboxes
listdirs $dir

#Keep track of where dispname and dispimage are located
set progdir [exec pwd]

# Set up bindings for the file manager.

bind all <Control-c> {destroy .}
# Return key is tied to topframe.dirname entry box
bind .topframe.dirname <Return>  "getdir"
# Double click on left mouse button
# selects a file or directory calling either selectfile
# or listdirs
bind .files.list <Double-Button-1> {set i [selection get]
                                    selectfile $dir $i}
bind .dirs.listdir <Double-Button-1> {set i [selection get]
                                      listdirs  $i}
```

7. Define the *dispimage* script to display a graphic. Tk can define two different types of graphics: photos and bitmaps. Photo covers most pictures, such as gif or ppm images, and bitmaps are usually icon art. Once the type is determined, the **image** command creates the image object giving it the name **imageName** (you can specify any name you want).

8. Then configure that image object to the image file. Define a label object in the window, **$w.image**, with the **label** command. With the **–image** option, identify the image object, **imageName**. Create the label **$w.image** with the **pack** command; it displays the image file.

The contents of the *dispimage* script is shown here:

```
# Script to display a graphic imagae - photo
set w .pict
catch {destroy $w}
toplevel $w

# Set window title and iconname
wm title $w "Display Image"
wm iconname $w "DisplayImage"

# Create button for quitting window
frame $w.buttons
pack $w.buttons -side bottom -fill x -pady 2m
button $w.buttons.wclose -text Close -command "destroy $w"
pack $w.buttons.wclose  -side left -expand 1

# Determing image type
if [regexp (\.bmp$) $file ] {
      set imagetype bitmap
    } else {
      set imagetype photo
    }

# Create image with name imageName.  Then configure that
# image name with the specified image file.  Then create a
# label in the window for that image name.
# Pack the label to display the image
image create $imagetype imageName
imageName configure -file $file
label $w.image -image imageName
pack $w.image -side top -anchor w
```

8

The contents of the *dispfile* script are shown here.

```
# Script to display the contents of a file.
set w .text
catch {destroy $w}
toplevel $w
wm title $w "Display File"
wm iconname $w "DisplayFile"

# Create quit button
frame $w.buttons
pack $w.buttons -side bottom -fill x -pady 2m
button $w.buttons.quit -text Quit -command "destroy $w"
pack $w.buttons.quit  -side left -expand 1

# Create disptext frame and scrollbar for displaying text
text $w.disptext -relief sunken -bd 2 \
         -yscrollcommand "$w.scroll set" -setgrid \
         1 -height 15 -width 70 -wrap word
scrollbar $w.scroll -command "$w.disptext yview"
pack $w.scroll -side right -fill y
pack $w.disptext -expand yes -fill both

# Function to load a text file
proc LoadFileText {win filename} {
    set fid [open $filename]
    $win.disptext delete 1.0 end
    while {![eof $fid]} {
     $win.disptext insert end [read $fid 10000]
    }
    close $fid
}

# Load the text file
LoadFileText $w $file
```

Mastery Check

1. Are Tk graphical objects organized hierarchically?

2. Can you use Tcl commands to control Tk operations?

3. How can you make a certain object respond to an event, such as a button to a mouse click?

4. Whereas most programs run by executing their statements sequentially, how is a Tk program driven? How are operations selected for execution?

5. How can you display different objects in the same space in a window, instead of using a different window for each set of objects? (For example, use a menu located at the top of a window to select different operations, each of whose objects is displayed in the same window space in which it is chosen.)

8

Part 3

GUI Programming

Module 9

GNOME

The Goals of This Module

- Develop GNOME desktop user interfaces
- Compile GNOME applications
- Learn to implement GNOME graphical objects, such as windows and buttons
- Use the GTK+ libraries to manage basic operations
- Manage program object interaction using slots and signals
- Learn to manage objects, such as menus, toolbars, and dialog boxes

The GNU Network Object Model Environment, known as GNOME, provides a powerful and easy-to-use desktop consisting primarily of a panel, a desktop, and a set of GUI tools with which program interfaces can be constructed. Its aim is not just to provide a consistent interface, but also a flexible platform for the development of powerful applications.

GNOME is completely free under the GNU Public License, with no restrictions. You can obtain the source directly from the GNOME Web site at **www.gnome.org**. GNOME uses the Common Object Request Broker Architecture (CORBA), which allows software components to interconnect, regardless of the computer language in which they are implemented or the kind of machine they are running on. The GNOME implementation of CORBA is called ORBit.

The core components of the GNOME desktop consist of a panel for starting programs, and desktop functionality. Other components normally found in a desktop, such as a file manager, a Web browser, and a window manager, are provided by GNOME-compliant applications. GNOME provides libraries of GNOME GUI tools that developers can use to create GNOME applications, and programs can be said to be GNOME compliant if they use buttons, menus, and windows that adhere to a GNOME standard.

GTK+ is the widget set used for GNOME applications, and its look and feel was originally derived from Motif. A widget set is the set of GUI objects that are available for use in a desktop: buttons, windows, and toolbars are all examples of widgets. The widget set is designed from the ground up for power and flexibility. For example, buttons can have labels, images, or any combination thereof. Objects can be dynamically queried and modified at run time. GTK+ also includes a theme engine that lets users change the look and feel of applications using these widgets. At the same time, the GTK+ widget set remains small and efficient.

The GTK+ widget set is entirely free under the Library General Public License (LGPL). The LGPL allows developers to use the widget set with proprietary as well as free software. The widget set also features an extensive set of programming language bindings including C++, Perl, Python, Pascal, Objective-C, Guile, and Ada. Internalization is fully supported, permitting applications based on GTK+ to be used with other character sets, such as those of Asian languages. The drag-and-drop functionality supports both XDND and Motif protocols, allowing drag-and-drop operations with other widget sets that support these protocols, such as Qt and Motif.

Hint

Though developed in ANSI C, there are wrappers available in other languages for the GNOME and GTK+ libraries. There are wrappers for most languages, including Ada, Scheme, Python, Perl, Dylan, Objective-C, and C++, of course.

Note

GNOME applications make use of GNOME, GTK+ Toolkit, GGTK Drawing Kit, and GNU libraries. For detailed descriptions of the functions, definitions, and structures contained in these libraries, it is strongly recommended that you use the extensive documentation available on the GNOME developer's Web site at **developer.gnome.org**. The Documentation section includes detailed tutorials, manuals, and reference works, including the complete reference for the GNOME, GTK, and GDK APIs.

Programs written to work on GNOME are essentially C programs that contain GNOME and GTK+ functions. The GNOME and GTK+ functions handle the GNOME desktop operations for a program. When programming for GNOME, you will make use of a very extensive set of functions and structures contained in many libraries—these functions and structures make up the different components that go into a GNOME application.

This module can provide only a general overview of these libraries and of how you use them to create GNOME programs. Though GNOME is not as easy to use as Tk, programming in GNOME requires the use of only a few basic functions to create simple user interfaces. You can think of GTK+ functions as lower level operations and GNOME functions as easy-to-use higher level operations. The GNOME functions usually incorporate several GTK+ functions, making GUI tasks relatively easy to program. A GNOME program is essentially a C program with GTK+ functions as well as GNOME functions. Because several basic GNOME operations are handled by GTK+ functions, this module begins by discussing basic GTK+ programming, and then discusses GNOME programs.

The GNOME libraries provide the highest level functions used in GNOME applications. Below them are the GTK+ libraries. GTK+ is the toolkit developed for the GNU Image Manipulation Program (GIMP).

9

GTK+ is made up of the GIMP Toolkit (GTK) and GIMP Drawing Kit (GDK) libraries.

GTK contains the functions and structures for managing widgets and user interface tasks. These functions and structures can be accessed directly in any GNOME program. In fact, a GNOME application is a GTK program with GNOME library functions. GTK functions and structures are C++ program objects, both designed to be used in a C++-style program.

GDK contains lower level functions that are used to connect GTK to the Xlib libraries. The Xlib libraries hold functions that perform the actual X Window System operations. Both GTK and GNOME also make use of the standard C functions provided by the Glib library. Table 9-1 lists the different GNOME components.

GNOME applications also make use of ORBit and Imlib (Image Library). With ORBit, programs can locate and request services from an object, even one located across a network. For example, an editor could request the use of a spreadsheet. Imlib contains functions for managing images in various formats, letting you display, scale, save, and load images into your program.

1-Minute Drill

● **What is the widget set that GNOME uses?**
● **What does GNOME stand for?**

GNOME Component	Description
GNOME libraries	Contain high-level GNOME functions
GTK (GIMP Tool Kit)	Contains widgets and GUI functions
GDK (GIMP Drawing Kit)	Provides a low-level wrapper for Xlib
Xlib	Provides X Windows operations
Glib	Contains the GNU C library of standard functions

Table 9-1 GNOME Components

● **GTK+**
● **GNU Network Object Model Environment**

GNOME Libraries

The GNOME libraries make it possible for GNOME applications to have the same kind of GUI interface with the same look and feel. Though a GNOME application is a GTK program with GNOME library functions, the GNOME library provides several complex higher level widgets, as well as many simple operations not included in the GTK+ libraries. Table 9-2 lists the GNOME libraries.

libgnome and libgnomeui are the two main libraries needed for any GNOME applications. libgnome is a set of functions designed to be independent of any particular GUI toolkit. These functions could be used in any kind of program, whether it be one with just a command line interface or even no interface. These functions are independent of any particular GUI toolkit. The libgnomeui library contains functions that provide GUI interface operations. These are tied to a particular GUI toolset, such as the GTK. It is possible to create a libgnomegui library that is tied to a different GUI toolset.

Library	Description
libaudiofile	Reads a wide variety of audio file formats (AIFF, AIFC, WAV, and NeXT/Sun).
libgdk_imlib	Includes functions to load multiple file formats (JPEG, GIF, TIFF, PNG, XPM, PPM, PGM, PBM, and BMP).
libgtk	This is the GTL Toolkit library. GNOME applications are written entirely using libgtk for all GUI elements (buttons, menus, scrollbars, and so on).
libgnome	Includes utility routines for the GNOME desktop environment, such as routines for configuration, help, managing mime types, and managing sessions. This library is independent of any GUI toolkit.
libgnomeui	Includes toolkit extensions to the GTK+ widget set for creating dialog boxes and message boxes, menu bars, toolbars, status lines, and so on. It also includes icons for use in dialog boxes, menu entries, and buttons; and it provides the GNOME canvas for the easy creation of complex interfaces, such as address books, calendar applications, and spreadsheets. This is a toolkit-dependent library currently using the GTK+ Toolkit.
libgnorba	A library for using the ORBit CORBA implementation with GNOME.
libzvt	A library containing a terminal widget.
libart_lgpl	Contains graphic functions used for GnomeCanvas.

Table 9-2   **GNOME Libraries**

9

The libgnome library provides many utility routines related to the GNOME desktop environment. Among the capabilities provided are config file support for applications to store persistent data, support for metadata (data attached to file objects, like the icon that will display for a particular file type), and support for loading help documents into the GNOME help browser. An interface is also provided so GNOME applications can talk to the GNOME session manager. Finally, there are routines to configure how different mime types are handled by GNOME and the GNOME file manager. Some of these functions are listed in Table 9–3.

The libgnomeui library contains the functions and structures you need to create GNOME user interfaces for your applications, and these functions are tied to the GTK+ toolkit. This library contains toolkit extensions to the GTK+ widget set, and programmers can easily create dialog boxes and message boxes, as well as menu bars, toolbars, and status lines. An extensive array of stock icons is provided for programmers to use in dialog boxes, menu entries, and buttons; and because all GNOME applications will use libgnomeui to create these common GUI elements, visual consistency is guaranteed. Similar in many ways to the Tk canvas, the GNOME canvas

GNOME Library Function Categories	Description
gnome-config	Provides simple access to configuration values
gnome-defs	Contains GNOME definitions for C++ linking
gnome-exec	Permits execution of programs from GNOME applications
gnome-help	Contains routines for displaying help
gnome-history	Keeps track of recently used documents
gnome-i18n	Provides support for localization and internationalization
gnome-mime-info	Contains routines to get information bound to a MIME type
gnome-paper	Contains paper dimensions and printing unit conversions
gnome-popt	Contains the command line argument parser
gnome-regex	Contains the regular expression cache implementation
gnome-sound	Includes sound-playing routines for GNOME applications
gnome-triggers	Contains a hierarchical signal mechanism for application events
gnome-url	Permits launching viewers for documents based on their URLs
gnome_lib	Initializes libgnome library

Table 9-3   GNOME Library (libgnome)

provides a framework for creating address books, calendar applications, and spreadsheets. The various kinds of functions you can find in this library are listed in Table 9-4.

GUI applications require extensive use of images to create a friendly and comfortable user interface. Traditionally, it has been difficult to load all of the common graphic file formats into X11 applications. The libgdk_imlib library addresses this issue by providing convenient and powerful functions to load multiple file formats (JPEG, GIF, TIFF, PNG, XPM, PPM, PGM, PBM, and BMP). These files are converted to an internal 24-bit RGB representation, and utility functions exist to scale as well as render from 24-bit RGB to a variety of other color depths (with dithering if desired). Input image files are cached internally by libgdk_imlib to improve performance in applications that repeatedly use images.

User Interface Function Categories	Description
gnome-app-helper	Enables simplified menu and toolbar creation
gnome-app-util	Includes utility functions for manipulating GnomeApp container widgets
gnome-canvas-util	Includes auxiliary canvas functions
gnome-dialog-util	Provides convenience functions for making dialog boxes
gnome-dns	Provides a nonblocking name-resolver interface
gnome-geometry	Includes window geometry utility functions
gnome-icon-text	Includes text-wrapping functions for icon captions
gnome-init	Initializes GNOME libraries
gnome-mdi-session	Includes routines providing GnomeMDI state saving and restoration
gnome-popup-help	Contains a popup help system for GtkWidgets
gnome-popup-menu	Includes routines for attaching popup menus to widgets
gnome-preferences	Contains routines for fetching and setting GNOME preferences
gnome-startup	Includes internal routines for session management
gnome-types	Contains some global types used by the GNOME libraries
gnome-winhints	Contains routines for manipulating GNOME-specific window manager hints
gtkcauldron	Produces gtk/GNOME dialog boxes from format strings

9

Table 9-4   **GNOME User Interface Library (libgnomeui)**

The libgtk library is the GTK Toolkit library. It is a professional-quality widget set that in many ways is superior to other widget sets. GNOME applications are written entirely using libgtk for all GUI elements (buttons, menus, scrollbars, and so on). The libgnorba library provides support for CORBA operations, such as obtaining references to objects and requesting new instances of objects. libzvt is a simple library containing a terminal widget. libart_lgpl holds graphic functions that can be used with the GnomeCanvas widget.

1-Minute Drill

● **Does GNOME have its own window manager?**

● **What two libraries are needed for any GNOME application?**

GTK+

GTK+ consists of an extensive set of functions for widgets of various types, such as menus, buttons, and windows. It also supports bindings that associate GUI events, such as mouse clicks, with objects, such as buttons. Check the online documentation for the GTK API at the **www.gtk.org** and **developer.gnome.org** Web sites. The documentation includes a comprehensive listing of all GTK functions, as well as a detailed tutorial on GTK programming. It is highly recommended that you make use of this documentation—due to size constraints, this book can present only brief introductions and list several of the common GTK functions. Also check the GTK header files for a detailed declaration of different functions and structures, including their arguments and return values.

Several basic functions and components are needed in any GTK program. You first need to include at least the *gtk.h* header file. Other GTK header files may be required, depending on the widgets and functions you are using. You then have to define pointers to the widgets you intend to define and use. Then you have to initialize the GTK library with the **gtk_init** function. Once that's done, you can define your widgets using GTK functions and assign their addresses to the pointers defined earlier. Then, you can use GTK functions to specify actions and attributes for the widgets, such as displaying them. For example, a close box event (**delete_event**) is connected to the window and

● No
● libgnome and libgnomeui

the **gtk_main_quit** function so that when a user clicks the Close box of the window, the program ends. Finally, you use the **gtk_main** function to run the widgets.

The following *base.c* program defines a simple GTK program that displays a simple window:

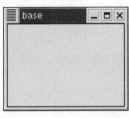

```
#include <gtk/gtk.h>
int main( int   argc, char *argv[] )
    {
        GtkWidget *window1;

        gtk_init (&argc, &argv);

        window1 = gtk_window_new (GTK_WINDOW_TOPLEVEL);

        gtk_signal_connect (GTK_OBJECT (window1), "delete_event",
                        GTK_SIGNAL_FUNC (gtk_main_quit), NULL);

        gtk_widget_show  (window1);

        gtk_main ();

        return(0);
    }
```

9

The *gtk.h* header file includes GTK variable, macro, and function definitions. **window1** is defined as a pointer to a structure named **GtkWidget**. The actual structure pointed to will later be determined by the function used to create a given structure. The **gtk_init** function creates initial settings, such as the default visual and color map, and it then calls the **gdk_init** function to initialize the GTK library and check for GTK arguments. The **gtk_window_new** function creates a new window structure, returning its address, which is then assigned to the window pointer. Window is now pointing to the GTK window structure. The GTK_WINDOW_TOP_LEVEL argument will place the window under the control of the window manager, using the window manager's defaults for displaying a window. The **gtk_widget_show** function then displays the window—notice that the window pointer is used as the argument to this function. Finally, the **gtk_main** function starts the interactive process, waiting for events to occur, such as button selections and mouse clicks.

You compile a GTK+ program using the gcc compiler and the GTK+ libraries. To specify the GTK+ libraries on the command line, you use the **gtk-config** command. This command determines the compiler options needed to compile a GTK+ program.

```
`gtk-config --cflags --libs`
```

gtk-config is a program that needs to be executed on the command line. To do this, you surround it and its arguments with back quotes. Back quotes are shell operators that are used to execute an enclosed command on the command line and place its returned values in the same place on that line. You can think of this operation as functioning somewhat like a macro, substituting returned values for the command executed. In this case, the **gtk-config** command with the **cflags** and **libs** arguments will place the compiler GTK flags and libraries you need on the command line for the **gcc** command. The **gcc** command is then executed with those flags and libraries.

```
gcc hello.c -o hello `gtk-config --cflags --libs`
```

The libraries usually used are listed in Table 9-5.

The program language types used in GTK+ programming can be categorized into fundamental, built-in, and object types. The fundamental types are basic types, such as standard C program types and the base class types for GTK+, like **GTK_TYPE_OBJECT**. The fundamental types

Library	Description
GTK (–lgtk)	GTK widget library
GDK (–lgdk)	Xlib wrapper
gmodule (–lgmodule)	Runtime extensions
Glib (–lglib)	GTK is built on top of Glib and always requires it
Xlib (–lX11)	Used by GDK
Xext (–lXext)	Shared memory pixmaps and other X extensions
math (–lm)	Math library

Table 9-5   Commonly Used GTK Libraries

are automatically defined by **gtk_init**. The built-in types include some basic enumerations, flags, and structures like **GdkWindow**—these are types that GTK+ need not understand to use. Object types consist of registered **GtkObject** types.

Signal and Events

GNOME programming works like other GUI programming—it is event oriented. In event-driven programs, you first define the objects that the user can operate on, and then you start the interaction function that continually check for certain events, such as mouse clicks and menu selections. When such an event is detected, it is passed to its appropriate function for handling. For example, if a user clicks an OK button, the mouse click is detected and control is passed to a function set up to handle a click on an OK button. When the function has finished, it returns control back to the interaction program.

GTK adds a further level of sophistication. When events occur on a certain widget, the widget will emit a signal that is then used to execute a function associated with both that signal and that object. For example, when you click a Close button, the Close button widget detects the mouse-click event and emits a "clicked" signal. The signal is detected and its associated function is executed.

You can also, if you wish, associate an event directly with a function. For this to work, the programmer has to connect a signal on a given object with a particular function. Functions associated with a particular signal are commonly referred to as "handlers" or "callbacks." When a signal is emitted, its handlers or callbacks are invoked. This process is referred to as "emission." Note that the signals referred to here are in no way like the signals used in UNIX systems.

To associate a particular event with the function you want executed for a given signal, you use either the **gtk_signal_connect** or the **gtk_signal_connect_object** function. When the signal is detected, its associated function is automatically executed. The **gtk_signal_connect** function is used for calling functions to which you may be passing arguments, and either **gtk_signal_connect** or **gtk_signal_connect_object** is used for calling functions that require no arguments. In the following **gtk_signal_connect** syntax statement, the **object** is the **GtkObject** you defined, such as a button. The **name** is the name of the signal, such as a

9

mouse click; **func** is the function you want executed whenever an event for this object occurs; and **func_data** are any arguments being passed to that function.

```
gint gtk_signal_connect( GtkObject  *object, gchar *name,
              GtkSignalFunc  func, gpointer   func_data );
```

When a signal is detected for the specified object, its associated callback function is called and executed, as shown in this syntax statement:

```
void callback_func( GtkWidget *widget, gpointer   callback_data );
```

Therefore, to associate a click on a button with the **hello** function, you would use the following **gtk_signal_connect** statement:

```
gtk_signal_connect (GTK_OBJECT (mybutton), "clicked",
              GTK_SIGNAL_FUNC (hello), NULL);
```

The object is **mybutton**, **clicked** is the click signal, and **hello** is a function the programmer wrote to be executed when this signal is detected. **GTK_OBJECT** and **GTK_SIGNAL_FUNC** are macros that perform type checking and casting to make sure the objects are passed with the appropriate types.

Certain objects have signals that can be associated with them. For example, the button object can be associated with a **clicked** signal or an **enter** signal. The **clicked** signal occurs when a user presses down and then releases the mouse button, whereas an **enter** signal occurs when the user moves the mouse pointer over the button object. The button signals are the following:

- **pressed**   Mouse button is pressed down when pointer is positioned on the button.

- **released**   Mouse button is released when pointer is positioned on the button.

- **clicked**   Mouse button is pressed down and released when pointer is positioned on the button.

- **enter**   Mouse pointer is moved onto the button.

- **leave**   Mouse pointer is moved off the button.

Ask the Expert

Question: Can I associate more than one callback function with an object and its signal?

Answer: Yes, you can associate as many callback functions with a particular object and a specific signal as you wish. They will be executed sequentially when the signal occurs.

Question: Once a callback function is associated with an object, can I disassociate it later?

Answer: You can, but you need to reference the tag for that function. The return value of the **gtk_signal_connect** function is an identifying tag for that function. Save this value to a variable of type **gint**. If you want to later disassociate that function from the particular object and signal, use the **gtk_signal_disconnect** function with the identifying tag and object as arguments.

```
void gtk_signal_disconnect( GtkObject *object,
                            gint id );
```

In the following example, the **myfunc** function is associated with a mouse click on the **button1** object. Its identifying tag is saved in the **myfuncid** variable, which is used in the **gtk_signal_connect** function to disassociate **myfunc** from the mouse-click operation.

```
gint myfuncid;

myfuncid = gtk_signal_connect (GTK_OBJECT (button1),
           "clicked", GTK_SIGNAL_FUNC (myfunc), NULL);
gtk_signal_disconnect (GTK_OBJECT (button1), myfuncid);
```

Question: Can I disassociate all the functions that may be associated with an object, at once?

Answer: Yes, you can. The function **gtk_signal_handlers_destroy** will disassociate all such associated functions and signals from a particular object:

```
gtk_signal_handlers_destroy(GtkObject *object);
```

9

You can also use the signal connection functions to connect events directly to an object and function, instead of using signals. Events are messages transmitted by the X11 server to indicate occurrences like mouse clicks and menu selections. In the **gtk_signal_connect** function, you use the name of the event instead of the signal. Callback functions for events include an added argument for the event.

The type for this parameter can be **GdkEvent** or one of several other event types. These are listed in Table 9-6.

```
void callback_func( GtkWidget *widget, GdkEvent  *event,
                    gpointer   callback_data );
```

For example, to associate a **button_press_event** with an OK button, you would use **"button_press_event"** as the signal name. The following example associates a **button_press_event** event on a button with the **button_press_callback** function:

```
gtk_signal_connect( GTK_OBJECT(button), "button_press_event",
                    GTK_SIGNAL_FUNC(button_press_callback), NULL);
```

The callback function used for the signal connection—in this case, **button_press_callback**—would have the event type **GdkEventButton** for its event argument.

```
static gint button_press_callback( GtkWidget  *widget,
                    GdkEventButton *event, gpointer data );
```

The following example associates a click on a window Close box with the **close-win** function. The object is **mywindow**, **delete_event** is the Close-box event, and **close-win** is a function the programmer wrote with code to be executed when this event occurs. When a user clicks the window's Close box, the **close-win** function is called.

```
gtk_signal_connect (GTK_OBJECT (mywindow), "delete_event",
                    GTK_SIGNAL_FUNC (close-win), NULL);
```

Event Type	GtkWidget Signal
GDK_DELETE	"delete_event"
GDK_DESTROY	"destroy_event"
GDK_EXPOSE	"expose_event"
GDK_MOTION_NOTIFY	"motion_notify_event"
GDK_BUTTON_PRESS	"button_press_event"
GDK_2BUTTON_PRESS	"button_press_event"
GDK_3BUTTON_PRESS	"button_press_event"
GDK_BUTTON_RELEASE	"button_release_event"
GDK_KEY_PRESS	"key_press_event"
GDK_KEY_RELEASE	"key_release_event"
GDK_ENTER_NOTIFY	"enter_notify_event"
GDK_LEAVE_NOTIFY	"leave_notify_event"
GDK_FOCUS_CHANGE	"focus_in_event", "focus_out_event"
GDK_CONFIGURE	"configure_event"
GDK_MAP	"map_event"
GDK_UNMAP	"unmap_event"
GDK_PROPERTY_NOTIFY	"property_notify_event"
GDK_SELECTION_CLEAR	"selection_clear_event"
GDK_SELECTION_REQUEST	"selection_request_event"
GDK_SELECTION_NOTIFY	"selection_notify_event"
GDK_PROXIMITY_IN	"proximity_in_event"
GDK_PROXIMITY_OUT	"proximity_out_event"
GDK_CLIENT_EVENT	"client_event"
GDK_VISIBILITY_NOTIFY	"visibility_notify_event"
GDK_NO_EXPOSE	"no_expose_event"

Table 9-6   GTK Events

9

Signals are stored in a global table. You can create your own signals with the **gtk_signal_new** function, and then use **gtk_signal_emit** to have an object emit a signal. **gtk_signal_new** will return an identifier for the new signal. You can use this with **gtk_signal_emit** to have your object emit that signal.

1-Minute Drill

- **What function do you use to connect objects with actions?**
- **What function do you use to disconnect objects from actions?**

GNOME Functions

GNOME programs build on GTK+ programs providing GNOME functions to let you more easily create GNOME interfaces that are consistent with the style for the GNOME desktop. To create a simple GTK program, you begin with GTK object definitions for your GNOME widgets and then use GNOME functions to initialize your program and define your widgets. GTK functions such as **gtk_signal_connect** are used to associate GUI events with objects, whereas GNOME functions such as **gnome_app_create_menus** create menus. In a GNOME program, you need to include an initialization function called **gnome_init**, which you place at the very beginning. To create a primary window for your application, you use **gnome_app_new**.

The following example shows the use of the **gnome_init** and the **gnome_app_new** functions. The **gnome_init** function takes as its arguments any initial arguments that the user must enter when the program starts, as well as an application ID and version number. The user's initial arguments are managed by the **argc** and **argv** special variables. **gnome_app_new** takes as its arguments the title you want displayed in the application window and the name of the application object. It returns the address of the new object, which, in this example, is assigned to the **app** pointer. **app** is a pointer to an object of type **GtkWidget**.

```
GtkWidget *app;

gnome_init ("", "0.1", argc, argv);
app = gnome_app_new ("Hello-World", "Hello App");
```

Other operations, such as displaying widgets and starting the interactive interface, are handled by GTK functions. **gtk_widget_show_all** will

---

- gtk_signal_connect
- gtk_signal_disconnect

display a widget and any other widgets it contains. **gtk_main** will start the interactive operations, detecting GUI events such as mouse clicks and key presses and executing their associated functions.

```
gtk_widget_show_all(app);
gtk_main ();
```

Compiling GNOME Programs

Given the extensive number of libraries involved in creating GNOME applications, the compiler command with all its listed libraries and flags can be very complex to construct. For this reason, GNOME provides the **gnome-config** script. You place a call to this script as an argument to the compiler operation instead of manually listing GNOME libraries and flags. **gnome-config** takes two options, **--cflags** and **--libs**. The **--cflags** option will generate all the flags you need, and the **--libs** option generates the list of necessary GNOME libraries. You do need to specify the libraries you want to use, such as gnomeui and gnome, as shown here:

```
gnome-config --cflags --libs gnome gnomeui
```

For the compiler operation, you would place the **gnome-config** operation in back quotes to execute it:

```
gcc myprog.c -o myprog `gnome-config --cflags --libs gnome gnomeui`
```

9

To simplify matters, you can place this operation in a Makefile. In a Makefile, the compiling is performed separately from the linking. For compiling, you would use a **gnome-config** script with the **--cflags** option, and for linking you would use the **--libs** option. In the following example, the **CFLAGS** and **LDFLAGS** macros are used to hold the compiling and linking results, respectively. Notice the use of back quotes in the code.

```
makefile
 CFLAGS=`gnome-config --cflags gnome gnomeui`
 LDFLAGS=`gnome-config --libs gnome gnomeui`

 all: bookrec

 bookrec: file.o calc.o
        cc $(LDFLAGS) main.o -o bookrec
```

```
main.o: main.c
     cc $(CFLAGS) main.c
file.o: file.c file.h
     cc $(CFLAGS) file.c
```

hello1.c

Project 9-1: GNOME Hello

The *hello1.c* program is a simple GNOME application in the "Hello World" tradition. The program creates a simple window with a button that displays a message on the standard output of your terminal window. When the user clicks the Close box (**delete_event**), the window closes.

GNOME functions begin with the term "gnome," whereas GTK functions begin with "gtk." Notice that the initialization function is a GNOME function, **gnome_init**. As explained earlier, GNOME programs are event driven: you first define your objects, such as windows, then set their attributes, and then bind signals from events such as mouse clicks to objects like windows and to functions that process these events. Such functions are often referred to as callback functions.

To compile this program, you can use the following compile command in a GNOME terminal window. Then, just enter **hello1** to run it. The **–o** option specifies the name of the program, in this case, *hello*. Be sure to use back quotes for the **gnome-config** segment. The following illustration shows the GNOME window and button.

```
gcc hello1.c -o hello1 `gnome-config --cflags --libs gnome gnomeui`
```

Step-by-Step

1. Define two callback functions: **hellomessage** and **closeprog**. **hellomessage** just outputs a simple text, "Hello World." **closeprog** invokes the **gtk_main_quit** function to end the program.

2. In the main function, define two **GtkWidget** pointers: **app** and **mybutton**. **app** should be a pointer to the main application window and **mybutton** to a simple button object.

3. Create a **gnome_init** function to initialize the GNOME interface.

4. Create a button object using the **gtk_button_new_with_label** function, and assign its address to the **mybutton** pointer, as shown in the following code line. The button will be displayed with the label "Click Me."

```
mybutton = gtk_button_new_with_label("Click Me");
```

5. Create an application window widget using the **gnome_app_new** function, and assign its address to the **app** pointer.

6. Use **gnome_app_set_contents** to place the button in the application window.

7. Use **gtk_signal_connect** to connect the application with a **delete_event** signal, which occurs when the user clicks the Close box. Set this to execute the **closeprog** function, which should use **gtk_main_quit** to end the program.

8. Use **gtk_signal_connect** to connect the button to the mouse click event (**clicked**), and set this to execute the **hello** function. Whenever the user clicks the button, "Hello World" should be displayed on the standard output.

9. Use the **gtk_widget_show_all** function to display the application window and the button it now contains.

10. Use **gtk_main** to start the interactive interface.

The contents of the *hello1.c* program are shown here:

```c
#include <gnome.h>

    void hellomessage( GtkWidget *widget, gpointer   data )
    {
        g_print ("Hello World\n");
    }

    gint closeprog ( GtkWidget *widget, GdkEvent  *event,
                                          gpointer   data )
    {
        gtk_main_quit();
    }
```

9

```
int main( int   argc, char *argv[] )
{
    GtkWidget *app;
    GtkWidget *mybutton;

    gnome_init ("", "0.1", argc, argv);

    mybutton = gtk_button_new_with_label("Click Me");
    app = gnome_app_new ("Hello-World", "Hello App");
    gnome_app_set_contents (GNOME_APP (app),  mybutton);
    gtk_signal_connect (GTK_OBJECT (app), "delete_event",
                        GTK_SIGNAL_FUNC (closeprog),NULL);

    gtk_signal_connect (GTK_OBJECT (mybutton), "clicked",
                  GTK_SIGNAL_FUNC (hellomessage), NULL);
    gtk_widget_show_all(app);
    gtk_main ();

    return(0);
}
```

GNOME App, Toolbar, and Menu Widgets

The **GnomeApp** widget is the basic widget for GNOME applications. This widget is the main window holding menus, toolbars, and data. You use the **gnome_app_new** function to create a new **GnomeApp** widget. This function takes as its argument the name of the application.

To add elements such as toolbars, menus, and status bars to the widget, you just use the appropriate function. For example, to add a menu, use **gnome_app_set_menus**, and to add a status bar use **gnome_app_set_statusbar**. To add just a single toolbar, use **gnome_app_set_toolbar**, and to add multiple toolbars use **gnome_app_add_toolbar**. A listing of GNOME widgets is provided in Table 9-7.

With the **gnome-app-helper** functions, you can generate menus and toolbars automatically using **GnomeUIInfo** structures. For toolbars and menus, you can create **GnomeUIInfo** structures for them with the appropriate values and then use **gnome_app_create_menus** to create menus and **gnome_app_create_toolbar** to create toolbars.

Widgets and Objects	Description
GnomeAbout	About box for an application
GnomeAnimator	Simple animations for GNOME applications
GnomeApp	Top-level GNOME container
GnomeAppBar	Statusbar/Progress/Minibuffer widget
GnomeCalculator	Calculator widget
GnomeCanvas	Generic engine for structured graphics
GnomeCanvasItem	Widget for creating and managing a canvas item
GnomeCanvasGroup	Functions and structures to bind a canvas item to a group
GnomeCanvasLine	Canvas line
GnomeCanvasPolygon	Canvas polygon
GnomeCanvasRE	Canvas rectangle and ellipse base class
GnomeCanvasRect	Canvas rectangle
GnomeCanvasEllipse	Canvas ellipse
GnomeCanvasText	Canvas text object
GnomeCanvasImage	Canvas image
GnomeCanvasWidget	Canvas widget
GnomeClient	Routines to provide session management support in your application
GnomeColorPicker	Widget for selecting colors
GnomeDateEdit	Date and time entry widget
GnomeDEntryEdit	Editing object for "dentries" (desktop files)
GnomeDialog	Transient (popup) dialog boxes
GnomeDockBand	Widget for implementing dock bands
GnomeDockItem	Dockable widget
GnomeDock	Widget supporting movable and detachable widgets
GnomeDruid	Main widget of the GNOME druid system
GnomeDruidPage	Virtual widget defining the druid page
GnomeDruidPageStart	A GnomeDruidPage for the beginning of a DRUID
GnomeDruidPageStandard	Standard GnomeDruidPage
GnomeDruidPageFinish	A GnomeDruidPage for the end of a DRUID
GnomeEntry	Entry widget with history tracking
GnomeFileEntry	Entry widget for file names

Table 9-7   GNOME Widgets and Objects

9

Widgets and Objects	Description
GnomeFontPicker	Button that displays the current font; click to select new font
GnomeGuru	Obsolete; use GnomeDruid instead
GnomeHRef	A link button
GnomeIconEntry	Selects an icon
GnomeIconTextItem	Canvas item for editable text captions in icon lists
GnomeIconList	List of icons with captions, with optional caption editing
GnomeIconSelection	Icon listing/chooser display
GnomeLess	Simple file content browser widget
GnomeMDIChild	Abstract multiple document interface child class
GnomeMDIGenericChild	Generic GnomeMDI child
GnomeMDI	GNOME multiple document interface
GnomeMessageBox	Message box display routines
GnomeNumberEntry	Entry line for number input
GnomePaperSelector	Paper selector
GnomePixmapEntry	Select large images
GnomePixmap	Displays and loads images (pixmaps)
GnomePropertyBox	Standardized dialog box for handling configuration
GnomeScores	Dialog box that displays high scores
GnomeStock	Default icons for toolbars, menus, and buttons
GtkClock	Text clock widget, capable of real-time, count-up, and count-down modes
GtkDial	Analog dial widget for number selection
GtkPixmapMenuItem	Special widget for GNOME menus
GnomeDockLayout	Widget for saving and retrieving the layout of a GnomeDock widget
GnomeProcBar	GNOME process bar

Table 9-7 GNOME Widgets and Objects *(continued)*

For simple menu entries, you can use one of many macros. Table 9-8 lists the GNOME menu macros.

With the GNOMEUIINFO_ITEM macro, you can add an item to a menu. The GNOMEUIINFO_SEPARATOR macro adds a separator line, and the GNOMEUIINFO_END macro specifies the end of a menu. In the following example, **label** is the text of the label, **tooltip** is the tooltip that will be displayed when the pointer moves over that item, and

File Menu Macros	Description
GNOMEUIINFO_MENU_NEW_ITEM(label, hint, cb, data)	"New" menu item (you need to provide label and hint yourself here)
GNOMEUIINFO_MENU_OPEN_ITEM(cb, data)	"Open" menu item
GNOMEUIINFO_MENU_SAVE_ITEM(cb, data)	"Save" menu item
GNOMEUIINFO_MENU_SAVE_AS_ITEM(cb, data)	"Save as" menu item
GNOMEUIINFO_MENU_PRINT_ITEM(cb, data)	"Print" menu item
GNOMEUIINFO_MENU_CLOSE_ITEM(cb, data)	"Close" menu item
GNOMEUIINFO_MENU_EXIT_ITEM(cb, data)	"Exit" menu item
Edit Menu Macros	
GNOMEUIINFO_MENU_CUT_ITEM(cb, data)	"Cut" menu item
GNOMEUIINFO_MENU_COPY_ITEM(cb, data)	"Copy" menu item
GNOMEUIINFO_MENU_PASTE_ITEM(cb, data)	"Paste" menu item
GNOMEUIINFO_MENU_SELECT_ALL_ITEM(cb, data)	"Select All" menu item
GNOMEUIINFO_MENU_CLEAR_ITEM(cb, data)	"Clear" menu item
GNOMEUIINFO_MENU_UNDO_ITEM(cb, data)	"Undo" menu item
GNOMEUIINFO_MENU_REDO_ITEM(cb, data)	"Redo" menu item
GNOMEUIINFO_MENU_FIND_ITEM(cb, data)	"Find" menu item
GNOMEUIINFO_MENU_FIND_AGAIN_ITEM(cb, data)	"Find Again" menu item
GNOMEUIINFO_MENU_REPLACE_ITEM(cb, data)	"Replace" menu item
GNOMEUIINFO_MENU_PROPERTIES_ITEM(cb, data)	"Properties" menu item
Settings Menu Macros	
GNOMEUIINFO_MENU_PREFERENCES_ITEM(cb, data)	"Preferences" menu item
Windows Menu Macros	
GNOMEUIINFO_MENU_NEW_WINDOW_ITEM(cb, data)	"New window" menu item
GNOMEUIINFO_MENU_CLOSE_WINDOW_ITEM(cb, data)	"Close window" menu item
Help Menu Macros	
GNOMEUIINFO_MENU_ABOUT_ITEM(cb, data)	"About" menu item
Menu Tree Macros	
GNOMEUIINFO_MENU_FILE_TREE (tree)	"File" menu
GNOMEUIINFO_MENU_EDIT_TREE (tree)	"Edit" menu
GNOMEUIINFO_MENU_VIEW_TREE (tree)	"View" menu
GNOMEUIINFO_MENU_SETTINGS_TREE (tree)	"Settings" menu
GNOMEUIINFO_MENU_FILES_TREE (tree)	"Files" menu
GNOMEUIINFO_MENU_WINDOWS_TREE (tree)	"Windows" menu
GNOMEUIINFO_MENU_HELP_TREE (tree)	"Help" menu
General Menu Macros	
GNOMEUIINFO_ITEM(label, tooltip, cb)	Adds a menu item with your own label
GNOMEUIINFO_SEPARATOR	Inserts a Menu separator line
GNOMEUIINFO_END	Specifies the end of the menu

9

Table 9-8   GNOME Menu Macros

callback is the function that is executed when the user clicks that item. You can add another argument for an icon image if you want an icon displayed in the menu item. This is usually an **.xpm** image.

```
GNOMEUIINFO_ITEM(label, tooltip, callback)
```

To specify an accelerator key for a particular item, you just place an underscore before the letter in the **label** for the key you want to use. An accelerator key is an alternative key you can use to access the menu item. This is usually an ALT key. In the following example, the menu item will have an Exit label with the "x" underlined, indicating that you can use an ALT-X key combination to access this item.

```
GNOMEUIINFO_ITEM("E_xit", "Exit the program", exitfunc)
```

The GNOMEUIINFO_ITEM macro generates the values to be used in a **GnomeUIInfo** structure. You can assign these values to such a structure. In the following example, a menu is created consisting of an array of **GnomeUIInfo** structures, and **GnomeUIInfo** macros are used to assign values to each **GnomeUIInfo** structure in this array. In this example, a simple File menu is created with two entries, one for Open and one for Exit. A line separator will be displayed between them.

```
GnomeUIInfo file_menu[] = {
        GNOMEUIINFO_ITEM("_Open", "Open a document", openfunc),
        GNOMEUIINFO_SEPARATOR,
        GNOMEUIINFO_ITEM("E_xit", "Exit the program", exitfunc),
        GNOMEUIINFO_END
        };
```

A number of macros are provided for standard menu items, like the Save and Open entries in a File menu. These take as their arguments the function to be executed when the item is selected (**cb**) and any icon image you want displayed for the entry (**data**). Here is the syntax for these macros:

```
GNOMEUIINFO_MENU_OPEN_ITEM(cb, data)
```

The following example creates the same simple File menu as in the previous example, but it uses specialized macros to create each item. Here, the GNOMEUIINFO_MENU_EXIT_ITEM macro creates the Exit entry for the menu:

```
GnomeUIInfo file_menu[] = {
        GNOMEUIINFO_MENU_OPEN_ITEM(openfunc),
        GNOMEUIINFO_SEPARATOR,
        GNOMEUIINFO_MENU_EXIT_ITEM(exitfunc),
        GNOMEUIINFO_END
        };
```

For submenus and for menus added to your menu bar, you use the **GNOMEUIINFO_SUBTREE(label, tree)** macro, where **tree** is the array of **GnomeUIInfo** structures to be used for that submenu.

The following example assigns the File menu defined earlier and an Edit menu to a menu bar. Again, these are **GnomeUIInfo** structures for which the macros generate values. Notice the use of underscores in the labels to designate ALT keys for accessing the menus.

```
GnomeUIInfo menubar[] = {
        GNOMEUIINFO_SUBTREE("_FILE", file_menu),
        GNOMEUIINFO_SUBTREE("_EDIT", edit_menu),
        GNOMEUIINFO_END
};
```

For particular menus on a menu bar, you use the menu tree macros, shown in Table 9-8. The **tree** argument is the array of **GnomeUIInfo** structures for the menu. For example, the File menu can be added to the menu bar with the following statement, where **tree** is the array of **GnomeUIInfo** structures for the File menu.

```
GNOMEUIINFO_MENU_FILE_TREE (tree)
```

The following example is a rewritten version of the menu bar assignment using specialized macros for the File and Edit menus:

```
GnomeUIInfo menubar[] = {
        GNOMEUIINFO_MENU_FILE_TREE(file_menu, NULL),
        GNOMEUIINFO_MENU_EDIT_TREE(edit_menu, NULL),
        GNOMEUIINFO_END
};
```

Once you have defined your menus, you can create them using the **gnome_app_create_menus** function. This takes as its arguments the GNOME application structure and the pointer to the **GnomeUIInfo**

9

structures you are using for your menu bar. In the previous example, this pointer was the array name **menubar**. Each of the elements making up the **menubar** array, in turn, references a **GnomeUIInfo** array for their menu.

```
gnome_app_create_menus (GNOME_APP (app), menubar);
```

mymenu.c

Project 9-2: File and Edit Menus

The program created in this project implements a GNOME application with two menus and a toolbar. File and Edit menus are implemented along with a toolbar featuring an Exit button, as shown in the following illustration.

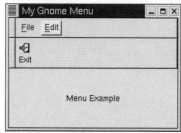

Step-by-Step

1. Define two callback functions: **copy_func** and **open_func**. In this program, they should just display a message; but in a complete program, they would perform file and copy operations.

2. Define a File menu with two items, one for Open and one for Exit. Make the File menu an array named **file_menu**. Use the **GNOMEUIIFO** macro to create the menu items, which will be elements of the **file_menu** array.

3. Define an Edit menu with one item for Copy. Make the Edit menu an array named **edit_menu**. Use the **GNOMEUIIFO** macro to create the menu item, which will be an element of the **edit_menu** array.

4. Define a menu bar with two menus, File and Edit. Make the menu bar an array named **menubar**. Use the **GNOMEUIINFO_MENU_**

FILE_TREE macro to add the menus to the menu bar, making them elements of the **menubar** array.

5. Create a toolbar with one button called **Exit**.

6. In the main function, create three pointers to widgets: **app**, **button**, and **label**.

7. Define the Application window with the **gnome_app_new** function and assign its address to the **app** pointer. Use a **gtk_signal_connect** function to bind a **delete_event** (close box click) on the Application window to the **gtk_main_quit** function to end the program.

8. Create a label with the **gtk_label_new** function, and assign its address to the **label** pointer. Place the label on the Application window with the **gnome_app_set_contents** function.

9. Use **gnome_app_create_menus** to place the menu bar and its menus (**menubar**) on the Application window (**app**).

10. Use **gnome_app_create_toolbar** to place the toolbar (**toolbar**) on the Application window (**app**).

11. Use **gtk_widget_show_all(app)** to display the Application window with its menus and toolbar.

12. In the **gtk_main** function, start an infinite loop that constantly checks for any of the bound signals (such as menu and toolbar selections) and executes their associated functions.

The contents of the *mymenu.c* program are shown here.

```
#include <gnome.h>
static void copy_func (GtkWidget *button, gpointer data)
        {
        g_print("Copy operation\n");
        }
static void open_func (GtkWidget *button, gpointer data)
        {
        g_print("Open operation\n");
        }
```

9

```
GnomeUIInfo file_menu[] = {
      GNOMEUIINFO_MENU_OPEN_ITEM(open_func,NULL),
      GNOMEUIINFO_MENU_EXIT_ITEM(gtk_main_quit,NULL),
      GNOMEUIINFO_END
      };

GnomeUIInfo edit_menu[] = {
      GNOMEUIINFO_MENU_COPY_ITEM(copy_func, NULL),
      GNOMEUIINFO_END
};

GnomeUIInfo menubar[] = {
      GNOMEUIINFO_MENU_FILE_TREE(file_menu),
      GNOMEUIINFO_MENU_EDIT_TREE(edit_menu),
      GNOMEUIINFO_END
};

GnomeUIInfo toolbar[] = {
      GNOMEUIINFO_ITEM_STOCK("Exit","Exit the application",
                  gtk_main_quit, GNOME_STOCK_PIXMAP_EXIT),
      GNOMEUIINFO_END
};

int
main(int argc, char *argv[])
{
      GtkWidget *app;
      GtkWidget *button;
      GtkWidget *label;

      gnome_init ("menu-sample", "0.1", argc, argv);
      /* Create a Gnome app widget */
      app = gnome_app_new ("Menu-App", "My Gnome Menu");
      gtk_signal_connect (GTK_OBJECT (app), "delete_event",
                  GTK_SIGNAL_FUNC (gtk_main_quit), NULL);

      label = gtk_label_new("Menu Example");
      gnome_app_set_contents (GNOME_APP (app), label);

      /*create the menus and toolbar */
      gnome_app_create_menus (GNOME_APP (app), menubar);
      gnome_app_create_toolbar (GNOME_APP (app), toolbar);

      gtk_widget_show_all(app);
      gtk_main ();
      return 0;
}
```

GNOME Icons

The libgnomeui library provides an extensive set of stock icons for use with menu items and toolbars. Table 9-9 lists some of the common stock icons. Stock buttons are also provided for such standard items as OK and

Toolbar Icons	Description
#define GNOME_STOCK_PIXMAP_NEW "New"	The New icon
#define GNOME_STOCK_PIXMAP_OPEN "Open"	The Open file icon
#define GNOME_STOCK_PIXMAP_CLOSE "Close"	The Close file icon
#define GNOME_STOCK_PIXMAP_SAVE "Save"	The Save file icon
#define GNOME_STOCK_PIXMAP_CUT "Cut"	The Cut edit operation icon
#define GNOME_STOCK_PIXMAP_COPY "Copy"	The Copy edit operation icon
#define GNOME_STOCK_PIXMAP_PASTE "Paste"	The Paste edit operation icon
#define GNOME_STOCK_PIXMAP_UNDO "Undo"	The Undo edit operation icon
#define GNOME_STOCK_PIXMAP_REDO "Redo"	The Redo edit operation icon
#define GNOME_STOCK_PIXMAP_PROPERTIES "Properties"	The Properties icon
#define GNOME_STOCK_PIXMAP_PREFERENCES "Preferences"	The Preferences icon
#define GNOME_STOCK_PIXMAP_HELP "Help"	The Help icon
#define GNOME_STOCK_PIXMAP_PRINT "Print"	The Print icon
#define GNOME_STOCK_PIXMAP_SEARCH "Search"	The Search icon
#define GNOME_STOCK_PIXMAP_BACK "Back"	The Back Browser button icon
#define GNOME_STOCK_PIXMAP_FORWARD "Forward"	The Forward Browser button icon
#define GNOME_STOCK_PIXMAP_FIRST "First"	The First Browser button icon
#define GNOME_STOCK_PIXMAP_LAST "Last"	The Last Browser button icon
#define GNOME_STOCK_PIXMAP_HOME "Home"	The Home Browser button icon
#define GNOME_STOCK_PIXMAP_STOP "Stop"	The Stop Browser button icon
#define GNOME_STOCK_PIXMAP_MAIL "Mail"	The Mail icon
#define GNOME_STOCK_PIXMAP_TRASH "Trash"	The Trash icon
#define GNOME_STOCK_PIXMAP_TRASH_FULL "Trash Full"	The Trash Full icon
#define GNOME_STOCK_PIXMAP_MIC "Microphone"	The Microphone icon
#define GNOME_STOCK_PIXMAP_CDROM "Cdrom"	The Cdrom icon
#define GNOME_STOCK_PIXMAP_ABOUT "About"	The About icon
#define GNOME_STOCK_PIXMAP_QUIT "Quit"	The Quit icon

9

Table 9-9   Stock Toolbar Icons, Menu Icons, and Buttons

Stock Menu Icons	Description
#define GNOME_STOCK_MENU_SAVE "Menu_Save"	A Menu Save Item icon
#define GNOME_STOCK_MENU_REVERT "Menu_Revert"	A Menu Revert Item icon
#define GNOME_STOCK_MENU_OPEN "Menu_Open"	A Menu Open Item icon
#define GNOME_STOCK_MENU_CLOSE "Menu_Close"	A Menu Close Item icon
#define GNOME_STOCK_MENU_QUIT "Menu_Quit"	A Menu Quit Item icon
#define GNOME_STOCK_MENU_CUT "Menu_Cut"	A Menu Cut item icon
#define GNOME_STOCK_MENU_COPY "Menu_Copy"	A Menu Copy Item icon
#define GNOME_STOCK_MENU_PASTE "Menu_Paste"	A Menu Paste Item icon
#define GNOME_STOCK_MENU_ABOUT "Menu_About"	A Menu About Item icon
#define GNOME_STOCK_MENU_PRINT "Menu_Print"	A Menu Print Item icon
#define GNOME_STOCK_BUTTON_HELP "Button_Help"	A Menu Help Item icon
#define GNOME_STOCK_BUTTON_UP "Button_Up"	A Button Up icon
#define GNOME_STOCK_BUTTON_DOWN "Button_Down"	A Button Down icon

Table 9-9 Stock Toolbar Icons, Menu Icons, and Buttons *(continued)*

Cancel buttons. In the previous program, a stock icon was used for the Exit button on the icon bar. The name of the stock Exit icon is **GNOME_STOCK_PIXMAP_EXIT**. For an entry in an icon bar, the **GNOMEUINFO_ITEM_STOCK** macro is used.

```
GNOMEUIINFO_ITEM_STOCK("Exit","Exit the App", gtk_main_quit,
                       GNOME_STOCK_PIXMAP_EXIT)
```

If you want to use a stock icon for something other than a **GnomeUIInfo** object, you need to generate a widget for it. For this, you use the **gnome_stock_pixmap_widget** function. **gnome_stock_pixmap_widget** takes as its arguments an address of a window and the name of an icon. You pass the address of the window widget and the string holding the name of the icon. The syntax for the function is shown here:

```
GtkWidget* gnome_stock_pixmap_widget (GtkWidget *window,const char *icon);
```

Hint

If you are manually creating menu items, you can use **gnome_stock_menu_item** to create a menu item with a specified icon. For stock buttons, you can use **gnome_stock_buttons**.

For a menu, you would use smaller icon stock items. These have the term **MENU** in them. You use them for the icon data argument in the menu and icon macros. For example, for the Copy entry in the Edit menu in the previous program, you could use the following, where **GNOME_ STOCK_MENU_COPY** is a smaller Copy icon for use in menus.

```
GNOMEUIINFO_MENU_COPY_ITEM(copy_func, GNOME_STOCK_MENU_COPY)
```

Dialog Boxes

With the GNOME dialog functions, you can easily create both modal and nonmodal dialog boxes. Though nonmodal dialog boxes tend to be more user friendly, modal dialog boxes are easier to program. To create a dialog box, you need to define a **GnomeDialog** widget using the **gnome_dialog_new** function. This function takes as its arguments the title of the dialog box and any buttons you want displayed on it. To use stock buttons, you can use any of the **GNOME_STOCK_BUTTON** definitions as arguments.

```
GtkWidget *mydialog;
mydialog = gnome_dialog_new("My Dialog", GNOME_STOCK_BUTTON_OK,
            GNOME_STOCK_BUTTON_APPLY, GNOME_STOCK_BUTTON_CLOSE, NULL);
```

9

For a simple modal dialog box, you use the **gnome_dialog_run_ and_close** function to execute the dialog box. A modal dialog box waits for a user to click a button or the window's Close box. It will return the number of the button selected (or −1 for a Close box).

If you have a dialog box where the user needs to click several buttons, you can use the **gnome_dialog_run** function. This function does not automatically close the dialog box at the first button click. Instead, it returns the number of the button click and remains displayed. You can use the returned value to execute any operations you have associated with that button, and then call **gnome_dialog_run** again to get the next button click.

An effective way to handle this is to place **gnome_dialog_run** in a loop and to exit the loop when the user clicks a Quit button or Close box. Then, use the **gnome_dialog_close** function to close the dialog box.

```
{
GtkWidget *mydialog;
 int drex;
 int dclose;
/*Create a new dialog, Be sure to include the NULL on the end*/
 mydialog = gnome_dialog_new("My Dialog",
                        GNOME_STOCK_BUTTON_OK,
                        GNOME_STOCK_BUTTON_APPLY,
                        GNOME_STOCK_BUTTON_CLOSE,
                        NULL);
/*add some content to the dialog here*/
dclose = 0;
  while (dclose != 1) {
        dres = gnome_dialog_run(GNOME_DIALOG(mydialog));
         switch(dres){
             case 0:              /* OK button */
             case 2:              /* Close button */
             case -1:             /* Close box */
                  dclose = 1;
                  break;
             case 1:              /* Apply button */
                g_print ("User pressed Apply");
                break
               }
     }
    /* close dialog */
   gnome_dialog_close(GNOME_DIALOG(dlg));
 }
```

For a nonmodal dialog box, you need to bind the click signal to the dialog box, and provide it with a function to manage the returned value for a clicked button. You use the **gtk_signal_connect** function to connect the clicking operation (**clicked**) with dialog buttons on your dialog box, and have the result passed to a function you define to manage the results.

```
gtk_signal_connect(GTK_OBJECT(mydialog),"
              "clicked",GTK_SIGNAL_FUNC(dialogres), NULL);
```

There are also several specialized dialog boxes, such as message boxes, property dialog boxes, and file dialog boxes. A **GnomeMessageBox** dialog box works the same way as a **GnomeDialog** dialog box. A message box is initially set up with a label and an icon determined by the message type. Table 9-10 lists the different message box types.

You create a message box using the **gnome_message_box_new** function. It takes as its first arguments the message text, then the type of message box, and then the buttons you want displayed on the message box, with the last argument being the NULL.

With the GnomePropertyBox dialog box, you can create notebook dialog boxes for different properties, options, or settings for an application. The notebook dialog box has pages with tabs you can click to display different kinds of properties. You create a property dialog box with the **gnome_property_box_new** function. This sets up a notebook and four buttons: OK, Apply, Close, and Help. OK and Apply will call the function you set up to manage the responses selected by the user, also known as the *apply handler*. OK will further close the dialog box. Close will simply close the dialog box, and Help will call the help function you set up for this dialog box. You can add pages to your property dialog box using the **gnome_property_box_append_page** function. This takes as its arguments the page number and the label. Each time the user makes a change on one of the dialog box's widgets, you use the **gnome_property_box_changed** function to mark the dialog box as changed. This enables the Apply and OK buttons to invoke the apply handler to enact the changes.

Message Boxes	Description
#define GNOME_MESSAGE_BOX_INFO "info"	Info box
#define GNOME_MESSAGE_BOX_WARNING "warning"	Warning box
#define GNOME_MESSAGE_BOX_ERROR "error"	Error box
#define GNOME_MESSAGE_BOX_QUESTION "question"	Question box
#define GNOME_MESSAGE_BOX_GENERIC "generic"	Generic message box

Table 9-10   Message Boxes

Entries

You use the **GnomeEntry** widgets for entering text, file names, images, icons, or numeric data. These widgets let you enter a line of information such as those used in forms. A box is displayed with a cursor inside, where you can type in your entry. To the left is a label for the box. This kind of widget is also known as a text box.

The **GnomeEntry** widget is used to hold text. First you create the **GnomeEntry** widget with the **gnome_entry_new** function, which takes as its argument an identifying string for this object. A **GnomeEntry** object holds a **GtkEntry** object that holds the actual text. To modify the text, you have to use a pointer directly to the **GtkEntry** text object. You can obtain this pointer using **gnome_entry_gtk_entry** functions. The following example creates a **GnomeEntry** widget using two pointers, **myentry** and **mytextentry**, to reference the widget itself and the text controls. First the **myentry** and **mytextentry** pointers are defined. Then the **gnome_entry_new** function creates a **GnomeEntry** widget and its address is assigned to **myentry**. Then the **gnome_entry_gtk_entry** function obtains the address of the element in the **myentry** widget that holds the text the user will enter. This address is assigned to the **mytextentry** pointer.

```
GtkWidget *myentry;
GtkWidget *mytextentry;
myentry = gnome_entry_new("text1");
mytextentry = gnome_entry_gtk_entry(GNOME_ENTRY(myentry));
```

The **GnomeFileEntry** widget works like the **GnomeEntry** widget, except that it also adds a Browse button and will accept file drops from the file manager. You create a **GnomeFileEntry** widget with the **gnome_file_entry_new** function. You use **gnome_file_entry_gtk_entry** to obtain a pointer to access the text used for the file name. To obtain the text of the file name, you can use **gnome_file_entry_get_full_path**.

GnomePixmapEntry is another text entry widget based on **GnomeFileEntry**. It displays a preview box for a selected image. You use **gnome_pixmap_entry_new** to create a new entry and **gnome_pixmap_entry_gtk_entry** to access its **GtkEntry** object. You can use **gnome_pixmap_entery_get_filename** to obtain the pixmap file name.

With the **GnomeIconEntry** widget you can select and display icons. It is based on the **GnomeFileEntry** widget and essentially adds a button that displays an icon. Clicking on the button displays a list of images from that icon's directory. Use **gnome_icon_entry_new** to create a new icon entry and **gnome_icon_entry_gtk_entry** to access its **GtkEntry** object. With **gnome_icon_entry_get_filename**, you can obtain the full name of the icon.

With the **GnomeNumberEntry** widget, you can enter double-precision numbers. **GnomeNumberEntry** consists of a **GnomeEntry** widget and a button that invokes a dialog box with a calculator. The user can use the calculator, and the result will be used to update the number entry. You use **gnome_number_entry_new** to create a number entry dialog box and **gnome_number_entry_gtk_entry** to access its **GtkEntry**. Use **gnome_number_entry_get_number** to obtain the value. For simple number entries, you would use the **GtkSpinButton** widget.

With the **GnomePixmap** widget, you can easily manage images. GNOME makes use of the Imlib image library. There are numerous **gnome_pixmap** functions available. These operate as higher level functions, allowing you to easily manage images without having to resort directly to the complexities of Imlib functions. With the **gnome_pixmap_ new_from_file** function, you can load an image and create a pixmap widget. The **gnome_pixmap_new_from_file_at_size** will perform the same operation, but will scale the image. The **gnome_pixmap_load** functions will perform operations on an existing pixmap widget.

9

GNOME Canvas

A canvas is a simple-to-use and very powerful graphic drawing widget. It contains support for Xlib graphics and anti-aliasing. You create a canvas widget with the **gnome_canvas_new** function. You need to make sure that the appropriate visual and color mapping is used. For this, you can use **gtk_widget_push_visual** and **gtk_widget_push_colormap**. If you want to enable anti-aliasing, you use the **gnome_canvas_new_aa** function to create the canvas widget. Anti-aliasing provides more display capabilities than the standard operations. The following example shows the creation of a canvas object for Imlib graphics.

```
GtkWidget *canvas;

gtk_widget_push_visual(gdk_imlib_get_visual());
 gtk_widget_push_colormap(gdk_imlib_get_colormap());
 canvas = gnome_canvas_new();
 gtk_widget_pop_visual();
 gtk_widget_pop_colormap();
```

Use the **gnome_canvas_set_pixels_per_unit** function to set the scale of the canvas, **gtk_widget_set_usize** to set the size of the widget, and **gnome_canvas_set_scroll_region** to set the region to scroll in.

To place objects on the canvas, you define **GnomeCanvasItem** objects and place them in groups. The default group is the root group, which you can access with the **gnome_canvas_root** function.

You create a canvas item with the **gnome_canvas_item** function. This function takes as its arguments the parent group for the object and the object type, followed by several attributes, such as location and color, with the last argument being a NULL. Different types of objects will have different sets of attributes. For example, the rectangle shown in the next example has two sets of x,y dimensions, shades, and color attributes.

```
GnomeCanvas *mycanvas;
GnomeCanvasItem *citem1;
citem1 = gnome_canvas_item_new(gnome_canvas_root(mycanvas),
        GNOME_TYPE_CANVAS_RECT,
        "x1", 1.0, "y1", 1.0, "x2", 23.0, "y2", 20.0,
        "fill_color", "blue", NULL);
```

To change any of these attributes, you use the **gnome_canvas_item_set** function. This function takes as its first argument the pointer to the canvas item, with the remaining arguments being the attributes just as they would be listed for **gnome_canvas_item_new**. Numerous functions are available for performing operations on objects, such as the **gnome_canvas_item_move** function that moves an object and the **gnome_convas_item_hide** function to hide it.

1-Minute Drill

● **What is an easy way to create menu entries for a menu?**
● **What functions do you use to create dialog boxes?**

Mastery Check

1. How do you invoke the GNOME libraries when compiling a GNOME program? How about GTK programs?

2. Can you associate more than one function with a particular object and signal?

3. What function would you use to connect a menu to a window?

4. Does GNOME provide operations for accessing different types of data?

9

● **Use the** GNOMEUIINFO_MENU **macros.**
● **The** gnome_dialog **functions.**

Module 10

KDE

The Goals of This Module

- Develop KDE user interfaces
- Compile KDE applications
- Learn to implement KDE graphical objects, such as windows and buttons
- Use the Qt libraries to manage basic operations
- Program object interaction using slots and signals
- Learn to manage objects such as menus, toolbars, and dialog boxes

347

KDE (K Desktop Environment) is organized on a C++ object model with C++ objects containing functions with which you can modify the object. Many of the functions are inherited from higher level KDE classes, while others are defined for a particular type of object. In a KDE program, you define an object and then use its public and private functions to modify it. For example, you can create a menu object and then use the menu object's functions to add new menu items to it. KDE uses the Qt toolkit, developed by Troll Tech (**www.trolltech.com**). This toolkit is actually used to display and manage GUI objects such as buttons and windows. The Qt toolkit operates much like the GTK+ toolkit in GNOME.

Because KDE applications are C++ object-oriented programs, they use a set of hierarchical object classes contained in the KDE and Qt libraries. Classes lower in the hierarchy will inherit members (functions) from predefined KDE classes higher in the hierarchy, and you can create your own classes and have them inherit members. KDE uses the Qt Toolkit and currently relies on it directly. Unlike GNOME, which can have its lower level functions managed by any toolkit, KDE relies solely on the Qt Toolkit. Currently, KDE programming is essentially Qt programming.

KDE and Qt programming rely on an extensive set of classes, each of which usually has a significant number of member functions that manage objects of that class. There are far more than can be listed within the size limitations of this book. For a complete listing of the KDE user interface classes, consult the documentation provided on the KDE developer's site, **developer.kde.org**. This site includes detailed tutorials and complete reference materials for the KDE API as well as KOM (KDE Object Manager) documentation and Qt reference material. Each class is described in detail, and class type declarations, including their member function declarations and definitions, are given. In addition, consult the KDE and Qt header files. The **.h** files contain a complete listing of the KDE and Qt classes, along with detailed comments describing their member functions.

A widget, like a window or a button, is just an object. You can define a window object using a KDE or Qt window class or a button using a KDE or Qt button class. There are several kinds of classes that you can use, depending on the type of window or button you want. To create a complex widget, such as a window that contains other widgets (perhaps toolbars and menus), you would define the subwidgets as children of the main widget. When you define a toolbar, you specify a particular window object as its parent. A subwidget can, in turn, have its own subwidgets—its own children. For example, a menu bar can have a window as its parent and individual menus as its children.

When you declare a C++ object, you usually include arguments in addition to the class and object name. These arguments are passed to a special function called a *constructor* that is executed when the object is defined, which performs any needed setup or initialization operations for the object.

For widgets, one of these arguments is usually the address of its parent widget. For example, a toolbar will be defined with one of its arguments being the address of a window object that is its parent. If the widget is a top-level object with no parent, the argument is NULL. With a series of simple object definitions, you can easily create a complex widget.

KDE Libraries

A KDE program is simply a C++ program that uses objects whose classes are defined in the KDE and Qt libraries. You use the g++ compiler on your source code files as you would any other C++ program. g++ is the C++ form of the gcc C compiler. There are several KDE libraries, each with an extensive set of classes. Currently, there are two versions of these libraries: those for KDE release 1.1 and those for the more recent KDE 2.0. Most programs will need at least the kdecore and kdeui libraries. kdeui holds the KDE user interface classes for KDE widgets (see Table 10-1). The 2.0 release of KDE also includes the KOffice suite. To compile programs that take advantage of KOffice components, you use the KOM libraries.

10

Widget	Description
DialogBase	A base class that provides basic functionality needed by nearly all dialog boxes
KApplet	The KDE Panel Applet class
KAuthIcon	The base class from which different authorization icon widgets that actually do something should be derived
KButton	The class that provides active raise/lower buttons

Table 10-1   Common KDE 2.0 kdeui (User Interface)

Widget	Description
KButtonBox	A container widget for buttons
KColorButton	A pushbutton to display or allow user selection of a color
KContainerLayout	An alternative layout manager widget
KCursor	A Qt QCursor wrapper allowing "themed" cursors
KDatePicker	A widget for selecting dates
KDialog	A dialog box with extended modeless support
KFontChooser	A widget for interactive font selection
KGradientSelector	A gradient selector widget
KIconLoaderButton	A button that uses KIconLoaderDialog
KIconLoaderDialog	A dialog box for interactive selection of icons
KKeyButton	A pushbutton that looks like a keyboard key
KLed	A round LED widget
KLedLamp	A CDE-style LED lamp widget
KLineEdit	A KDE line-input widget
KLineEditDlg	A dialog box for users to enter a single line of text
KMenuBar	A floatable menu bar
KMessageBox	An easy MessageBox dialog box
KNumCheckButton	A different type of Check button
KPopupMenu	A pop-up menu with a title
KProgress	A progress-indicator widget
KRadioGroup	A class for a group of radio buttons in a toolbar
KRuler	A ruler widget
KSelector	A 1-D value selector with contents drawn by the derived class
KSeparator	A standard horizontal or vertical separator
KStatusBar	A KDE status bar widget
KStatusBarItem	An internal class for use in KStatusBar
KStatusBarLabel	An internal class for use in KStatusBar
KTMainWindow	A KDE top-level main window
KToolBar	A floatable toolbar with auto-resize
KToolBarButton	A toolbar button
KToolBarItem	A toolbar item
KToolBoxManager	A class for own window management
KTopLevelWidget	An old KDE top-level window
KUIActions	A unified user-interface action manager
QXEmbed	Embedded Qt

Table 10-1   Common KDE 2.0 kdeui (User Interface) *(continued)*

KDE Applications and Widgets

To create a KDE application, you simply create an object of type
KApplication in your program before you define any other KDE objects.
The class declaration for **KApplication** is contained in the *kapp.h* file.
The definition of a **KApplication** object takes as its arguments **argc**
and **argv**. These operate as they do in C programs, referencing any
command line arguments the user enters. The following example
defines an application object called **myapp**:

```
KApplication myapp( argc, argv );
```

Declarations for different kinds of KDE and Qt objects are located in
separate header files. Whenever you define an object of a particular type,
be sure to include the header file that has its class declaration. For example,
to create a main application window, you use **KTMainWindow** class,
and you need to include the *ktmainwindow.h* header file.

```
#include <ktmainwindow.h>
```

The header files are also extremely helpful as a reference source.
They list all the member functions for a particular class and include
detailed comments describing each function and its use. The header files
will be located in the KDE *include* directory. Currently for Red Hat, this
is the standard *include* directory, */usr/include*. On OpenLinux and other
distributions, it may be the special KDE directory, such as */opt/kde/include*.

To define a main window for your application, use the **KTMainWindow**
class. The following example defines a main window object called **mywin**.

```
KTMainWindow mywin;
```

If you create an application in which the main window is the primary
interface, and you want the application to close when that window closes,
you have to make it the main widget for the application. To do this, you
use the application object's **setMainWidget** function. The main widget
could be any widget you want. Be sure to pass the address of the widget.
You do this by preceding it with the address operator, the ampersand (**&**).

10

The following example sets the main widget to be the **mywin** window. The address of the **mywin** widget is passed: **&mywin**.

```
myapp.setMainWidget(&mywin);
```

Hint

If you are using a pointer to a widget, as in the program examples later in this module, you need only pass the pointer without using the address operator. A pointer already holds the address.

When you define a widget, you will also be defining any of its member functions contained in its class declaration. See the **developer.kde.org** documentation for a complete description of all KDE class declarations, including their member functions. Many of these member functions are designed to let you change the display features of a widget, such as its color or initial size. For example, to control the display size of the **KTMainWindow** widget, you use its **setGeometry** function, as shown here:

```
mywin.setGeometry(100,100,200,100);
```

You have to explicitly instruct KDE to show any widget that you want displayed. To do this, you use your widget's **show** member function. For example, to have the **mywin** window display, you execute its **show** function, as shown here:

```
mywin.show();
```

Once you have defined all your widgets and made any modifications, you can then run the application. You do this with the **KApplication** object's **exec** member function.

```
myapp.exec();
```

When the user closes the application, control returns to the main function, which can then terminate the program. Usually the return statement with the **exec** function will return any errors that **exec** may return.

```
Return myapp.exec();
```

The following program creates a simple KDE application that displays a window. Figure 10-1 shows the window displayed by this program.

```
#include <kapp.h>
#include <ktmainwindow.h>

int main( int argc, char **argv )
{
  KApplication myapp( argc, argv );  ◄─── Define myapp application
  KTMainWindow mywin;  ◄───
  mywin.setGeometry(100,100,200,100);

  myapp.setMainWidget(&mywin);  ◄─── Defines mywin window
  mywin.show();
  return myapp.exec();
}
```

1-Minute Drill

● **Are KDE programs written in C++?**

● **What class do you use to define the main window of an application?**

10

Figure 10-1 KDE Window

● Yes
● KDMainWindow

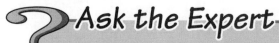

Ask the Expert

Question: How do I compile a KDE program?

Answer: You compile a KDE program just as you would compile any C++ program. Use the **g++** command and specify the KDE and Qt libraries to use.

Question: What if I receive an error that the compiler cannot find a header (.h) file?

Answer: This usually means that the compiler does not know where the KDE or Qt libraries are located on your system. You can use the **-I** option to specify a directory for header files and the **-L** option to specify the directory that contains libraries. For example, if your KDE header files are located in the */opt/kde/include* directory, you would use the following option:

```
-I/opt/kde/include
```

Question: Is there an easier way to specify the location of header files and libraries?

Answer: Yes, many systems will have set up the KDEDIR and QTDIR shell variables. KDEDIR would contain the path names for the KDE commands, headers, and libraries, and QTDIR would contain the path names for Qt. To specify the header files for KDE, you would use the following:

```
-I/$KDEDIR/include
```

Be sure to include the **$** before **KDEDIR**. If **KDEDIR** is not already defined, you can define it yourself, assigning the location (if you know it) of the KDE components:

```
KDEDIR = /opt/kde
```

On Red Hat Linux, the Qt libraries for 6.0 are placed in the */usr/lib/qt* directory, and KDE libraries are mixed with other libraries in the */usr/lib* directory. You will not have to specify a KDE library; and for Qt, you specify the */usr/lib/qt* directory. Caldera OpenLinux, along with other distributions, currently defines the KDE libraries to be in the */opt/kde* directory.

In the following example, both the KDE and Qt libraries are specified for the *myapp.cpp* KDE program.

```
g++ -I$KDEDIR/include -L$KDEDIR/lib -I$QTDIR/include -L$QTDIR/libs
            -lkdecore -lkdeui -lqt myapp.cpp
```

Question: How do I set these library and directory specifications in a makefile?

Answer: Remember that a makefile is set up to compile a program composed of several different source code files. Each file is compiled separately and then the compiled versions are combined by the Linker into an executable application file. For compiling the source code files, you would need to specify the header files, as shown here.

```
g++ -c -I$KDEDIR/include -I$QTDIR main.cpp
```

To create an application with the linker, you need to specify the KDE library's directory and the specific KDE libraries you want to use, along with the Qt library. In this example, the kdecore and kdeui libraries are used. These are the KDE core library and the KDE user interface library. Qt is the Qt library.

```
g++ -L$KDEDIR/lib -I$QTDIR/lib -lkdecore -lkdeui -lqt -o myapp main.o mydata.o
```

10

Signals and Slots

KDE and Qt use signals and slots to allow one widget to communicate with another. Signals and slots are member functions defined in a class that have special capabilities. *Signals* are emitted by an object when it is activated by some event occurring on it. For example, when a user clicks a button object, the button will emit a **clicked** signal. This signal can then be picked up by any other object set up to receive it. Such an object will have *slots* that are designated to receive the signal. A slot is just a member function that executes when the object receives a certain signal.

In effect, slots operate like event handlers, and signals can be thought of as events; but KDE and Qt do not operate like standard event–driven GUIs. Instead, the process of event handling is implemented as messages are sent and received by objects. Instead of focusing on the processing of an event when it occurs, objects manage their own event tasks as they occur, whether that be receiving or sending signals. A KDE widget emits a signal when an event occurs on it or when it changes state for some reason. There are several possible signals, among the more common of which are the **activated** and **clicked** signals. So, when an **activated** signal occurs on a menu item widget, the processing function will execute the corresponding function for that item. For example, given a window with a menu that has an Exit item, when a user clicks an Exit item in the File menu, a function to exit the program should be executed. The Exit item emits a signal that is then received by the main window object, which then executes the slot function associated with the Exit item.

The connection between the signal from an emitting object to a slot function in a receiving object is created with the object's **connect** function. The **connect** function sets up a connection between a certain signal in a given object with a specific slot function in another object. Its first argument is the object, the second is the signal, and the last is the callback function. To specify the signal, you use the **SIGNAL** macro on the signal name with its parameters. For the callback command function, you use the **SLOT** macro. Using **connect** operations, you can also connect a signal to several slots and connect several signals to just one slot. In the following example, the clicked signal on the **buttonhi** object is connected to the **myhello** slot function in the **mywin** object:

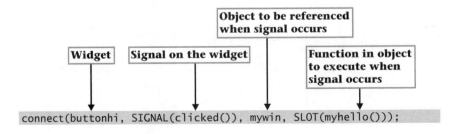

Classes composed of several widgets, such as an application window, will often have connections from signals from the different widgets to the main widget. Connect operations are usually placed with the class declaration of the main widget for connecting signals from its subwidgets to itself. In this case, the main widget (object) can then be referenced with the C++ **this** pointer reference, which always references the class being declared, as shown next.

```
connect(buttonhi, SIGNAL(clicked()), this, SLOT(myhello()));
```

Tip

Any class that includes slots or signals must also include a special reference named **Q_OBJECT**. This enables the Meta-Object Compiler preprocessor (described next) to set up any signals and slots declared in the class.

Meta-Object Compiler: MOC

Though the code for entering signal and slot functions, as well as that for making the connections, may appear straightforward to the programmer, it actually requires much more complex C++ coding. Signal and slot functions need to be preprocessed by the Meta-Object Compiler (MOC) to generate the C++ code that can implement the signal and slot message–connection process. You then include the output of MOC in your source code file for compiling. This means that you should place the class declarations for any classes that have signals and slots in separate header files. You can then preprocess these header files and include the output in the source code.

You cannot combine the member function definitions with the class declaration. To compile, the class declaration has to first be preprocessed by MOC before it can be combined correctly with the member function definitions. This necessitates placing the class declaration in a separate file from the member functions so that the class declaration can be separately preprocessed by MOC.

Table 10-2 lists the different MOC options.

10

Option	Description
–o *file*	Write output to *file* rather than to **STDOUT**.
–f	Force the generation of an **#include** statement in the output. This option is only useful if you have header files that do not follow the standard naming conventions.
–I	Do not generate an **#include** statement in the output. You should then **#include** the meta-object code in the **.cpp** file.
–nw	Do not generate any warnings.
–ldbg	Write **lex** debug information on **STDOUT**.
–dbg	Treat all nonsignal members as slots, for internal debugging purposes.
–p path	Makes the MOC prepend **path/** to the file name in the generated **#include** statement.
–q path	Makes the MOC prepend **path/** to the file name of Qt **#include** files in the generated code.

Table 10-2 MOC Options

To declare a class that contains either signals or slots, you would first declare the class in a header file like *myobj.h*. You do not place the definitions of any of the member functions in the header file, only the class declaration. Note that the class declaration will include declarations of the member functions, structures, and variables. In a separate source code file, you would place the definition of member functions, like *myobj.cpp*. A member function definition is the actual code for the function.

For these definitions to be correctly compiled, you have to include the MOC preprocessed version of its object declaration, not the actual declaration itself. To generate the preprocessed MOC versions, you use the class declaration header file and the **moc** command, like this:

```
moc myobj.h -o myobj.moc
```

In the particular source code files in which you are defining member functions for this object, you would include the MOC version of the header file that contains the object declaration, not the header file itself. So you would include *myobj.moc* in the *myobj.cpp* source code file, not *myobj.h*.

However, for any other source code files in which you are generating an object of that class, say with a **new** operation, you just include the header file, not the MOC file. So, for any source code file in which you only need the class declaration, you include the header file, such as *myobj.h*.

For example, suppose in the *main.cpp* file a **myobj** object is generated as a variable, whereas in a *myobj.cpp* file there are function definitions for member functions for the **myobj** class. Furthermore, suppose the class definition for **myobj** is in the *myobj.h* header file and the MOC version of *myobj.h* is in the *myobj.moc* file. In the *main.cpp* file, you would include the *myobj.h* file (not *myobj.moc*), but in the *myobj.cpp* file you would include the *myobj.moc* file (not *myobj.h*).

hellowin.cpp

Project 10-1: A KDE Window

hellowin.cpp is a simple program that displays a button in the main window and then displays a message box with "Hello World" when clicked. The **Hellowin** class will have two slots declared: **myhello** (to display the message) and **myexit** (to exit the program). The declaration should also include **Q_OBJECT**. Q_OBJECT is a special object used by KDE to connect to the Qt toolkit objects. The declaration for **Hellowin** will be placed in the *hellowin.h* header file, and all the member function definitions will be placed in the *hellowin.cpp* file.

To compile this program, you first need to preprocess the *hellowin.h* header file with MOC. Then, you can compile the *hellowin.cpp* file. Notice that this file should include the *hellowin.moc* file, not the *hellowin.h* file. The compile operations are shown here:

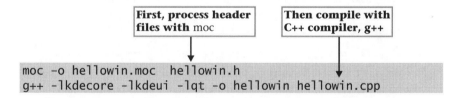

First, process header files with moc	Then compile with C++ compiler, g++

```
moc -o hellowin.moc  hellowin.h
g++ -lkdecore -lkdeui -lqt -o hellowin hellowin.cpp
```

Depending on your system, you may also need to specify the location of the KDE libraries and header files. These are usually held in a KDE directory specified in the **KDEDIR** system variable. Use the **–L** option with the */lib* directory to specify the libraries, and **–I** options with the */include* directory for header files, as in **–L$KDEDIR/lib** and **–I$KDEDIR/include**. If **KDEDIR** is not set, then check with your system administrator or with your Linux distribution manual for the location of the KDE libraries and header files. An example of the

10

compile operation specifying the location of the KDE **include** and **lib** directories is shown here:

```
g++ -L$KDEDIR/lib -I$KDEDIR/include -lkdecore -lkdeui -lqt -o hellowin hellowin.cpp
```

Note

A better way of organizing this would be to place the member function definitions in a separate source code file of their own, leaving the main function in its own source code file. In this case, you would include *hellowin.h* with the main function and *hellowin.moc* with the member function definitions.

The displaying of the "Hello World" message will be handled by a **KMsgBox** object. This class implements a simple dialog box with messages and several buttons, if you want them. In addition to a simple message dialog box, **KMsgBox** also supports dialog boxes with Yes and No buttons and Yes, No, and Cancel buttons. Be sure to include *kmsgbox.h*. For About dialog boxes you can use **KAboutDialog**.

Step-by-Step

1. Create the *hellowin.h* header file that will hold the class definition of the **Hellowin** class.

2. Include header files that contain class definitions for objects such as windows, buttons, and message boxes. In this case, include the header file for the main window, *ktmainwindow.h*; for a button, use *qpushbutton.h*; and for a message box, use *kmsgbox.h*.

3. Define the **Hellowin** class, derived from the **KTMainWindow** class. Give the **Hellowin** class two slots (functions) called **myhello** and **myexit**. Define two pointers to buttons: **buttonhi** and **buttonExit**.

4. The *myhello.cpp* file will hold the main program. Begin it by including header files and the *hellowin.moc* file, which needs to be separately generated by the MOC preprocessor.

5. Define a constructor function for the **Hellowin** class, **Hellowin::Hellowin**. When an object of that class is defined, this function is automatically executed.

6. Create a button object using **QPushButton**, and assign it to the **buttonhi** pointer. Set its size and then display it. It is connected to the **myhello** slot so that when it is clicked, the **myhello** function is executed.

7. Create another button object using **QPushButton**, and assign it to the **buttonExit** pointer. Set its size and then display it. Connect it to the **myexit** slot so that when it is clicked, the **myexit** function will be executed.

8. Define a **closeEvent** function for the **Hellowin** class. This function should simply end the program by invoking the **kapp->quit** function.

9. Define the **myhello** function for the **Hellowin** class. This should displays a separate message box with the message "Hello World."

10. Define the **myexit** function for the **Hellowin** class, and set it to close the **Hellowin** window.

11. In the main function, define a **KApplication** called **myapp**. Define a **Hellowin** object called **mywin**. Then set the size of the object.

12. Use the **setMainWidget** function for **myapp** to make the **mywin** object the main application window.

13. Use **mywin.show** to show that window.

14. Use **myapp.exec** to run the application.

The code for the *hellowin.h* file is shown next. Figure 10-2 shows both the main window with its Exit and Hello buttons and the hello window displayed by this program.

10

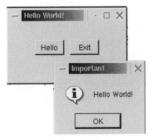

Figure 10-2   KDE windows and buttons

```
#include <kapp.h>
#include <ktmainwindow.h>
#include <qpushbutton.h>
#include <kmsgbox.h>

class Hellowin : public KTMainWindow
{
  Q_OBJECT
public:
  Hellowin ();
  void closeEvent(QCloseEvent *);
public slots:
  void myhello();
  void myexit();
private:
  QPushButton *buttonhi;
  QPushButton *buttonExit;
};
```

The following is the code for the *hellowin.cpp* file:

```
#include <kapp.h>
#include <ktmainwindow.h>
#include <qpushbutton.h>
#include "hellowin.moc"
#include <kmsgbox.h>

Hellowin::Hellowin () : KTMainWindow()
{
  buttonhi = new QPushButton("Hello", this);
  buttonhi->setGeometry(45,30,50,25);
  buttonhi->show();
  connect(buttonhi, SIGNAL(clicked()), this, SLOT(myhello()));

  buttonExit = new QPushButton("Exit", this);
  buttonExit->setGeometry(105,30,50,25);
  buttonExit->show();
  connect(buttonExit, SIGNAL(clicked()), this, SLOT(myexit()));
}

void Hellowin::closeEvent(QCloseEvent *)
{
  kapp->quit();
}
```

```
void Hellowin::myhello()
{
  KMsgBox::message(0,"Important","Hello World!");
}

void Hellowin::myexit()
{
  close();
}

int main( int argc, char **argv )
{
  KApplication myapp ( argc, argv, "Hello World!" );
  Hellowin mywin;
  mywin.setGeometry(100,100,200,100);

  myapp.setMainWidget( &mywin );
  mywin.show();
  return myapp.exec();
}
```

Menus

To create menus, you create a KDE menu bar and then add Qt menus
with their menu items to it. You will need to include the *qpopupmenu.h*
header file for the menus and the *kmenubar.h* header file for the menu bar,
as shown here:

```
#include <qpopupmenu.h>
#include <kmenubar.h>
```

You then define a menu bar object, or a pointer to one, and do the
same for your menus. The class for a menu bar is **KMenuBar**, and the
class for a menu is **QPopupMenu**. The following example defines
pointers to a menu bar and a menu:

> **Define a pointer to a**
> KMenuBar **type of object**

```
KMenuBar *mymenubar;
QPopupMenu *myfilemenu;
```

10

If you defined pointers, you can create the menu and menu bar objects with the **new** operation, as shown here. **KMenuBar** takes as its argument its parent. When defined in a class like a window, where you want the class itself to be the parent, you use the **this** pointer.

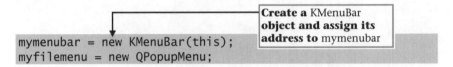

```
mymenubar = new KMenuBar(this);
myfilemenu = new QPopupMenu;
```

Create a KMenuBar **object and assign its address to** mymenubar

You can then add the menu to the menu bar with the menu bar's **insertItem** member function. The first argument is the label you want displayed on the menu bar for the menu, and the second argument is the address of the menu object. The following example adds **myfilemenu** to **mymenubar**:

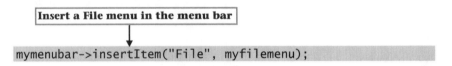

Insert a File menu in the menu bar

```
mymenubar->insertItem("File", myfilemenu);
```

Then, to add items to a particular menu, you use the menu object's **insertItem** member function. Its first argument is the label you want displayed for the item, and the next two arguments are references to a slot function to be executed when the item emits a signal. (This is the same as the slot arguments in the **connect** function.) The second argument for **insertItem** is the address of the object that holds the slot function, and the third argument is the slot function in that object to be executed.

The following example creates an Exit item in the **myfilemenu** menu and connects it to the **myexit** slot function in the current object (denoted by the **this** pointer):

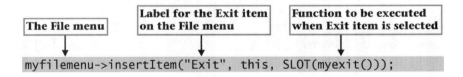

The File menu   Label for the Exit item on the File menu   Function to be executed when Exit item is selected

```
myfilemenu->insertItem("Exit", this, SLOT(myexit()));
```

Status and Toolbars

The KDE status bar widget is **KStatusBar**. To create a status bar, you create a **KStatusBar** object and assign its address to a pointer you want to use to reference the object. **KStatusBar** takes as its argument the address of its parent. In the following example, the parent is the class it is being defined in, which is referenced with the special **this** pointer (commonly used for subwidgets):

```
statusbar= new KStatusBar(this);
```

To set the text you want initially displayed on the status bar, you use the **KStatusBar** class's **insertItem** method. This takes as its first argument the text you want displayed and as a second argument an identifier. To change the status bar message, you use the **changeItem** function.

```
statusbar->insertItem("My hello program", 0);
statusbar->changeItem("My New Hello Program", 0);
```

To attach the status bar to the window object, you use the **KTMainWindow** class's **setStatusBar** function. This takes the address of the status bar object and an identifier as its arguments.

```
setStatusBar(statusbar, 0);
```

Then, to have the status bar displayed, you use the **show** function.

```
statusbar->show();
```

10

To create a toolbar, you define a **KToolBar** object, assigning its address to a pointer you want to use to reference the object. In this example, the user creates a toolbar object and assigns its address to **mytoolbar**:

```
mytoolbar = new KToolBar(this);
```

For a toolbar, you also need to manage the icons you want to use in it. To load icons, you use a **KIconLoader** object that you create with a **getIconLoader** method, as shown here:

```
KIconLoader *myloader = myapp->getIconLoader();
```

The **KIconLoader** object will load and cache the toolbar icons, searching for them in specified KDE icon directories. Be sure to include the *kiconloader.h* header file.

To add a button to the toolbar, you use the **insertButton** method. This takes as its first argument the icon you want to use for the button. For this argument, you have to first load the icon using the **KIconLoader** object's **loadIcon** method. This method takes as its argument the file name of the icon. The following example loads the file for the Exit icon:

```
loader->loadIcon("filenew.xpm")
```

The second argument is the command identifier, the third is a flag to indicate whether the button is enabled, and the last is the ToolTip text. The following example adds an Exit button to a toolbar with the hint "Exit program":

```
mytoolbar->insertButton(loader->loadIcon("exit.xpm"), 0, TRUE,
                                          "Exit Program");
```

Hint

It is helpful to allow for international support by wrapping the ToolTip text in the **klocale->translate** function, like this:

klocale->translate("Exit Program")

To connect an icon in the toolbar with an object's slot function, you use the toolbar object's **addConnection** function. This takes as its first argument the identifier of the icon on the toolbar. The identifier is the number you used as the second argument with the **insertButton** function when you added the icon to the toolbar. The remaining arguments are similar to those for the **connect** function: the signal, the object holding the slot function, and the slot function.

```
mytoolbar->addConnection(0, SIGNAL(clicked()),this, SLOT(myexit()));
```

Use an **insertButton** operation for each button you want to add. Once you have added your button, use the **KTMainWindow** object's **addToolBar** function to add the toolbar to the window. Then use the toolbar object's **setBarPos** function to position it and the **show** method to display it.

```
addToolBar(toolbar);
toolbar->setBarPos(KToolBar::Top);
toolbar->show();
```

1-Minute Drill

● **What function do you use to create an item in a menu?**

● **What is a slot?**

hellowin2.cpp

Project 10-2: KDE Menus and Toolbars

This project illustrates the use of complex widgets. *The hellowin2.cpp* program creates a window with a toolbar, menus, and a status bar. The toolbar will have two icons, one for exiting the program and one for displaying the "Hello World" message. The status bar will display a program description. And the menu bar will have a File menu with entries for displaying a "Hello World" dialog box and also for exiting the program.

Step-by-Step

1. Create the *hellowin.h* header file that will hold the class definition of the **Hellowin** class.

10

● insertItem.
● A member function in an object designed to execute when the object receives a specified signal.

2. Include header files containing class definitions for objects, such as windows, buttons, and message boxes. In this case, include the header file for the main window, *ktmainwindow.h*; for a button, use *qpushbutton.h*; and for a message box, use *kmsgbox.h*.

3. Define the **Hellowin** class, deriving it from the **KTMainWindow** class. The **Hellowin** class should have two slots (functions) called **myhello** and **myexit**. Define several pointers to KDE objects, including pointers to buttons (**buttonhi** and **buttonExit**), a pointer to a menu bar (**mymenubar**), a pointer to a menu (**filemenu**), a pointer to a toolbar (**mytoolbar**), and a pointer to a status bar (**mystatusbar**). The class also needs to contain a constructor function executed when it is defined (**Hellowin**) and a function for ending the program (**closeEvent**).

4. The *hellowin.cpp* file will hold the function definitions for the **Hellowin** class. Include header files and the *hellowin.moc* file, which needs to be separately generated by the MOC preprocessor.

5. Define a constructor function for the **Hellowin** class, **Hellowin::Hellowin**. When an object of that class is defined, this function will be automatically executed.

6. In the constructor function, create a toolbar object using the **KToolBar** class. Then make a pixmap image accessible for use in the toolbar. Create a **KIconLoader** object with a **myloader** pointer holding its address. Then use the **loadIcon** function in that object to load an image (*stamp.xpm*) into a **QPixmap** object called **hellopic**.

7. Create a button in the **mytoolbar** toolbar using the *stamp.xpm* image contained in **hellopic**. The text for the button should be "Hello window."

8. In the **mytoolbar** object's **addConnection** function, associate a mouse click (**clicked**) with the **Hellowin** class's **myhello** slot and the first toolbar button (*stamp.xpm*).

9. Another image, called *exit.xpm*, is then placed in the **exitpic** **QPixmap** object. Use this image to create another toolbar button labeled "Exit Program." The **addConnection** function associates with a **clicked** signal and the **myexit** function, which will exit the program.

10. Position the toolbar as a floating toolbar, and add it to the **Hellowin** object with the **addToolBar** function.

11. Define a status bar and assign its address to the **mystatusbar** pointer. Insert a simple message: "My hello program."

12. Create a menu object using **QPopupMenu**, and assign its address to the **filemenu** pointer. Insert two items, one labeled "Hello" and one "Exit." Set the "H" to be underlined in the Hello item, and the "x" to be underlined in the Exit item.

13. Create a menu bar called **mymenubar**. Insert the **filemenu** menu object in it, and label it "FILE."

14. Define the **closeEvent** function, which calls **kapp->quit** to end the program.

15. Define the **myhello** function for the **Hellowin** class, and set it to display a separate message box with the message "Hello World."

16. Define the **myexit** function for the **Hellowin** class, and set it to close the **Hellowin** window.

17. Create the **main.cpp** file, which will hold the main function for the program. Begin it by including header files and the **hellowin.moc** file, which needs to be separately generated by the MOC preprocessor.

18. In the main function, define a **KApplication** called **myapp**. Create a **Hellowin** object called **mywin**, invoking its **Hellowin** constructor function at the same time. Set the size of the object.

19. Use the **setMainWidget** function for **myapp** to make the **mywin** object the main application window.

20. Set *mywin.show* to shows that window.

21. Use *myapp.exec* to run the application.

Following is the code for the *hellowin2.h* file. Figure 10-3 shows the windows displayed by this program, including the menu bar with the File menu, the toolbar with Exit and Hello window buttons, and the status bar.

10

Figure 10-3 KDE menu, toolbar, and status bar

```
/************* hellowin2.h ******************/
#include <kapp.h>
#include <ktmainwindow.h>
#include <qpushbutton.h>
#include <kmenubar.h>
#include <ktoolbar.h>
#include <kstatusbar.h>
#include <qpopupmenu.h>

class Hellowin : public KTMainWindow
{
  Q_OBJECT
public:
  Hellowin();
  void closeEvent(QCloseEvent *);
public slots:
  void myhello();
  void myexit();
private:
  QPushButton *hellobutton;
  QPushButton *exitbutton;
  KMenuBar *mymenubar;
  QPopupMenu *filemenu;
  KToolBar *mytoolbar;
  KStatusBar *mystatusbar;
};
```

Here is the code for the *hellowin2.cpp* file.

```
/************* Hellowin.cpp ******************/
#include "hellowin2.moc"
#include <kmsgbox.h>
#include <kpixmap.h>
#include <kiconloader.h>


Hellowin::Hellowin() : KTMainWindow()
{

mytoolbar = new KToolBar(this);
KIconLoader *myloader = kapp->getIconLoader();

QPixmap hellopic = myloader->loadIcon \
    ("/opt/kde/share/toolbar/stamp.xpm", 0, 0);
mytoolbar->insertButton(hellopic,1, TRUE,"Hello window", 0);
mytoolbar->addConnection(1, SIGNAL(clicked()),this, SLOT(myhello()));

QPixmap exitpic = myloader->loadIcon("exit.xpm", 0, 0);
mytoolbar->insertButton(exitpic,0, TRUE,"Exit Program", 0);
mytoolbar->addConnection(0, SIGNAL(clicked()),this, SLOT(myexit()));

mytoolbar->setBarPos(KToolBar::Floating);
addToolBar(mytoolbar, 0);
mytoolbar->show();

mystatusbar = new KStatusBar(this);
mystatusbar->insertItem("My hello program", 0);
setStatusBar (mystatusbar);
mystatusbar->show();

filemenu = new QPopupMenu();
filemenu->insertItem("&Hello", this, SLOT(myhello()));
filemenu->insertItem("E&xit", this, SLOT(myexit()));

mymenubar = new KMenuBar(this);
mymenubar->insertItem("&FILE", filemenu);
}

void Hellowin::closeEvent(QCloseEvent *)
{
  kapp->quit();
}

void Hellowin::myhello()
{
  KMsgBox::message(0,"World Message","Hello World!");
```

10

```
}
void Hellowin::myexit()
{
  close();
}
```

And here is the code for the *main.c* file.

```
#include <kapp.h>
#include <ktmainwindow.h>
#include "hellowin2.h"

int main( int argc, char **argv )
{
    KApplication myapp( argc, argv, "Hello World!" );
  Hellowin *mywin = new Hellowin();
  mywin->setGeometry(100,100,200,100);
  myapp.setMainWidget( mywin );
  mywin->show();
  myapp.exec();
  return 0;
}
```

To compile the program, it is best to use a makefile, as shown next.

Note

Notice how the MOC file is created with an entry for the header files in the makefile.

```
Hellowin2: main.o hellowin2.o hellowin2.moc
    g++ -L$KDEDIR/lib -lkdecore -lkdeui -lqt
                    -o hellowin2 main.o hellowin2.o

hellowin2.o: hellowin2.cpp
    g++ -c -I/$KDEDIR/include -I/$QTDIR/include hellowin.cpp

main.o: main.cpp
    g++ -c -I/$KDEDIR/include -I/$QTDIR/include  main.cpp

hellowin2.moc: hellowin2.h
    moc hellowin2.h -o hellowin2.moc
```

Qt Programming

KDE currently relies directly on the Qt Toolkit. Using just Qt objects, you can create an interface with a look and feel similar to KDE. You can create a Qt application using just Qt objects and the Qt libraries. This section provides a basic introduction to Qt programming. Both the KDE development site at **developer.kde.org** and the Qt Web site at **www.trol.com** provide very detailed documentation and tutorials on Qt programming. It is strongly recommended that you consult these resources for a detailed presentation of Qt programming and API references.

Qt Applications

A Qt program is a C++ program. The Qt libraries provide extensive definitions of Qt classes with which you can define Qt objects in your Qt program. You can also use these classes to create your own classes, inheriting their parents' predefined capabilities. Table 10-3 lists the commonly used Qt widgets.

Widget	Description
QCheckBox	A check box with a text label
QComboBox	A combined button and popup list
QFrame	The base class of widgets that can have a frame
QLabel	A label that displays static text or a pixmap
QListBox	A list of selectable, read-only items
QListView	A list/tree view
QMainWindow	A typical application window, with a menu bar, some toolbars, and a status bar
QMenuBar	A horizontal menu bar
QPopupMenu	A popup menu widget
QProgressBar	A horizontal progress bar
QPushButton	A push button with a text or pixmap label

Table 10-3   Common Qt Widgets

10

Widget	Description
QRadioButton	A radio button with a text label
QScrollBar	A vertical or horizontal scrollbar
QSizeGrip	A corner grip for resizing a top-level window
QSlider	A vertical or horizontal slider
QStatusBar	A horizontal bar suitable for presenting status messages
QTextBrowser	A rich text browser with simple navigation
QTextView	A sophisticated single-page rich text viewer
QToolBar	A simple toolbar

Table 10-3   Common Qt Widgets *(continued)*

To create a Qt application, you have to define a **QApplication** object. Each application has to have at least one **QApplication** object. This **QApplication** object is used to manage application features such as the font and cursor. To include the **QApplication** class declaration in your program, you just need to include the *qapplication.h* file.

```
#include <qapplication.h>
```

You can then choose to include various objects in your application, such as windows, buttons, and menus. To define a particular object, you first declare its class; then, as you would traditionally declare a variable, you define an object of that class. In non–C++ terms, you can think of the *class* as the *type* and an *object* as a *variable* of that type.

Qt provides numerous class declarations, each placed in its own header file. To declare a class, you just have to include its header file. For example, to declare the **QPushButton** (a button), you include the *qpushbutton.h* file.

```
#include <qpushbutton.h>
```

Widgets, such as buttons, will automatically implement default features with which they can maintain their own look and feel. You can modify these features, changing aspects like the color or the text displayed.

When you define a widget object, you also have to provide as arguments the name you want to give to the object, and the widget's parent. If it is not part of another widget, then you can use NULL, 0, to indicate that it has no parent. The arguments are passed to a constructor function that will be executed to perform certain initialization operations on the widget. For example, the following definition of the **mybutton** button widget will display "Click Me" and indicate that it has no parent:

```
QPushButton mybutton( "Click Me", 0 );
```

A Qt program is essentially a C++ program, so you define your classes and any member functions, and then define the main function where the program starts. This is where you place the definition for your **QApplication** object. This definition has to occur before any other Qt widget (object) definitions. For the **QApplication** widget definition, you include the **(argv, argc)** arguments, which have the same functionality as in other C++ programs. Other widgets will take different sets of arguments.

The following example defines the **QApplication** widget called **myapp** and a button widget called **mybutton**.

```
          ┌────────────────────────────────┐
          │ Define a Qt application object  │
          │ and a Qt button widget          │
          └────────────────────────────────┘
QApplication myapp( argc, argv );
QPushButton mybutton( "Click Me", 0 );
```

To make a widget into the application's main widget, you use the **QApplication** object's **setMainWidget** member function. The main widget is the one that you will use to control closing the application. When you close the main widget, you close the application. The main widget is usually the application's main window, so that closing that window will close the application. The argument for this function is the address of the widget, which you can obtain with the **&** operator.

```
myapp.setMainWidget( &mybutton );
```

Once you have defined your widgets and changed any features, you then need to specify that the widget is to be displayed. You do this with

10

the widget's **show** member function. The following example will display the **mybutton** button:

```
mybutton.show();
```

When you have finished constructing your application and specifying the widgets to be displayed, you can then turn control over to Qt to manage the execution of the application with the **QApplication** widget's **exec** member function. This function runs the application and displays all the widgets. Qt will manage events, invoking the appropriate widget connected to them. When the user closes the application's main widget, control returns to the program. You can then end the program with a final **return** statement in the main function.

```
myapp.exec();
return 0;
```

The following program illustrates the basic structure of a Qt program.

```
#include <qapplication.h>
#include <qpushbutton.h>

int main( int argc, char **argv )
{
    QApplication myapp( argc, argv );
    QPushButton mybutton( "Click Me", 0 );
    mybutton.resize( 100, 30 );

    myapp.setMainWidget( &hello );
    mybutton.show();
    return myapp.exec();
}
```

Qt Signals and Slots

Traditionally, GUI toolkits use a type of event that activates callback functions. When an event occurs, its associated callback function is executed.

Qt replaces this approach with a system of signals and slots. The event activation process is reformulated as a message communication process between two objects. Since they are merely communicating messages, signals and slots can be made very robust. They can take a varying number of arguments of different types, and you can connect any number of signals to the same slot. Signals and slots can be used in any classes that inherit from the **QObject** class, such as **QWidget**. Any object can contain both signals to send messages and slots to receive messages.

When an event occurs on a widget, it will emit a signal. That is all it does. It does not set up a connection to another object. To be able to receive a message from a signal, an object must set up a slot. A slot is just a member function that is executed when the object receives a signal. Conceptually, slots are used to obtain information about a change in other objects. A slot does not know if there are actually any signals connected to it, and a signal does not know if there are any slots to receive it.

You use the **connect** function to set up a connection between a signal in one object and a slot in another. You can connect as many signals as you want to a single slot, and a signal can be connected to any number of slots. Each object can have signals to send messages and slots to receive messages. The **connect** functions will set up a connection between two objects, connecting a signal from one to a slot in another.

In the following example, the **clicked** signal for the **mybutton** object is connected to the **quit** slot of the **myapp** object:

```
QObject::connect( &mybutton, SIGNAL(clicked()), &myapp, SLOT(quit()) );
```

When an event occurs on an object, the **emit** operation uses the **signal** function to send out a message. When a signal is emitted by an object, any slots connected to it are immediately executed. Slots are simply member functions in a class that differ only in that they can be connected to a signal. They also can be called as regular functions. You make slots **protected**, **private**, or **public** and thereby control what objects can have their signals connect to them.

10

```
private signals:
    void mysignal();
private slots:
    void myslot1();
    void myslot2();
```

The signal and slot terms in a class definition will be replaced with code acceptable to the C++ compiler by the MOC preprocessor. Any source code files that contain classes with signal and slot definitions have to be preprocessed by the MOC. In addition, any class with slots and signals has to include the term **Q_OBJECT** in its class declaration—this is used by MOC. MOC also generates code that initializes the meta-object. The meta-object contains names of all signal and slot members, along with pointers to these functions.

Windows

To create an application window, you use the **QMainWindow** class. The following example creates a new application window and assigns its address to the **mw** pointer:

```
QMainWindow * mywin = new QMainWindow;
```

A **QMainWindow** widget includes several member functions for setting different features. With the **setCaption** member, you can set the window title.

```
mywin->setCaption( "My Document" );
```

To have your application close automatically when you close your last open window, you can connect the application widget's **lastWindowClosed** signal to its **quit** slot, as shown here.

```
myapp.connect( &myapp, SIGNAL(lastWindowClosed()), &myapp, SLOT(quit()) );
```

The following program shows the implementation of a Qt window:

```
#include <qapplication.h>
#include <qmainwindow.h>

int main( int argc, char **argv )
{
    QApplication myapp( argc, argv );
    QMainWindow mywin;
    mywin.setCaption( "Document 1" );
    myapp.connect( &myapp, SIGNAL(lastWindowClosed()), &myapp, SLOT(quit()) );
    myapp.setMainWidget( &mywin );
    mywin.show();
    return myapp.exec();
}
```

Parent-Child Objects

You construct a Qt interface using objects that you place in hierarchical structures, with lesser objects designated as dependent on a major object. For example, a window would be a major object that in turn would have lesser objects such as menus, toolbars, and slider bars dependent on it. The major object is the parent, and the lesser objects are its children. When you create a major widget like a window, you can also create lesser widget toolbars that you can then attach to the window. You do this by making the lesser widget, such as the toolbar, a child of the major widget (like the window). A child widget can, in turn, be a parent to its own child widgets. In constructing an interface, you place widgets in a hierarchical structure of parent widgets and their children.

To create a complex widget, such as a window with its dependent children, you first define the parent widget. Then, when you define a widget that you want to be a child of that parent, you place the address of the parent widget as an argument in the widget's definition.

The following example defines a button widget named **quit** and makes it a child of the window widget. The window widget now includes the button widget. Notice that the **&** operator is used to obtain the address of the parent widget.

```
QPushButton mybutton( "Quit", &mywin );
```

The window widget now includes the button widget. Notice that the **&** operator was used to obtain the address of the parent widget.

When you display the parent widget, all its child widgets are automatically displayed. In the following example, the **show** member function for the window widget will also "show" the **mybutton** button:

```
myapp.setMainWidget( &mywin );
mywin.show();
```

The following program shows a button as a child of a window. Figure 10-4 shows the window displayed by this program along with the Click Me button.

10

Figure 10-4 Qt window and button

```
#include <qapplication.h>
#include <qmainwindow.h>
#include <qpushbutton.h>
#include <qfont.h>

int main( int argc, char **argv )
{
    QApplication myapp( argc, argv );
    QMainWindow *mywin = new QMainWindow;
    QPushButton mybutton( "Click Me", mywin );

    mywin->setCaption( "My Document" );
    myapp.connect( &myapp, SIGNAL(lastWindowClosed()), &myapp, SLOT(quit()) );
    myapp.setMainWidget(mywin);
    mybutton.setFont( QFont( "Times", 14, QFont::Bold ) );

    mywin->show();
    return myapp.exec();
}
```

Layout Widgets

With layout widgets, you can easily position the child widgets (such as buttons or text) on a parent widget (such as a window). In addition to positioning, layout widgets provide default sizes, resizing, and updating of the widgets' display. There are several easy-to-use widgets available. **QHBox** positions widgets in a horizontal row, **QVBox** positions them vertically in a column, and **QGrid** positions them in a table. For more detailed control, you can use **QGridLayout**, **QHBoxLayout**, and **QVBoxLayout**.

1-Minute Drill

- **Can you create a user interface using just the Qt toolkit?**
- **In what kind of relationship are Qt widgets organized in a program?**

- **Yes**
- **Hierarchical parent-child**

Creating Your Own Widgets

Creating your own widgets is a simple matter of defining a Qt-compliant class and then creating an object of the class. Such a class has to be derived from a Qt base class, such as **QWidget**. You specify such a derivation by making the Qt the base class for your new class. In the following example, the user creates a **MyWidget** class, deriving it from the **QWidget** class. **Mywidget** will inherit member functions and variables from the **QWidget** class.

```
class MyWidget : public QWidget
{
};
```

You can declare whatever public and private members, including functions and variables, you may want for your class. The definitions of member functions are usually placed after the class definition.

A common member function found in most classes is the constructor. This function bears the same name as the class and is automatically invoked whenever an object of that class is defined. You can think of a constructor as a kind of initialization function that takes care of any initial setup tasks you want performed on a new object of this class. In the following example, a constructor function is declared in the **MyWidget** class.

```
class MyWidget : public QWidget
{
public:
    MyWidget( QWidget *parent=0, const char *name=0 );
};
```

In the constructor functions for your own Qt widgets, you need to include an argument for the address of the widget you want to be the parent. The default is NULL, 0. If the parent is NULL, it automatically becomes a top-level widget, rather than a child of another. The second argument is the name to be given to the particular widget of this class being created. Instead of writing the code to handle the parent and name, you can just pass them on to the **QWidget** constructor that is inherited by your class. To do this, you place the **QWidget** constructor with its

10

arguments in your class's constructor function, attaching it after the function arguments.

```
MyWidget::MyWidget( QWidget *parent, const char *name )
        : QWidget( parent, name )
```

In the constructor function, you would place the definitions for any child objects that you want to make up your widget. For example, if you are creating a window widget, you would write a constructor function for it in which you would define components like a menu, toolbars, or a status bar. You can set features for these widgets, such as size and color, and also set up any signal and slot connections for them as needed.

The following example is a constructor function definition for **mywidget**:

```
MyWidget::MyWidget( QWidget *parent, const char *name )
        : QWidget( parent, name )
{
    QPushButton *quit = new QPushButton( "Quit", this, "quit" );
    quit->setFont( QFont( "Times", 18, QFont::Bold ) );
    connect( quit, SIGNAL(clicked()), qApp, SLOT(quit()) );
}
```

Suppose you want to construct your own application window with menus and toolbars that you design. **QMainWindow** only provides a bare window. To create an application window with your own menus, toolbars, and other widgets, you would define a new window class of your own and have it inherit from the **QMainWindow** class. Your new window class will include the **QMainWindow** members as well as any new classes you define in it.

The following example creates a new window class called **MyAppWindow** that is based on the **QMainWindow** class:

```
#include <qmainwindow.h>

class QToolBar;
class QPopupMenu;

class MyAppWindow: public QMainWindow
{
```

```
    Q_OBJECT
public:
    MyAppWindow ();
    ~ MyAppWindow ();
protected:
    void closeEvent( QCloseEvent* );
private slots:
    void newfile();
    void openfile();
private:
    QToolBar *mytoolbar;
    QMenuBar *mymenubar;
};
```

The **MyAppWindow** class is based on **QMainWindow** and
will inherit its public members. The class includes a constructor and a
destructor for setting up the window and shutting it down. It also has a
toolbar and menu bar, declared as private members. This class definition
includes slots that will be executed when a certain object emits a signal.
For example, when a user selects a **New** item on a menu or clicks on a
New button on the toolbar, the **newfile** function (slot) is executed.

The "private slots:" label is not a C++ term. It needs to be
preprocessed by the MOC to generate readable C++ code. To indicate
that this class has MOC terms in it, the **Q_OBJECT** term was placed in
the class definition.

You may need to reference actions on your main application widget. For
example, if you make a window the main widget for your application, you
may want to be able to close the application by just clicking a Quit button
on the window's toolbar. To do this, you have to connect the toolbar's Quit
button to the application's **quit** function. This involves creating a **clicked**
signal connection from the button to the application's **quit** slot. However,
the window widget will not know the name of the application widget. To
handle this problem, Qt creates a special pointer called **qApp** that references
a program's application widget. The window widget will use **qApp** to
reference the application widget and its **quit** function.

In the following example, the **connect** function connects a clicked
signal on a window toolbar's Quit button with the application's **quit**

function (slot). When the user clicks the Quit button on the window's toolbar, the entire application will close.

```
connect(quit, SIGNAL(clicked()), qApp, SLOT(quit()) );
```

Dialog Boxes

To create a simple dialog box, you can use the **QMessageBox** widget. You can then generate dialog boxes with different features by using the **QMessageBox** member functions (methods). For example, if you just want to display a message, receiving no information back from the user, then you can use the **QMessageBox** widget's **about** function. It simply takes the parent object, the message title, and the message as its arguments. You can use escape sequences for newlines and tabs: **\n** and **\t**.

```
QMessageBox::about( this, "Qt Message box example",
                "This example demonstrates simple use of ",
                "The message box.");
```

For dialog boxes where you want the user to select one of several buttons, you use the **QMessageBox** object's **information** function. This takes several arguments: its parent object, its title, the message text, and the buttons you want displayed. For separate lines on the message, place each line in its own string.

The following example creates a simple message box with two lines of text and three buttons: OK, Cancel, and Apply.

```
QMessageBox::information( this, "Save notice",
                "The document has been changed since "
                "the last save.", "OK",
                "Cancel", "Apply",0, 1 )
```

The message box will return the number of the button selected. You can then use this result to select the action you want to take, as shown next.

```
res =  QMessageBox::information( this, "Save notice",
                   "The document has been changed since "
                   "the last save.", "OK",
                   "Cancel","Apply",0, 1 )
     switch( res) {
     case 0:
          myok();
          break;
     case 1:
     default:
          break;
     case 2:
          myapply();
          break;
     }
```

Mastery Check

1. Where can you find a complete listing of all KDE class declarations and their member functions?

2. What kind of object do you need to always define first in a KDE program? What header file is its class definition contained in?

3. Do you need both Qt and KDE libraries to compile a KDE program?

4. How does one KDE object communicate with another?

5. What is the MOC preprocessor used for?

6. What objects would you use to create a set of menus for an application?

10

Part 4

Appendix

Appendix A

Mastery Check Answers

Module 1: Introduction to Linux Programming

1. What are the four general categories of Linux programming?

Shell programming languages, higher level languages, programming for graphical user interfaces (GUIs), and standard programming using system calls.

2. Can you create GUI programs without programming desktops like GNOME and KDE?

Yes; use Tk with Tcl.

3. What programming language would you use to create filters?

GAWK

4. What programming tasks require that you know another language?

Programming in GNOME requires that you know C, and KDE requires that you know C++.

5. What institution created Linux?

None; it was created by Linus Torvalds.

Module 2: BASH Shell Scripts

1. How can you run a BASH shell script from within the TCSH shell?

Invoke the BASH shell at the beginning of the script with the following:

```
#!/bin/bash
```

2. What would a **read** command in a shell script input if the script argument is *?

The **read** command would read all the file names and directory names in the current working directory. When used on the command line, the * is a file name matching operator that will match on and generate a list of all file and directory names. This list of file and directory names becomes the arguments for the script.

3. Could you assign the text of several lines to a variable?

Yes, by quoting the end of each line with a backslash (\), literally quoting the newline character. All the lines are read as one line.

4. How do you reference the different arguments of a script as a single argument?

Yes, use the **$*** special variable, which holds a list of all the arguments that the user entered. **$#** is the number of arguments.

5. Can you define global variables?

Not as such. You can export a variable, generating a copy of it and its value in a subscript. But changing the value of the copy does not change the original.

6. What is the difference between == and = ?

== is used to compare numeric values and check whether they are equal, whereas = is used to compare strings to determine whether they are the same.

Module 3: BASH Shell Control Structures

1. Can you nest **if** structures?

Yes; use the **elif** command in place of the **else** followed by the new **if** structure. Use **else** on the last **if** structure.

2. How do you implement a default selection in a **case** operation?

Use the keyword *default* in place of the case for the last entry in the **case** structure.

A

3. How could you read the arguments of a script one by one, processing each in turn?

Use the **for** structure with an empty list. It will automatically read the arguments the user entered.

4. What command could you use to automatically detect options entered on the command line?

Use an **if** command, as shown, with a test to check whether the value of **$#** is zero. **$#** is the number of arguments the user entered.

```
if [ $# -eq 0 ]
    then
    echo No arguments entered
    exit 1
fi
```

5. Could your program execute any commands after the user forces it to terminate with a CTRL-C?

Yes; you can trap this event using the **trap** command and then list commands you want executed when the event occurs. The following example traps the CTRL-C event (2) and executes an **echo** command to display a message followed by an **exit** command to end the program.

```
trap 'echo "Goodbye"; exit 1' 2
```

Module 4: TCSH Shell Programming

1. What command do you use to read input in a TCSH shell script?

Invoke the TCSH shell at the beginning of the script with the following code. Keep in mind that all TCSH shell scripts need to have a # symbol in the first column of the first line of the script.

```
#!/bin/tcsh
```

2. Can you reference multiple elements in an array at once?

Yes, you can reference a set or range of elements. The first example that follows references the range of elements from 3 to 7 (3, 4, 5, 6, and 7), and the second example references individual elements 2, 7, and 9.

```
$weather[3-7]
$weather[2,7,9]
```

3. How can you determine the number of arguments that a user enters on the command line when running a script?

Use the **#argv** special variable. This holds the number of arguments the user entered.

4. How can you define a variable that can be referenced in subshells?

Define the variable with the **setenv** command, instead of **set**. This variable is then known to any subshells and its value can be changed in them.

5. What is the difference between the =, ==, and =~ operators?

The = is an assignment operator, the == is a comparison operator used to determine whether two operands are equal, and the =~ is a pattern-matching operator that checks to determine whether a pattern exists in a string or variable.

6. How would you check to see whether the argument a user supplies to a script is a directory name?

Use the **if** command to test the argument with the **–d** operator.

```
if ( -d $argv[1] ) then
    echo argument is a directory
endif
```

A

Module 5: GAWK

1. Can you use regular expressions in test expressions?

Yes.

2. What is the difference between the symbols ~, =, and == ?

~ checks for a pattern in a field. = is used to assign values to variables. == is a comparison test used in control structures to test for equality.

3. The **for-in** control structure is designed to work with what kind of arrays?

With associative arrays.

4. What function could you use to assign each word in a sentence to an element in an array in a single operation?

The **split** function.

5. What special GAWK variable would you use to create a GAWK operation that would display just the fourth through the seventh lines of a file?

Use the **NR** variable (the number of the current record) with the comma operator (,)and specify the beginning and ending record numbers of the range, as in **NR==1,NR==3** for records 1, 2, and 3.

Module 6: Perl

1. What symbols do you use to read input from a file?

Place the file name within the < and > symbols.

2. If a **print** command has no argument, does it output anything?

It outputs the contents of the **$_** variable, usually the current record that has just been read.

3. How do you assign a list of values to an array?

You can simply assign the list of values to the array in a single assignment operation. You can also assign values to a range of elements or to a set of elements, as shown here:

```
@mynums[2..4] = (92, 55, 8);
@mynums[0, 3] = (1700, 34);
@mynums = (23, 41, 92, 7);
```

4. Can you delete elements in an associative array?

Yes; use the **delete** function, like so:

```
delete(%myarr,"Sacramento");
```

5. How can you find out what strings are used to index an associative array?

Use the **keys** function.

6. If a script attempts but fails to open a file, how can you end the program at that point?

Use an **if** structure to test for this fact using a not operator (**!**) on the **open** function. This will be true if the **open** operation fails and returns a 0. If true, execute a **die** command to end the program.

```
if (!(open (REPS, "< $filen"))) {
    die "Can't open $filen";
}
```

Module 7: Tool Command Language (Tcl)

1. How do you sort a list of numbers?

Use the **lsort** function with the **–integer** option:

```
lsort -integer (89 45 100 67 )
```

2. What operation would you use to read a record consisting of a line that has fields separated by a colon delimiter?

A **split** operation. In this example, *sun:rain:storm* is split into a list with three elements **{sun rain storm}**:

```
split sun:rain:storm :
```

3. How do you open a file for both reading and writing?

Use the **r+** option with the **open** command, like so:

```
set myfile [open  $filen r+]
```

A

4. What control structure reads items in several lists at once, assigning each to a variable in turn?

The **foreach** structure, as shown in the following example:

```
foreach {cityval indexval} {Chicago 4 NewYork 7 LA 3}
   {
     set $city(indexval) cityval
   }
```

5. Could you design a script that would automatically download files from an FTP site?

Yes; use an **expect** script.

Module 8: Tk

1. Are Tk graphical objects organized hierarchically?

Yes.

2. Can you use Tcl commands to control Tk operations?

Yes. Tk functions are designed to be invoked from within a Tcl script.

3. How can you make a certain object respond to an event, such as a button to a mouse click?

Bind the object to the mouse click action using the **bind** command.

4. Whereas most programs run by executing their statements sequentially, how is a Tk program driven? How are actions selected for execution?

A Tk program is event driven. Bind operations connect actions to objects. For example, clicking an object will execute a function that has been bound to that object with a mouse click.

5. How can you display different objects in the same space in a window, instead of using a different window for each set of objects? (For example, use a menu located at the top of a window to select different operations, each of whose objects is displayed in the same window space in which it is chosen.)

Use frames that will be displayed in the same place on the window. A frame is bound to a menu entry, usually a tag, and then invoked and displayed when the entry is clicked. Clicking a menu entry for another frame would erase the previous one and display the new one.

Module 9: GNOME

1. How do you invoke the GNOME libraries when compiling a GNOME program? How about GTK programs?

For GNOME you use the *gnome-config* program with the **--cflags** and **--libs** options:

```
gnome-config --cflags --libs
```

Place the entire invocation within back quotes to execute it on the command line:

```
gcc hello.c -o hello `gnome-config --cflags --libs` gnome gnomeui
```

For GTK, you use the *gtk-config* program:

```
gtk-config --cflags --libs
```

2. Can I associate more than one function with a particular object and signal?

Yes; they are executed sequentially.

3. What function would you use to connect a menu to a window?

Once you have defined a component, such as a menu bar for menus, you need to connect it to a window. Use the **gnome_app_create_menus** function to do this:

```
gnome_app_create_menus (GNOME_APP (app), menubar);
```

A

4. Does GNOME provide operations for accessing different types of data?

GNOME provides structures and functions for accessing text, images, and numbers. These functions end with the term *entry,* such as **gnome_number_entry_gtk_entry** for accessing numbers and **gnome_file_entry_gtk_entry** to access text of a file.

Module 10: KDE

1. Where can you find a complete listing of all KDE class declarations and their member functions?

At **developer.kde.org**.

2. What kind of object do you need to always define first in a KDE program? What header file is its class definition contained in?

The **KApplication** object. Its class definition is located in the *kapp.h* header file.

3. Do you need both Qt and KDE libraries to compile a KDE program?

Yes.

4. How does one KDE object communicate with another?

Through signals and slots. Signals are emitted when events occur on an object. Slots are functions defined in a KDE object that execute when such signals are received.

5. What is the MOC preprocessor used for?

The Meta-Object Compiler generates code to manage signal and slot connections.

6. What objects would you use to create a set of menus for an application?

The **KMenuBar** and **QPopupMenu** objects.

Index

A

G